GCSE
HUMANITIES FOR AQA

Jonathan Plows
Meirion Williams

Hodder Murray

A MEMBER OF THE HODDER HEADLINE GROUP

The publishers would like to thank the following for permission to reproduce material in this book:

p. 2 *l* Ilpo Musto/Rex Features, *r* Les Wilson/Rex Features; **p.3** *l* The Travel Library/Rex Features, *m* Photodisk, *r* educationphotos.co.uk/Walmsley; **p.5** Sipa Press /Rex Features; **p.8** *t* © Michael St. Maur Sheil/CORBIS, *m* Terrance Klassen/Alamy, *b* The Art Archive/Museo Prenestino Palestrina/Dagli Orti; **p.11** *l* © Tiziana and Gianni Baldizzone/CORBIS, *r* Sipa Press/Rex Features; **p.13** Mary Evans Picture Library; **p.20** *tl* ©The Image Works/TopFoto, *tr* © Joe McDonald/CORBIS, *ml* © Clay Perry/CORBIS, *mr* ©Topham/Photri, *bl* Peter Frischmuth/Still Pictures, *br* © David Turnley/CORBIS; **p.23** © Kevin Fleming/CORBIS; **p.33** © Crispin Hughes/Photofusion; **p.48** educationphotos.co.uk/walmsley; **p.49** Rex Features; **p.51** Mary Evans Picture Library; **p.52** © Bettmann/CORBIS; **p.53** © Bettmann/CORBIS; **p.54** © Bettmann/CORBIS; **p.55** © Bettmann/CORBIS; **p.56** © Bettmann/CORBIS; **p.57** © Bettmann/CORBIS; **p.60** © Bernard Bisson/CORBIS SYGMA; **p.62** © Bettmann/CORBIS; **p.64** *l* © Bettmann/CORBIS, *r* © Tim Page/CORBIS; **p.66** Eddie Adams/AP/EMPICS; **p.68** © Bettmann/CORBIS; **p.69** © Robert van der Hilst/CORBIS; **p.71** *l* The Art Archive/Musée des Beaux Arts Valenciennes/Dagli Orti, *r* Chad Ehlers/Getty Images; **p.73** *t* Sipa Press/Rex Features, *b* © Yann Arthus-Bertrand/CORBIS; **p.74** *tl* Worldwide Picture Library/Alamy, *tr* © Gustavo Gilabert/CORBIS SABA, *b* © COLLART HERVE/CORBIS SYGMA; **p.75** HERBERT GIRADET/Still Pictures; **p.79** © David Turnley/CORBIS; **p.81** © Natalie Fobes/CORBIS; **p.82** ©Greenpeace/Greig; **p.86** *(top to bottom)* 1 © Andy Hibbert; Ecoscene/CORBIS, 2 Photodisk, 3 © Najlah Feanny/CORBIS SABA, 4 © Anthony Cooper; Ecoscene/CORBIS, 5 © Steve Lindridge; Eye Ubiquitous/CORBIS; **p.88** Photodisk; **p.94** *l* © Kendra Luck/San Francisco Chronicle/Corbis, *r* © Tom Ives/CORBIS; **p.98** *t* © K.M. Westermann/CORBIS, *b* © Carl & Ann Purcell/CORBIS; **p.99** *both* Mick Gleave; **p.103** © GIRY DANIEL/CORBIS SYGMA; **p.104** © NASA/Reuters/Corbis; **p.106** *t* EPA/EMPICS, *b* Sam Morgan Moore/Rex Features; **p.109** *t* © Bettmann/AP/EMPICS, *b* © David Zimmerman/CORBIS; **p.110** © Greenpeace-Steve Morgan; **p.118** © Bettmann/CORBIS; **p.121** © CORBIS; **p.122** Homer Sykes/Alamy; **p.123** © Bob Krist/CORBIS; **p.132** ©LWA-Dann Tardif/CORBIS; **p.133** © Jose Luis Pelaez, Inc./CORBIS; **p.135** News Team International/Darren Quinton; **p.137** *l* © HELLO! Ltd, *r* Advertising Archives; **p.142** EPA/EMPICS; **p.144** © Hulton-Deutsch Collection/CORBIS; **p.145** Akg-images; **p.147** Akg-images; **p.148** © Commission for Racial Equality; **p.149** AFP/Getty Images; **p.151** *tl* Guiseppe Aresu/Rex Features, *tr* Jonathan Banks/Rex Features, *bl* PA/EMPICS, *br* Getty Images; **p.153** geogphotos/Alamy; **p.158** PA/EMPICS; **p.161** © Bettmann/CORBIS; **p.163** EPA/EMPICS; **p.164** Reproduced with kind permission from Amnesty International UK; **p.166** © Howard Davies/CORBIS; **p.167** © Lee Besford/Reuters/Corbis; **p.173** *A* © Joel Stettenheim/CORBIS, *B* © Peter Turnley/CORBIS, *C* © Royalty-Free/Corbis, *D* © Owaki - Kulla/CORBIS, *E* © Kevin Fleming/CORBIS, *F* Gerhard Jaegle/Still Pictures, *G* © Mark Peterson/CORBIS, *H* © Liba Taylor/CORBIS; **p.181** *t* © Philip Gould/CORBIS, *b* Michael Dunlea/Rex Features; **p.187** Rex Features; **p.188** © Eva-Lotta Jansson/Corbis.

AQA for the question on culture and beliefs taken from AQA Humanities GCSE 2004 Paper 1; BBC for the table 'Different ways of making a moral decision' adapted from the BBC Education Website www.bbc.co.uk/education/asguru/generalstudies/, reproduced with kind permission of the BBC; Bloomsbury for the extract from *Holes* by Louis Sachar, Bloomsbury; Bully OnLine for the quote from the Code of Advice from www.bullyonline.org Copyright © Tim Field 1998-2005; CMG Worldwide, Inc. for the extract from a speech given by Malcolm X; Gillon Aitken Associates for 'I was bullied continually from 10-15', Sarah May, The Sunday Telegraph, 5th September 1999; Greenpeace for the by-catch case study adapted from material from the Greenpeace website; How Stuff Works for the diagram of the inside of a hydroelectric plant from http://people.howstuffworks.com; the Independent for the article 'Oceans turn to acid as they absorb global pollution', Geoffrey Lean © The Independent (01/08/2004); NARA for remarks by President Eisenhower, The President's News Conference of April 7, 1954, Public Papers of the Presidents: Dwight D. Eisenhower, 1954, Washington, DC: Office of the Federal Register, National Archives and Records Service, (Now National Archives and Records Administration), 1960; Telegraph Group Limited for 'Playground bullies are likely to have violent children ', Roger Highfield, The Daily Telegraph, 10th March 1999; the Times for 'Michael Howard Conservative Politician' (02/01/2004), 'Report of court case' (29/01/2002) and '13 year old school girl overdose' (23/09/2004); Trinity Mirror plc for the extract from the Sunday Sun 'Police stop march' (24/04/05); UNICEF for the table on development indicators for Kenya, India and MEDCs from UNICEF report 'Child Rights and Child Poverty in Developing Countries'; Vintage (Random House) for the map adapted from *Guns, Germs and Steel*, Jared Diamond, 1998; Wendy Wallace for 'Is there a bully in your home?', The Times (08/12/2004); the World Wildlife Fund for the quote from the WWF website; Writer's House for extracts from speeches given by Dr Martin Luther King.

Every effort has been made to trace all copyright holders, but if any have been inadvertently overlooked the Publishers will be pleased to make the necessary arrangements at the first opportunity.

Although every effort has been made to ensure that addresses are correct at time of going to press, Hodder Murray cannot be held responsible for the content of any websites mentioned in this book. It is sometimes possible to find a relocated web page by typing in the address of the home page for a website in the URL window of your browser.

Orders: please contact Bookpoint Ltd, 130 Milton Park, Abingdon, Oxon OX14 4SB. Telephone: (44) 01235 827720. Fax: (44) 01235 400454. Lines are open 9.00 – 6.00, Monday to Saturday, with a 24-hour message answering service. Visit our website at www.hoddereducation.co.uk

© Edward Waller, Jonathan Plows, Mick Gleave & Meirion Williams 2005
First published in 2005 by
Hodder Murray, an imprint of Hodder Education,
a member of the Hodder Headline Group
338 Euston Road
London NW1 3BH

Impression number   10 9 8 7 6 5 4 3 2 1
Year   2010 2009 2008 2007 2006 2005

Cover image by David Angel at DebutArt.
Typeset in 12pt Adobe Garamond by DC Graphic Design Limited, Swanley, Kent.
Printed in Italy.

A catalogue record for this title is available from the British Library

ISBN-10: 0340 88583 1
ISBN-13: 978 0340 88583 3

Contents

INTRODUCTION

This book supports the aims of your AQA GCSE Humanities course – to help you understand better some of the important issues facing human beings in the twenty-first century. You will probably find that as you become more aware of why groups of people behave the way they do, you will also understand yourself better.

About the book

The book is divided into sections. The first three sections cover the core unit. This takes you through a study of:

• Culture and beliefs
• Conflict and co-operation
• Environmental issues.

The next four sections cover the following optional units from the specification:

• Patterns of family life
• Prejudice and persecution
• Power and democracy
• Global inequality.*

Each section is broken down into smaller topics that cover a key issue and contain the features described on the opposite page.

At the end of the core unit, there are some examination questions, example answers and advice from examiners (pages 112–15). Some questions give you a previous answer to mark and comment on. In this way, you can form a good idea of what standard is expected of you, and this will hopefully help you to improve your own standard.

Towards the end of the book there is a section on coursework, which gives you advice on how to do your coursework and improve your research, evaluation and communication skills.

The use of examples and case studies

We often hear people say, 'I have the right to my own opinion', and this is true. But with that right comes the responsibility to take the trouble to check that the opinion can be supported by evidence.

In your physical science subjects (biology, chemistry and physics) and in maths, you can set up an experiment to test a theory and see if the evidence supports it. In Humanities, on the other hand, there would probably be a few complaints if you tried to do the same thing. Imagine, for example, the outcry if you decided to put a random group of young children in a house on their own for a month to see whether and how they would survive! So we have to scour the world for examples and case studies that have occurred 'naturally' and use these as the evidence for our theories. Most sections in the book have at least one case study to demonstrate a theory or opinion about human behaviour.

People love stories and gossip. We often like to have a story to tell about a friend or someone we know. These are known as anecdotes. Many of us enjoy gossip about celebrities in newspapers or magazines. Stories are fun, but if we are to understand what makes us do the things we do (our behaviour) then we need to look for patterns in behaviour. We need more than an anecdote.

This book combines story telling (case studies, examples) with looking for patterns. The case studies and examples have been chosen because we think they are typical or represent a pattern. In other words, we think there are lots of other case studies/examples/statistics that would reinforce the point being made just as well as the one we have chosen. One of the challenges in studying Humanities is to test whether the evidence in the case studies provides sufficient 'proof'.

Features of the book

- **Topic questions**, which pose a question around a central issue.

- **Key questions**, which focus on the key ideas you need to understand, followed by an explanation of why it is important to study this topic.

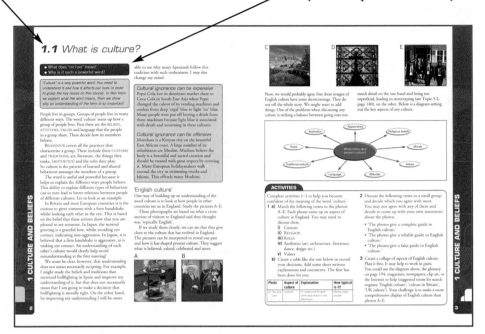

- **Investigations** give you ideas for extension and research work, which could lead on to coursework assignments.

- **Case studies, examples and sources**, which illustrate the key ideas and help you to test them out.

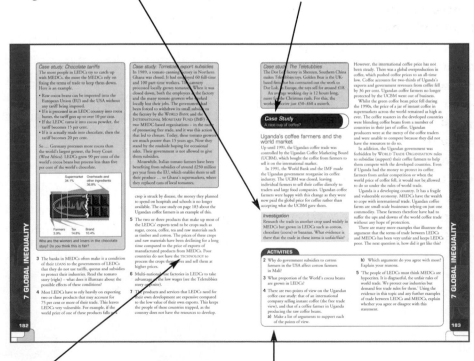

- **Key words and concepts** are highlighted in SMALL CAPITALS the first time they appear in a section and are defined in the glossary.

- **Activities**, which check your basic understanding of the key concepts and give you practice in applying these to analyse, interpret or evaluate a case study, source or example.

1.1 *What is culture?*

- What does 'CULTURE' mean?
- Why is it such a powerful word?

'Culture' is a very powerful word. You need to understand it and how it affects our lives in order to grasp the key issues on this course. In this topic we explain what the word means, then we show why an understanding of the term is so important.

People live in groups. Groups of people live in many different ways. The word 'culture' sums up how a group of people lives. First there are the BELIEFS, ATTITUDES, VALUES and language that the people in a group share. These decide how its members behave.

BEHAVIOUR covers all the practices that characterise a group. These include their CUSTOMS and TRADITIONS, art, literature, the things they make, (AESTHETICS) and the roles they play. So culture is the pattern of learned and shared behaviour amongst the members of a group.

The word is useful and powerful because it helps us explain the different ways people behave. This ability to explain different types of behaviour can in turn lead to better relations between people of different cultures. Let us look at an example.

In Britain and most European countries it is the custom to greet someone with a firm handshake whilst looking each other in the eye. This is based on the belief that these actions show that you are pleased to see someone. In Japan, the normal greeting is a graceful bow, whilst avoiding eye contact, indicating non-aggression. In Japan, it is believed that a firm handshake is aggressive, as is making eye contact. An understanding of each other's culture would clearly help avoid misunderstanding at the first meeting!

We must be clear, however, that *understanding* does not mean necessarily *accepting*. For example, I might study the beliefs and traditions that surround bullfighting in Spain and improve my understanding of it, but that does not necessarily mean that I am going to make a decision that bullfighting is morally right. On the other hand, by improving my understanding I will be more

able to see why many Spaniards follow this tradition with such enthusiasm. I *may* also change my mind.

Cultural ignorance can be expensive
Pepsi Cola lost its dominant market share to Coca Cola in South East Asia when Pepsi changed the colour of its vending machines and coolers from deep 'regal' blue to light 'ice' blue. Many people were put off buying a drink from these machines because light blue is associated with death and mourning in these cultures.

Cultural ignorance can be offensive
Mombasa is a Kenyan city on the beautiful East African coast. A large number of its inhabitants are Muslim. Muslims believe the body is a beautiful and sacred creation and should be treated with great respect by covering it. Many European holidaymakers walk around the city in swimming trunks and bikinis. This offends many Muslims.

'English culture'
One way of building up an understanding of the word culture is to look at how people in other countries see us in England. Study the pictures A–E.

These photographs are based on what a cross-section of visitors to England said they thought was 'typically English'.

If we study them closely, we can see that they give clues to the culture that has evolved in England. The pictures can be interpreted to reveal our past and how it has shaped present culture. They suggest what is believed, valued, celebrated and more.

A

B

C  D  E

Now, we would probably agree that these images of English culture have some shortcomings. They do not tell the whole story. We might want to add things. One of the problems when discussing any culture is striking a balance between going into too much detail on the one hand and being too superficial, leading to stereotyping (see Topic 5.2, page 140), on the other. Below is a diagram setting out the key aspects of any culture.

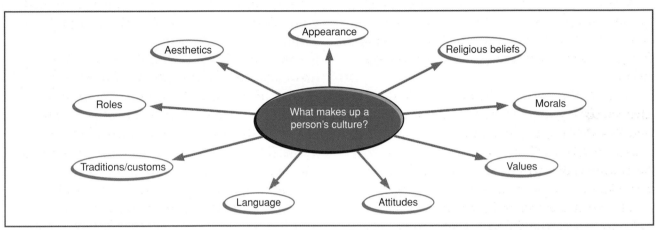

ACTIVITIES

Complete activities 1–3 to help you become confident of the meaning of the word 'culture'.

1 a) Match the following terms to the photos A–E. Each phrase sums up an aspect of culture in England. You may need to discuss these.
- **i)** Custom
- **ii)** RELIGION
- **iii)** ROLES
- **iv)** Aesthetics (art, architecture, literature, dance, design etc.)
- **v)** Values

b) Create a table like the one below to record your decisions. Add some short written explanations and comments. The first has been done for you:

Photo	Aspect of culture	Explanation	How typical is it?
a) Tea and cake	Custom	A traditional English drink and snack in the afternoon	Mainly older people

2 Discuss the following views in a small group and decide which you agree with most. You may not agree with any of them and decide to come up with your own statements about the photos.
- 'The photos give a complete guide to English culture.'
- 'The photos give a reliable guide to English culture.'
- 'The photos give a false guide to English culture.'

3 Create a collage of aspects of English culture. Plan it first. It may help to work in pairs. You could use the diagram above, the glossary on page 194, magazines, newspapers, clip art, or the Internet to help (suggested terms for search engines: 'English culture', 'culture in Britain', 'UK culture'). Your challenge is to make a more comprehensive display of English culture than photos A–E.

1.2 Why do people live in groups?

In this topic you will find out why people live in groups. This will help you begin to understand the need for CO-OPERATION and NORMS in any culture.

In Topic 1.1 (pages 2–3), we explained that the word 'culture' could be used to describe a group of people who have certain beliefs and behaviours in common. But why do people live in groups anyway?

The explanation lies in the nature of human beings.

On our own, we are weak. If we look at the evidence of Early Man (over 1–2 million years ago) we can see that human beings alone were no match for the animals they hunted, such as sabre-toothed tigers, cave lions and woolly mammoths. So they got together in groups to improve their chances of survival. They also found they could search for fruits and berries more efficiently in small groups than on their own. Once they learned to act together, they could not only survive, but also begin to thrive.

The strength of human beings comes from our ability to work together in groups. When we are alone, we sense our weakness. We become afraid and want to feel we belong.

Co-operation and its consequences

Living in groups, or tribes, however, meant that Early Man had to co-operate. This meant in turn that other aspects of culture became important.

• To co-operate, you need to have an agreed way of doing things. These are known as norms. For example, in many early cultures, it was the norm to share out all food and other produce fairly within the group. Norms would guide the individuals in the group so they knew what to do as a team. They would be passed on from one generation to the next. Some norms would become a formal set of rules. These would then be enforced through SANCTIONS (rewards or punishments).

• People would learn their roles. This would build up trust within the group and give each individual a sense of belonging. The tribes that co-operated best became the most successful.

• The drive to co-operate better led to improved ways of communicating. This is why language developed.

Finding food

One example of co-operation was the way people within a tribe would share their knowledge about the animals and plants around them. In this way, they could improve their knowledge of the animals' feeding habits, making it easier to hunt them. They would also learn more quickly which plants were poisonous, which ones could be used for medicine, which ones were good to eat and when they should be harvested.

Fire

Another example of co-operation is how groups of humans shared the discovery of how to make fire. Fire gave groups:

• protection from predators, as most animals were afraid of fire. This gave groups more choice about where they camped

• confidence to migrate into colder regions, as fire would keep them warm

• the ability to cook food. Cooked food is safer and much softer to eat.

This meant the youngest and oldest members of the group had more chance of survival.

ACTIVITIES

1 How important was co-operation for the survival of Early Man? Give your reasons.
2 Study the cave painting and caption opposite. How would co-operation within a group have allowed art to develop?

1 CULTURE AND BELIEFS

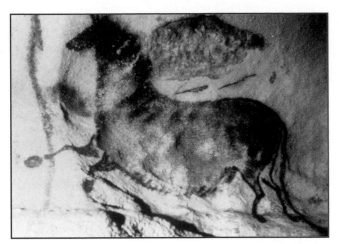

Modern humans, known as Homo sapiens, have only been around for the past 120,000 years. By 40,000 years ago, they had learned how to make tools out of bone, antler, ivory, stone and wood. By 17,000 years ago, they were producing fine artwork like this cave painting found in Lascaux, in South West France.

Living in groups today

So humans co-operated in groups to ensure their survival. You could be thinking now, 'OK, this may well be true of our ancestors, but how does it help to explain why we live in groups today? Surely I am not struggling to survive?'

Today we are usually in several groups at the same time: our FAMILY, school, workplace, PEER GROUP, sports team, and our local, national and international COMMUNITY. We belong to each group because they still help to satisfy our needs and desires better than if we tried to live independently. You only have to study where your food, clothes and other possessions come from to realise we have become a world community where we depend on each other.

Learning how to co-operate

We are not born knowing how to co-operate, however. We learn to do so as we grow up. First, our parents teach us through smiles, frowns and other sanctions what is and is not 'acceptable'. They show us how to play and share. We learn that we have to give to the group in order to receive from the group.

In each group we have a set of rules or norms, both written and unwritten, and in each one we have a role to play so that the group achieves its purpose. People depend on us and we depend on them. It makes us feel secure to feel we identify with/belong to a group. The more we fear being on the outside, alone, the more we seek to identify with 'our group'. By learning to co-operate we develop the ability to work in groups and so play our part in providing for each other.

Sadly this is not everyone's experience, however, as the story below shows.

> ### Hayley's story
> Hayley was neglected as a baby. If she cried, she would be shouted at, even smacked. As a child, her parents did not play with her, take her for walks or read to her. Most days she played out until late. She was shouted at if she got into trouble. Her parents took little interest in what she did at school. She began to get into trouble at school for disrupting lessons. She began shouting at her teachers. She started truanting. When she was 15, Hayley left home and moved into a flat with some 20-year-olds who regularly took drugs. She had a baby. If the baby cried, she shouted at him.

ACTIVITIES

3 Suggest reasons why Hayley was disruptive at school. Use the following words to help you answer:

Love; Co-operation; Norms; Sanctions; Learn

4 What help should be given to Hayley and her baby? Why? Who should give it?

5 Use the information in this topic to provide evidence to support your answers to the following questions:

a) Why does co-operation require trust?

b) How difficult would it be to live totally independently today?

c) What are the disadvantages of living in groups?

d) How important is it for a group to have sanctions for people who break the norms?

e) How might a culture be affected if the experiences described in Hayley's story become widespread?

1.3 Why are there different cultures?

- Why did the early groups of people develop different languages, beliefs and ways of behaving?

Having studied why people live in groups in Topic 1.2 (pages 4–5), in this topic we will look at why these groups have developed different cultures around the world. By learning why there are different cultures, you can begin to understand some reasons why people have different values and attitudes about the way we should live.

All children have the right to an education.

The voting age should be reduced to 16.

The tradition of ARRANGED MARRIAGES should be stopped.

Families should be responsible for looking after their elderly relations.

There should be capital punishment for 'terrorists'.

People should do more to reduce GLOBAL WARMING.

People in the West should do more to help eliminate hunger.

All countries should accept genuine ASYLUM SEEKERS.

More should be done to reduce under-age drinking of alcohol.

ACTIVITIES

1 On your own:
   a) Organise the beliefs above into those you agree with and those you disagree with.
   b) Put them into a rank order, starting with the issues you consider most important. Give reasons for your order.
   c) Now, in small groups, discuss and complete the following tasks:

   - How do your views compare on which beliefs you agree and disagree with?
   - As a group, come to a decision on which beliefs your group agrees with and which it opposes.
   - Now compare your rank orders of importance. How much agreement is there?
   - Reach a group decision on rank order.

Appoint/elect someone to keep a record of the discussion and decisions. They will then report back for the group at the whole-class discussion.

2 As a group or class, discuss the following questions about activity 1c):
   a) What difficulties were there in completing activity 1c)?
   b) What aspects of culture can help explain your differences of opinion? (Beliefs, values, traditions?)
   c) What part did co-operation and COMPROMISE play in your discussions?
   d) On which issue(s) was it easiest to be tolerant of opposing views? Why?

It is likely that there was some disagreement in your group in activity 1. Around the world there are differences both between and within cultures on these and other beliefs. Your experience of this activity will help you understand this quotation from Lester Pearson:

'We are moving into an age when different CIVILISATIONS will have to learn to live side by side in peaceful interchange, learning from each other, studying each other's history and ideals of art and culture to enrich each other's lives. The alternative in this overcrowded little world is misunderstanding, tension, clash and catastrophe.'

Lester Pearson, former Prime Minister of Canada and NOBEL PEACE PRIZE winner, 1957

Emergence of different cultures

Human beings have basic physical needs that must be satisfied if they are to survive: food, water, shelter. We also have emotional needs such as love, security and identity. Living in groups makes it easier to provide for these needs as we showed in Topic 1.2 (pages 4–5). Different groups have found very different ways of achieving these goals. This has led to the emergence of many different cultures with different beliefs and values.

How has this come about? To answer this we need to look at the map below and learn a little history.

ACTIVITIES

3 What would be your three main pieces of advice to help 'different civilisations learn to live side by side'?

4 'We are all IMMIGRANTS.' How true is this statement? Use the map to support your answer.

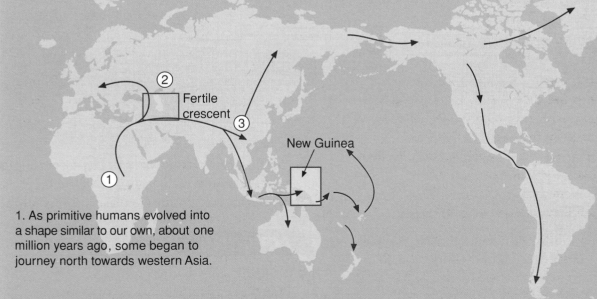

2. In western Asia they divided, some turning northwest towards Europe (earliest remains 500,000 years old).

3. Others crossed Asia to the east. From there they migrated southeast to Australia or northeast, across the Bering Straits to America. They could do this either by walking over a land bridge of ice 1,610 km (1,000 miles) wide, during the last Ice Age which ended about 10,000 years ago, or by boat across the sea which was only 80 km (50 miles) wide. They then travelled on down the west of North and South America. Here the earliest remains are only about 12,000 years old.

Fertile crescent

New Guinea

1. As primitive humans evolved into a shape similar to our own, about one million years ago, some began to journey north towards western Asia.

From about seven million years ago, there have been various types of human being evolving and spreading around the world. Evidence in the form of human fossils and bones and crude tools have helped us piece together the map shown above. This traces the MIGRATION of human beings from their origins in eastern Africa.

A map of the world showing how human beings have spread across the continents from Africa, based on skeleton remains. (Adapted from: *Guns, Germs and Steel* by Jared Diamond)

Natural environment

Groups adapted in order to survive. In adapting, they were beginning to develop their own distinct culture. Local materials would be used for clothing and shelter; animals and plants that thrived locally would be hunted or gathered. The beliefs and languages that developed would reflect their particular natural ENVIRONMENT. The power of the environment to influence culture can be seen in New Guinea today.

Case study: Cultural groups in New Guinea

New Guinea is a large island near the equator north of Australia (see map on page 7). There are 6,000 languages spoken in the world and 1,000 of them (one sixth) are to be found on this island, the size of Texas! How can this be explained?

The island is very rugged and very mountainous. There are mangrove swamps at sea level and dense tropical rainforest covers most of the island. There are glaciers capping the highest mountains. It has one of the heaviest annual rainfalls in the world of nearly three metres, so there are many very fast flowing rivers. These have divided the slopes into deep gorges and valleys. It is usual for a three mile journey to take all day.

Since travel is so difficult, the people living in one valley are rarely in contact with those living in the next valley, let alone those up the mountains or by the sea. So over time the population has divided into thousands of separate cultural groups. Each has adapted to living in different natural environments: by the sea, in the deep tropical valleys and high in the mountains, developing its own distinct language, traditions, norms and values.

The variations in culture around the world are simply a larger version of the variations that have occurred on this one island.

'House' design

Natural environment influenced the shelters people developed, some examples of which are shown in the photos (right).

Beehive hut in West Ireland, about 3000BCE – made from local stone and built layer by layer with no mortar.

Tipi in North America – made from the tanned hides of bison or elk. They were designed to be transportable because the Indians lived off these animals and had to follow the herds as they migrated in search of grazing grounds as the seasons changed.

Mud from the banks of the Nile was shaped into bricks, dried out and used to build homes in Ancient Egypt. The dry climate was essential for this.

ACTIVITIES

5 Using the New Guinea case study as an example, explain why are there so many different languages around the world.
6 How do you think the different 'house' designs shown in the pictures above were influenced by differences in the natural environment?

1 Research building designs and materials in different cultures today and make a presentation of your findings. How big are the differences you found? How far do they reflect differences in environment and climate?

Wealth and technology

Some natural environments turned out to be more helpful to human development than others. This is a major cause of differences between cultures. While some human groups struggled to survive in harsh environments, others thrived in 'kinder' environments.

Case study: The Fertile Crescent

One 'kinder' environment is an area stretching from the Eastern Mediterranean to the Persian Gulf, known as the Fertile Crescent (see map, page 7). Here, vegetation grows very easily in the warm, wet winters and hot, dry summers. Large areas of land are relatively flat. This is the region where human beings first learned how to farm successfully. For example, the first farmers grew wheat and rye 13,000 years ago in Syria.

When a culture turned to farming for its food instead of hunter-gathering, some very important changes in their way of life took place.

- Instead of wandering around hunting wild animals, they could now settle in one place.
- This made it more worthwhile designing permanent buildings.
- Storing food surpluses became possible. This allowed some people to be released from farming and to develop other skills.

This is why it was the cultures of this region who invented writing and made huge progress in maths and building design. They created the first cities, civilisations and EMPIRES in the world.

Evidence suggests that the earliest writing developed in three fertile areas – Egypt, Mesopotamia (Iraq, Syria, Iran) and Harappa (Pakistan) between 3500BCE and 3100BCE.

Other environments

As groups migrated to other parts of the world, such as to Australia or down the western coastline of the Americas, they became very cut off from the peoples in Europe and Asia.

They would not have heard about any of the important developments, so they could not share what had been learned. Also the environments they learned to survive in were very different. They found fewer plants that could be farmed to make food and far fewer animals that could be domesticated (for example, no sheep, horses or donkeys).

In some, wildlife and game were plentiful, so there was no pressure to look for alternative sources of food or to develop farming. In others, the environment was too harsh for farming to work. So in Australia and the Americas they remained hunter-gatherers.

Back in Africa, where Homo sapiens had originated, the Sahara Desert and the equatorial rainforests proved to be huge barriers to communication and trade. The widely different natural environments provided few animals to domesticate, or crops for farming. So, in Africa too, many cultures remained hunter-gatherers.

Peoples in Arctic regions, Africa, Australia and America developed their own distinct cultures due to their isolation and did not develop powerful civilisations like the ones that grew up in Asia and Europe.

Even the apparent exceptions, like the empires of the Incas and Aztecs in South and Central America, were held back by their lack of crops and farm animals. This limited the development of technology and communications and contributed to their defeat by the Europeans in the sixteenth century.

Spread of ideas

Cultures living in 'kinder' natural environments used their domesticated horses to help them travel between settlements. New ideas spread across Asia and Europe; trade increased. Places on the same latitude would benefit most from learning about improved farming methods because they had similar climates.

Progress

These cultures grew wealthier. They could use this WEALTH to develop their art and TECHNOLOGY. This in turn led to progress in architecture, sciences and government.

Although cultures traded with each other, they also competed with each other for power. This encouraged the development of more things to trade on the one hand and more powerful weapons of war on the other.

Farming could support a denser population than hunting and gathering. The cultures that adopted the best farming methods became the most populated. This enabled them to have the biggest armies.

This competition for power strengthened the mistrust and fear between the different cultures, such as the rivalries between the Phoenicians, Greeks and Romans to control the lands around the Mediterranean 2,000–3,000 years ago.

Conclusion

So, even though human beings had learned that living in groups and co-operating was the best way to survive, they learned to do this in different ways. Some were more successful than others. At the same time they learned to be cautious, even hostile, towards 'outsider' groups.

As a result, men and women in different cultural groups have developed different roles, norms, beliefs, languages, and traditions.

ACTIVITIES

7 There are three main reasons why different cultures have emerged. These are:

- different environments
- differences in wealth
- different technology.

These reasons are all linked. Draw a diagram with notes to explain the links between the reasons and why they caused different cultures to emerge. You can use the words listed below to help you:

Crops for farming; Horses/cattle; Settlements; Surplus; Wild animals for hunting; Latitude; Trade; Technology; Size of population; Isolation

8 'The reason that some cultures are more wealthy and powerful today than others is mainly down to luck.' How far does the evidence in this topic support this opinion? Discuss this in groups, then write up the discussion.

9 Why did the cultures that developed farming methods gain an advantage over those that remained mainly hunter-gatherers?

Investigation

2 Research one or more of the following peoples. They each have, or had, their own distinct culture.
  a) Yanomami of South America (see Topic 3.2, page 76)
  b) Bushmen of the Kalahari
  c) Inuit of North America
  d) Native Americans of the plains

For each culture:

- identify and describe the people's natural environments
- explain how well the culture has adapted to its environment
- explain what you consider to be the strengths and weaknesses of the way the people adapted
- identify what problems the people face today.

1.4 How is culture acquired?

- What is the NATURE V NURTURE debate?
- What is meant by SOCIALISATION?

By learning about the nature v nurture debate and what is meant by socialisation, you will become more aware of the way people are shaped by the culture they are born into. You can, as a result, become more self-aware.

The questions dealt with in this topic are: 'How do we actually "get" our culture? Are we born with it or do we learn it somehow as we grow up?' This is part of what is known as the 'nature v nurture' debate.

Nature v nurture

Which has the more powerful influence on us as a person: our GENES or the people and physical environment around us? Simply put, the two sides of the debate are as follows:

- nature – supporters of this side argue that genes are a major influence on our INTELLIGENCE and behaviour, and therefore our culture
- nurture – supporters argue that our intelligence, behaviour and culture are learned through a complex process known as socialisation.

ACTIVITY

1 In Source A, the man of the Wodaabe and the Western European model both use make-up. Which is regarded as normal and which is regarded as abnormal behaviour in England? Give reasons for your answer.

We want to be scientific in our reasoning, but it is difficult to set up experiments in a laboratory to find answers that help us decide which side of the debate to support. However, look at the following evidence (Sources A–I, pages 11–14), which has been collected over the last 100 years or so.

Think about it
If nurture (socialisation) is more influential than nature (genes), then our parents have a big role to play in influencing us. Should parents be held more responsible for their children?

If intelligence, criminal and addictive behaviour are due to our genes, then what should happen to those people with 'deficient genes'?

Other reasons why this is an important debate should emerge as you research the arguments in this section.

Source A

Wodaabe man of Niger (western Africa) preparing for a party.

A western European model.

Source B

As a result of evolving separately, the tribes in New Guinea developed more than language differences (see Case Study on page 8). For example, GENDER ROLES are different. In her famous research, the ANTHROPOLOGIST Margaret Mead described three tribes. These are some of her findings.

• The Arapesh expected both men and women to be gentle and play an equal part in bringing up their children.

• The Mundugumor, however, were the opposite. Both men and women were forceful and women detested having and looking after children.

• The Tchambuli were different again. The women were self-assertive, practical and ran the HOUSEHOLD. They shaved their heads and did not wear any necklaces, rings or bracelets. The men wore lovely ornaments, did the shopping, gossiped and loved dancing.

ACTIVITIES

2 Look up the following terms in the glossary and learn their meanings:

Genes; Socialisation; MALE; FEMALE; MASCULINE; FEMININE; Gender roles; Intelligence

3 a) Create a table like the one below. Put the terms you looked up in activity 1 into the columns you think are correct. In the fourth column, add the reasons for your choice.

Nature	Nurture	Both	Reasons

b) Decide whether Source A (page 11) supports the nature or nurture argument, or both, and add to the table. Then select an appropriate statement from the list below to write into the 'Reasons' column.

• 'Masculine behaviour is different in different cultures.'

• 'It is not natural for men to wear make-up.'
• 'Gender roles are learned through socialisation.'
• 'Gender roles are determined by our genes.'
• 'The way each person's brain works is determined by our genes.'

c) Now do the same with Source B.

d) Study the following sources C–I (pages 13–14) and add each source to your table with reasons for your decisions, just as you did for Sources A and B, creating your own sentences for the 'Reasons' column.

e) When you have completed d) reflect on the nature v nuture debate. Write down your own opinion about which has the most powerful influence on us as a person (you may well be undecided). What are the most important pieces of evidence on both sides?

Source C

The 'Jim Twins'

Studies of twins who have been brought up apart could help resolve the debate. If twins have identical behaviour, even though they have been socialised differently, then this would suggest that nature is more powerful than nurture in determining our behaviour and culture. Thomas Bouchard, a psychologist at the University of Minnesota in the USA, conducted the most famous of these studies. One of the cases he researched was that of the 'Jim Twins'.

Born in 1940, Jim Springer and Jim Lewis were adopted by different families four weeks after birth. In 1979, they were reunited for the study at the age of 39. The Jim twins caused a public stir, as they shared remarkably similar lives. Similarities were striking and included the following:

- did well in maths at school and had problems with spelling
- the same hobbies: mechanical drawing and carpentry
- similar habits: chewing their fingernails, chain smoking Salem cigarettes
- headaches at the same time daily
- the same colour and model Chevy car
- first wives named Linda and second wives named Betty.

Other similarities included naming their dogs Toy, their sons James Allan and taking holidays in the same place each year. Their IQ scores were as close as one person would get doing the test twice.

Source D

Eyesight

A recent study of British twins has revealed that the need to wear glasses is largely genetic. Only 15 per cent of short-sightedness is caused by environmental influences such as using computers or reading a lot of small print.

Source E

There have been a number of reports of feral children – children who have grown up without the usual human parenting. Here is one of the more famous cases. More can be researched on the Internet.

Kamala and Amala, the 'Wolf Girls'

Two young girls were discovered under the care of a she-wolf in 1920, in Midnapore, India. The girls were taken to an orphanage. Kamala, aged eight and Amala, aged 18 months, behaved exactly like small wild animals.

- They slept during the day and woke by night. They slept curled up together in a tight ball and growled and twitched in their sleep.
- They remained on all fours, enjoyed raw meat, and would bite and attack other children if provoked. They had spent so long on all fours that their tendons and joints had shortened to the point where it was impossible for them to straighten their legs and even attempt to walk upright.
- They could smell raw meat from a distance.
- They had an acute sense of sight and hearing.
- Amala died one year later, but Kamala lived for nine years in the orphanage until she died of illness at the age of 17.
- Kamala found it very difficult to learn to speak. She only learned a few words.

1 CULTURE AND BELIEFS

Source F

Intelligence: a summary of views

- Intelligence testing is a very sensitive area of research and debate. Some scientists believe you can measure intelligence just as you can measure eyesight. In the early part of the last century they put forward the idea that you can control the human race by selective breeding (eugenics). If intelligence is genetically determined, for example, what is the point of education for those with a low IQ? Why not breed them out?

- In 1994, Hernstein and Murray's book, *The Bell Curve*, argued that differences in IQ scores between racial groups reflect BIOLOGICAL differences. Belief in the Bell Curve and in the genetic, rather than social, basis for intelligence has encouraged many racist ideas.

- Other scientists argue that genes work by interacting with the environment; so social factors will also influence intelligence.

- Intelligence tests may be more of an assessment of social factors, such as your educational background. For example, the US military tested recruits to assign rank and found that black applicants scored lower than whites. However, an analysis of the recruits found this to be due to educational differences; black recruits scored very low until the 1950s, when an increase in score corresponded to improved educational standards for all.

- Many researchers believe there is more than one way of measuring intelligence.

- It is impossible to devise questions without some cultural or gender bias. For example, boys tend to do better in spatial tests whereas girls score higher on linguistic tests.

- Diet is also an important factor. Good nutrition enables an individual to function well both physically and mentally.

Source G

Aggressive genes?

For 26 years, researchers followed the fate of 1037 children born in 1972 in Dunedin, New Zealand. They found that children were much more likely to grow up to be aggressive and antisocial if they had inherited a 'short' version of a gene called 'MAOA', which affects how the brain works.

But carriers only went off the rails if they had had an awful, abusive upbringing. Carriers with good parenting were usually completely normal, the New Zealand study showed.

Source H

Smoking

Maternal smoking during pregnancy is associated with low birth weight in the baby – a clear example of the effects of nurture. However, recent research shows that most of this effect is confined to that half of women who have deficiency variants of two genes, CYP1A1 and GSTT1.

Source I

A gene's influence

Recent research in Italy shows that families in which the women are very fertile also contain a high frequency of homosexual men. It is suggested that the link is a gene responsible for both.

Nature and nurture: the debate continues

Some of the evidence in the sources you have studied shows that socialisation plays at least some part in making us the person we are. Exactly what the balance is, however, between nature and nurture is still open to debate. This is a voyage of discovery. Human beings do not have the whole answer to this important issue and more research is needed. Whatever the outcome of this debate, there is no doubt that much of our culture is learned. So, now let us look at how it is learned.

How does socialisation work?

Primary socialisation

Evidence shows that our family, or others immediately involved in looking after us in our first months and years, play a central part in moulding us (see Topic 4.3, page 124). It is from our immediate family that we learn to talk, walk and use various objects such as a spoon. They are also the ones who first teach us what is right and wrong behaviour and how to relate in a 'proper' way to different people such as grandparents, friends, strangers and so on.

So already we are learning norms, MORALS, values, language (the 'what' of culture) through our family (the 'how' of culture). The family is the primary agent of socialisation. Methods of learning include:

- *imitation*, copying mummy when washing
- *identification*, baby follows older brother around
- *role learning*, for example, helping to clear away at the end of a meal
- *conditioning*, rewards and sanctions applied to encourage or discourage certain behaviours.

A child is learning the basics of co-operation, and the blueprints of how to behave, so these blueprints are the ones most firmly imprinted in his or her brain. Once these blueprints have been established, research shows that it is very difficult to override them with new ones.

This is one of the key reasons why it has proved so hard to re-socialise feral children when they are found. They have already been socialised, but not in a human way.

ACTIVITIES

4 List the four methods by which a child learns through primary socialisation and give one more example for each.

5 'Give me a child until she/he is five and I will give you the woman/man.' Explain this statement using your understanding of primary socialisation. Refer to Source E, page 13, about feral children. Does this source support it? Give your reasons.

Other agents of socialisation are shown in the diagram below.

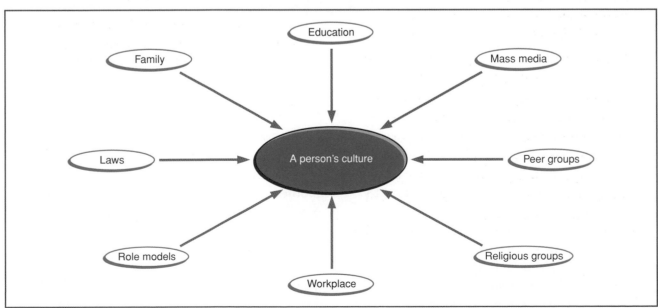

How do we acquire our culture?

Secondary socialisation

These are the other agents of socialisation identified in the diagram on page 15 and explained in the diagram below.

- **Education:** Schools teach about and model a culture's values, traditions, attitudes and language.

- **The mass media:** If businesses are prepared to spend so much money on advertising, then the mass media must be having some influence on our values, attitudes and behaviour in relation to the products being advertised. If that is the case, then is it not reasonable to argue that the headlines, articles and pictures on the TV, Internet and in newspapers and magazines are likely to be part of our socialisation too?

- **Peer groups:** This is particularly powerful during teenage years. The desire to belong to a group is strong.

- **Religious groups:** In some cultures, these affect almost everyone (see Topic 1.5, page 19).

- **The workplace:** The way we are organised at work and our relationships within it contribute to our socialisation. The hours we work and the type of work we do are also important influences.

- **Role models:** Senior or famous members of a culture play a key part in maintaining or adapting it. They may reinforce or challenge behaviour, values and traditions that others want to copy.

- **Laws:** These are formal norms with sanctions. They can help influence attitudes and behaviour. For example, laws against DISCRIMINATION (see Topic 5.5) at work have helped improve the treatment of women, homosexuals and ethnic minorities.

These influences are not all of equal importance for all cultures. For example, the mass media is clearly more powerful in a culture where everyone can read and each household has access to a TV and radio. Religious organisations have real influence on culture in some parts of the world. Examples include South America (Catholic Christian) in the Middle East (Islam) and parts of the US (evangelical Christian).

The different agents of socialisation can also CONFLICT with each other. For example, in England, a young person may learn to conform to one set of norms with their family concerning such values as swearing and sexual relationships, but experience another set of norms with their peers or on the TV. As we mature we usually (but by no means always) learn to manage these conflicting pressures. In such a SOCIETY, individuals have to work out their own beliefs and values. As you will see in Topic 1.5, (pages 19–23) there are some cultures that go out of their way to exclude the mass media from the socialisation process.

In order to show how socialisation works, we shall consider the way we learn our gender roles. There is often much confusion between the nouns *gender* and *sex*. The word 'gender' refers to the way we are expected to think and behave by our culture according to whether we are male or female. In other words, it is to do with our ideas of masculine and feminine. 'Sex', on the other hand, covers our biological and INNATE CHARACTERISTICS. It is simply whether we are male or female.

We are born into a culture that already has a set of beliefs and values so all the people who are involved in the raising of a child will have ideas about how children should behave. As soon as we are born, we are sent signals as to what is expected of us by our parents and other family members. As we go through life, gender role norms are usually then reinforced by secondary socialisation.

The table below shows some familiar examples of the ways gender roles can be socialised.

LANGUAGE	IMAGES	ROLES
'Go and help mummy/daddy'	Blue theme in bedroom and for clothes for a boy; pink themes for a girl	Boy helps dad wash the car Girl helps mum wash up
GIRLS: 'Isn't she sweet!' 'Girls should not be rowdy' 'She is so kind' 'Doesn't she look pretty!'	TOYS FOR GIRLS: Pram/doll Role-play set: nurse, hairdresser Make-up kit	OCCUPATIONS, 2004: Hairdressers: 92 per cent female Nurses: 89 per cent female Taxi drivers: 92 per cent male MPs: 82 per cent male High court judges: 94 per cent male Surgeons: 90 per cent male 70 per cent of women are in the worst paid jobs
BOYS: 'He's a real lad' 'He's so forceful' 'Isn't he big and strong!'	TOYS FOR BOYS: Action man figures Tractor/farm set Skateboard/football kit/bike/violent video games *James Bond* film poster	OPTIONS, 2004: Average option figures at 14 in state schools: Electronics: 97 per cent boys Textiles: 93 per cent girls

ACTIVITIES

6 Divide into small groups and consider the following statements:

- All boys are interested in is sport.
- Girls should wait for boys to invite them out.
- Boys show off more than girls.
- Girls are better at modern languages than boys.
- Girls are more concerned about their appearance than boys.
- Boys should pay for girls when they take them out.
- Girls are less confident than boys.
- Boys are better at maths.
- Girls are more caring than boys.
- Groups of boys are more rowdy than groups of girls.

a) For each statement, take it in turns to say whether you agree or disagree.

b) Record the group's views, including whether you all agreed or not.

c) Reflect: are you guilty of stereotyping each other? In other words, do your answers suggest that you have 'hidden' expectations based on your assumptions about how males and females should behave? Where have these assumptions come from?

7 Study the table above and use examples to show how primary socialisation can affect our career choices.

Different gender roles

The norms in England for gender, however, are not the same for every cultural group. The fact that gender roles can vary from culture to culture is further evidence that gender is learned rather than biologically inherited.

ACTIVITY

8 Read the description in Source J about the Arapesh people of New Guinea.

a) Write a short profile (around 60 words) of a 'typical' 15-year-old boy in your local community.

b) In groups, show your profiles to each other. Discuss the differences with Source J and write down a summary of them.

Source J

Based on Margaret Mead's research (see Source B, page 12).

If an Arapesh teenage boy behaved aggressively he would be OSTRACISED from the group for displaying 'deviant' (abnormal) behaviour. Those who shared and co-operated best within the group were the ones given the highest honours and respected most. Mead described the typical Arapesh woman and man as caring, co-operative, gentle, loving, sharing, and selfless.

ACTIVITY

9 Read Source K about teenage girls in Fiji.

a) What evidence is there that Fijian girls' eating habits have changed?

b) What effect has the arrival of TV had on the socialisation of Fijian girls?

Source K shows how some of the agents of primary and secondary socialisation give us our culture. The research opportunities suggested in 'Investigations' (right) will help you extend your understanding of these influences.

Source K

Anne Becker has studied eating habits in Fiji since 1988. In a recent report she explained that the traditional Fijian preference has been for a 'robust, well-muscled body' for both sexes. There was no dieting to lose weight. The family and community elders were the main influences on the children.

In 1995, Fiji's only TV station went on air and started broadcasting programmes from the UK, US and New Zealand such as *Seinfeld*, *ER*, *Melrose Place* and *Xena: Warrior Princess*. Since then there has been a sharp rise in signs of disordered eating amongst young girls. Her research showed that 15 per cent of the girls reported they had vomited to control weight and 74 per cent of them felt they were 'too big or fat'.

She added that 'The teenagers see TV as a model for how one gets by in the modern world. They believe the shows depict reality.'

Investigations

1 Obtain a shopping catalogue and analyse the adverts for children's toys.

a) Are these advertisements a form of primary or secondary socialisation? Give your reasons.

b) How does the catalogue use colour to suggest which pages are for boys' toys and which are for girls?

c) Why are there children shown playing with many of the toys?

d) What later roles are the toys preparing children for? Explain.

2 Study a week's films on TV by using a guide and identify those that promote 'masculine' and 'feminine' roles. How do these films affect our socialisation?

3 a) Collect information about numbers of students at a coeducational school taking options. Identify those options where there seems to be a male/female bias.

b) Design a questionnaire to find out the main influences on the students' choices.

1.5 How important are beliefs to a culture?

- How can the culture of the Amish be described and explained?
- How far do the Amish live out their beliefs in daily life?

You can use the case study of the Amish to consolidate what you have learned about the theory of culture (what it is and how you acquire it).

You can also use it as a model for a future study of another culture.

Case Study
The Amish culture

Introducing the Amish

Imagine what it would be like if you had never watched television or if you had never heard music on a CD/tape player. What would your life be like if you did not have a telephone, or a fridge, or a washing machine in your home, or have the use of a car?

This is how the Amish live. They refuse to have or use any of these items in their lives.

Why?
It is not because they are poor. It is because they believe it is wrong to have them.

Why?
Read on.

Today, most Amish live in Pennsylvania, Ohio and Indiana in the USA. They choose to live separately from other US citizens and have a distinct culture.

The information on pages 20–23 gives you some clues about the Amish. You can research their culture further either on the Internet, where there is a range of useful sites, or through your library. You may design your own research or use the activities below depending on the guidance you receive. The film *Witness*, set in the 1980s is well worth watching, as is the documentary *The Devil's Playground*.

ACTIVITIES

1 Start by studying the six photos A–F and their captions on page 20 . On your own or with a partner, write down any questions about the Amish culture that are prompted by these pictures. You can then plan how to research answers to them.

2 Having studied the information on pages 20–22 about the Amish, sort the following sentence starters and enders:

a) The Amish do not wear buttons because	i) they believe it will cause their communities to drift apart and pursue material wealth.
b) The Amish will not join the US army because	ii) it is a sign they are married.
c) The Amish do not educate their children beyond 14 years of age because	iii) they believe it will cause conflict and make it more difficult for them to concentrate on following Jesus' teachings.
d) The Amish do not live with people from other cultures because	iv) it is a way of enforcing their norms.
e) The Amish do not have modern technology because	v) they believe that they, the people, are the Church.
f) The Amish use shunning as a sanction because	vi) they believe these are proud and they want to be humble.
g) Some Amish men grow beards because	vii) they are pacifists. They believe this is what God and Jesus want us to be.
h) The Amish do not have church buildings because	viii) they believe they will get distracted by worldly ambition and 'the ways of the English', and not stay close to God's way.

A

Amish men are wearing traditional black suits and hats. Women are also in traditional black, with aprons and bonnets.

B

The Amish pursue a life based around farming, using horses and simple farm machinery.

C

This woman is making quilts, a traditional Amish occupation for women. You can also see her bonnet and traditional clothes.

D

The Amish have a very clear DIVISION OF LABOUR. The men do the barn raising whilst the women prepare and serve the food.

E

Amish women making pretzels. Can you see any electrical items?

F

Children are taught from a very young age to help out on the farms and around the home. They stop going to school at the age of 14.

Background to the Amish

In Europe in the early sixteenth century, the Catholic Christians, led by the Pope in Rome, had a powerful influence over people's daily lives, including kings and queens and their governments. It was also a period of conflict between different groups of Christians (known as the Reformation).

In Switzerland, one of these groups of Christians was led by Jacob Amman. They wanted to practise Christianity differently to the way the Pope and the kings and queens of Europe at that time thought was right. They wanted to:

- simplify prayer and church service
- wait until children grew up before baptising them.

For this, the Catholic Christians persecuted them. For example, many were put in sacks and thrown into rivers.

So they gave up trying to live in Europe and, in the seventeenth century, fled to North America, where they settled in Pennsylvania. Here they could rebuild their way of life based on farming and their Christian beliefs. The way they live has scarcely changed since those days.

Today, they live separately from other cultures in small, tight-knit communities. Amongst themselves, they speak a form of German. Most Amish have very little to do with anyone outside of the Amish faith. Those who are not Amish are still referred to as the 'English'. Eighty per cent of the Amish live in Pennsylvania, Ohio and Indiana.

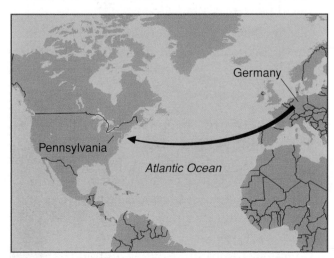

Map showing migration of Amish from Europe to Pennsylvania, USA, in the seventeenth and eighteenth centuries, where many settled.

What are Amish principles?

The Amish believe that living how God wants them to is essential. They believe God wants them to submit to his guidance and serve others – giving up any selfish thoughts. This way of life is called *Gelassenheit* and is summed up in Source A below. The Amish believe that modern technology such as electricity, television, cars and the telephone all undermine these principles. This is because they are means of bringing the outside world into the community. If they used modern technology, they believe their communities would drift apart.

ACTIVITY

3 What reasons can you give for the Amish being afraid that modern technology such as electricity, television, cars and the telephone will cause their communities to 'drift apart'?

Source A

The basic beliefs of the Amish

The Amish say:

- the Bible is God's inspired word
- God loved the world so much that he gave his only son, Jesus, to die on the cross for the sins of the world, so we must be humble at all times and try to live as Jesus said we should in his Sermon on the Mount
- we are committed to peace at all times, the use of violence is never an option
- faith calls for a lifestyle of discipleship, good work, serving others and holy living
- the Church is separate from the state. The Church is the people, not a building.

Rules

Amish communities live by a set of rules. These are called *Ordnung*. These rules are guidelines for living, covering all aspects of Amish life, including clothing, leisure activities, work, worship and giving birth. Every rule has a reason that links back to their beliefs. See Source B for some Amish rules.

Source B

Some Amish rules

Beards

A man does not shave his beard after he becomes married. Moustaches, on the other hand, have a long history of being associated with the military and therefore are forbidden as they symbolise violence and pride.

Clothes

Women and girls wear dresses made from one solid colour. They always wear long sleeves, and their skirts must be longer than halfway between their knees and the floor. They cannot cut their hair. It is always worn in a bun on the back of their heads. If they are married, they wear a black bonnet on their heads. If they are single, they wear a white one.

Buttons are not allowed because the Amish believe they are a sign of pride. This reminds them of the time when many of the Catholics who persecuted them were rich and wore expensive clothing with 'show-off' buttons.

Men must wear a solid coloured shirt, dark trousers, braces and a straw or broad-rimmed hat. The Amish feel that these clothes separate them from the world.

ACTIVITY

4 How do Amish beliefs in Source A (page 21) explain their rules for beards and clothes (Source B)?

Shunning

Since they will never use violence, the Amish use shunning as a sanction to enforce their beliefs and rules. If someone is shunned, no one buys from, sells to, or even eats at the same table as the shunned person. All members that leave the Amish Church and those who marry an outsider are shunned. This idea also comes from the Bible:

'But now I am writing to you that you must not associate with anyone who calls himself a brother but is sexually immoral or greedy, an idolater or a slanderer, a drunkard or a swindler. With such a man do not even eat.'

1 Corinthians 5:11

Tourism

The oldest and second largest Amish community in Lancaster, Pennsylvania, has become the centre of 'Amish tourism'. It is near many cities – close enough for people to take day trips there.

On the one hand, tourism is resented because:

- it means the community becomes crowded. Their farm and schoolwork is disrupted
- tourists take photos of the Amish – something that the Amish believe should be avoided, as it is a sign of pride to have your photo taken.

However, tourism has also benefited the community through:

- bringing money into the community
- increasing 'outsider' understanding of the Amish way of life, which in turn means the government tolerates them and does not interfere. For example, Amish children can legally stop going to school at 14.

Teenagers

When they turn 16, the Amish community allows teenagers the freedom to explore the customs of the outside 'English' world – including alcohol, drugs and sex – before deciding whether to join the Amish Church for life and be baptised, or leave the community altogether. This period is called *Rumspringa* – the Pennsylvania Dutch (i.e. German) word for 'running around'.

Source C

The Devil's Playground

Rumspringa is the focus of *The Devil's Playground*, a documentary by filmmaker Lucy Walker. It tells of hundreds of Amish teenagers from ten different states who congregate in 'barn hops' and 'hoedowns'. Large fields are filled with cars and horses and buggies. Many get drunk.

One of the teenagers in *The Devil's Playground* is 16-year-old Gerald of Indiana, who moves out of his parents' house to live in a trailer. In the film he says: 'I didn't tell my parents for like a month. If I was living at home, I couldn't have 200 channels of DirecTV, a stereo and Nintendo, and a fridge full of beer.'

Faron is an 18-year-old with an increasingly serious drug problem. His music idol is the late rapper Tupac Shakur. Yet Faron says he hopes to follow his father into the Amish ministry.

Despite the freedom to experiment, or maybe because of it, 85–90 per cent of the teenagers actually decide to return to the Amish ways and join the Church by getting baptised. You can read more on the Internet and view video clips by putting *The Devil's Playground* into a search engine.

Amish teenagers during *Rumspringa*.

ACTIVITIES

5 According to Source C, what does *The Devil's Playground* tell us about the influence of the following agents of socialisation on Amish youth? Give your reasons.

The mass media; Peer groups; Religion; The family

6 Having studied all the information and sources about the Amish on pages 19–23, use the spider diagram of what culture is on page 3 as a model to create your own concept map of the Amish culture. An example of how you might start this is given below:

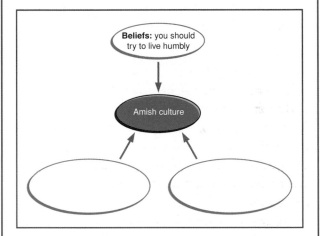

7 What are the main religious beliefs of the Amish and how do they influence other aspects of their culture (apart from wearing beards – see activity 4)? Refer to examples in the information and sources on pages 19–23 to support your answer.

8 Why is interaction with the 'outside' culture in the USA such a problem for the Amish?

9 Does this study of the Amish support or challenge the argument that nurture is more important than nature in making us who we are?

10 What do you consider are the strengths and weaknesses of the Amish culture? Give your reasons.

1.6 Is there an English culture?

- Has England become a multi-cultural society?
- Do the English have a common set of beliefs?
- What happens to different cultures when they interact with each other?

By looking at the sources and information in this topic, you will discover some of your own history, whether your family migrated here generations ago or whether you are a more recent arrival.

Over the past 2,000 years, many different ETHNIC GROUPS have occupied what is known as 'the British Isles'. A 'British' identity was only created in 1707 with the Union of England, Wales and Scotland, and Great Britain is made up of these three countries.

Current maps of 'the British Isles' are thus a little confusing. Understandably, people living in the REPUBLIC of Ireland do not quite understand why they are included!

How British are the British Isles?

But is there a single CULTURAL IDENTITY in England and Britain? To answer this, we need to go back further.

Early history

People have been living on and moving in and out of these islands for at least 10,000 years. These early settlers had migrated from central Asia. They did not see themselves as 'British' or 'English'. They simply saw themselves as members of one of the many tribes that had migrated from mainland Europe and lived in competition with each other.

ACTIVITIES

Look at the map below.

1 When was the United Kingdom first legally established?

2 What is the difference between Great Britain, the United Kingdom and the British Isles?

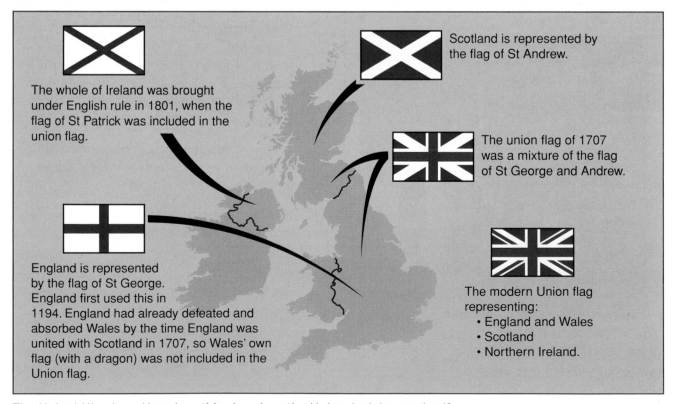

The whole of Ireland was brought under English rule in 1801, when the flag of St Patrick was included in the union flag.

Scotland is represented by the flag of St Andrew.

The union flag of 1707 was a mixture of the flag of St George and Andrew.

England is represented by the flag of St George. England first used this in 1194. England had already defeated and absorbed Wales by the time England was united with Scotland in 1707, so Wales' own flag (with a dragon) was not included in the Union flag.

The modern Union flag representing:
- England and Wales
- Scotland
- Northern Ireland.

The United Kingdom. How does this show how the Union Jack has evolved?

ACTIVITY

3 In pairs, brainstorm what would be the most likely causes of conflict between the early tribes settling in these islands. Refer back to Topic 1.3, page 10 for some clues. Discuss as a class.

By the time of the Roman invasions of 2,000 years ago, the Celts had established themselves as one of the leading groups of tribes with a distinct culture.

The Celtic tribes

Celtic tribes spread from central Europe from 500BCE onwards. They settled in areas now known as France, Belgium, Britain, Ireland and Spain.

- Daily life – the Celts lived in large family groups. They made clothes from woollen material woven into tartan patterns. They also became outstanding metalworkers. Celts living in central Europe improved their metalworking skills by learning from tribes living in western Asia. These skills were then passed on to other Celtic tribes across Europe. They used these skills to make beautiful images of sacred birds and animals in bronze and gold.
- Religion – the Celts believed in many gods and goddesses, who they worshipped in temples. Druid priests (Ancient Celtic priests) taught about the importance of life after death.
- Food – the Celts were good hunters. They also knew how to grow crops. They invented a harvesting machine that the Romans thought was such a good idea that they copied and developed it further.

ACTIVITIES

4 Give two examples of Celtic beliefs and two examples of other aspects of Celtic culture.

5 Describe and explain two ways cultures benefited from interacting with each other.

The Roman invasions

The Romans invaded Britain in the first century BCE and again in the first century CE. The Romans saw Britain as a useful source of metals (especially tin), corn, meat, skins and wool. The Celts fought hard to stop the Romans taking over their lands.

There were uprisings and rebellions. The Romans wanted to bring this to an end and to start trading with the Celts. This quote from a Roman General to his advisers sums up their thinking:

> If we are to end the fighting and remain in control, we must encourage the Celts to become more like us. We must offer their leaders gifts like mirrors, furniture and new cooking tools. We must make sure they see how much better we live. When they see our superior buildings, stone streets, public baths, large town villas with under-floor heating, our painted and plaster-covered walls, they'll realise that it is worth accepting our laws and other customs. They'll accept the need to speak our language. Most will then want to stop fighting us and join us instead.

This plan eventually worked. The Celtic islanders actually became Romans, both culturally and legally. Roman CITIZENSHIP gave the Celts political status. By 300CE, almost everyone in 'Britannia' was Roman, even though they were descended from Celts and still mostly speaking 'Celtic' dialects. Roman rule brought cultural change but without any mass MIGRATION.

However, Rome only ever conquered half the island. The future Scotland and parts of Wales remained beyond Roman control.

ACTIVITIES

6 Get into pairs. Imagine you are Celts. You have heard a report of what the Roman General said (above). Prepare a speech to make at your tribal gathering – either for or against co-operating with the Romans. Use arguments based on the information in the speech above and your knowledge of the Celts.

7 What was likely to happen to the Celtic culture if they did/did not co-operate with the Romans?

The English language

The Romans never managed to conquer the Celts in Scotland, Ireland, Wales and Cornwall. In these areas, the Celts remained fiercely independent, keeping their own language and culture for many centuries to come.

Angles, Saxons and Jutes

After the Romans finally left in the fifth century CE, many tribes from northern Europe began invading Britain.

The Angles, Saxons and Jutes landed and settled in the eastern and southern parts of Britain. These tribes came from areas in what is now known as northern Germany and the Netherlands. They mixed with each other over the years, leading to a common Anglo-Saxon culture. Their language became known as 'Angle-ish' or English. Their land in the south and east became known as 'Angle-land' – England.

Vikings

Meanwhile, the Vikings from Norway, Sweden and Denmark (also known as the Norsemen – the men from the north) began arriving in the eighth century CE. They invaded large parts of northern Britain where their language and culture became the main influence. For over 200 years on and off there were battles between Viking descendants and their Anglo-Saxon rivals for control of the island.

Normans

Finally, in 1066, the Norman invasion led to the defeat of both the Saxons and the Vikings. The Normans took strict control of the people they had defeated. Norman language (old French) and culture now became dominant over nearly all of Britain. One example of this can be seen in the way words for our food change from farm to table (from peasant worker to nobleman). 'Pig', 'cow' and 'sheep' are Anglo-Saxon words. These are the words used on the farm. When the meat arrives at the table, they become 'pork', 'beef' and 'mutton'. These are French-based words (*porc*, *boeuf* and *mouton*).

The English language we speak today has grown from the mixing of languages spoken by all these invaders.

ACTIVITIES

8 What is the origin of the word 'English'?

9 Why do you think people in different parts of England speak English with different accents and dialects?

10 How true is it to say that English is a pure language? Explain your answer.

11 How important is a common language in developing a common culture?

Source A

LATIN (ROMAN) VERBS	FRENCH	MEANING	ENGLISH WORDS
duco, duxi, ductus	duc	lead	conduct, induction, duke
mitto, misi, missus	metre, mis	send	mission, message, emit
scribo, scripsi, scriptum	ecrire	write	inscribe, scripture, script

Source B

Some regional dialects in spoken English

Na then, me China Plate, would ya loike ter Scapa Fla daahhhn ter the bloomin' Noah's Ark for a ball of chalk wif me? (Cockney: London)

Noo then, me skip, ood yoo loike ter goo dowl ter the park for a walk with me? (Birmingham)

'Na' then, mi bonnie lad, ood thee li' ta nip on darn ta t' park for eur walk wi' mee? (Yorkshire)

Neeo then, wor bairn, wud yee leek tuh gan doon tuh the wreck fo' a wark wi' wor? (Newcastle)

ACTIVITIES

12 Look at Source A. Can you think of five more French words that are linked to English words?

13 With a partner, try speaking aloud the phrases in Source B in the different dialects. Now try translating the phrase. Which did you find easier to translate – why?

Other settlers

Huguenots

During the sixteenth and seventeenth centuries, over 60,000 Protestant (Huguenot) refugees from Belgium, Holland and France fled to Britain to escape religious PERSECUTION.

They settled in London and in towns like Norwich and Canterbury. Most finally settled in Spitalfields in the East End of London and in Soho in London's West End. Some were expert in making clocks and scientific instruments. Others were goldsmiths, silversmiths, merchants and artists.

Their skills at weaving silk and velvet helped expand the silk weaving industry in Spitalfields that already employed many Irish workers. During the eighteenth century, wealthy members of the Huguenot and Jewish communities gave a lot of money to support the army.

Germans

Between 1850 and 1914, the number of Germans who chose to live in Britain rose from 4,000 to 40,000. They brought with them new ideas in banking and other industries. Companies that are world famous today, like ICI (chemicals), Siemens (cables and insulators) and Berger (paint) were all started by Germans settling in Britain during this time.

Russian and Polish Jews

Between 1870 and 1914, about 120,000 Russian and Polish Jews fled to Britain to escape racist and religious persecution. Many settled in London, Manchester and Leeds where they were free to practise their religious traditions. Some set up their own textile businesses, providing good clothing that ordinary people could afford. Many went to work in factories where they often played a leading role in trade union struggles for better working conditions, and against unemployment.

Irish

Irish labourers worked on the construction of new roads, canals and railways during the Industrial Revolution in the eighteenth and nineteenth centuries.

Sailors

As the British Empire developed so did trade, bringing new peoples to Britain. Lascars (sailors from South East Asia and India) came along with seamen from countries like China, West Africa, and those known today as Somalia and the Yemen.

Textile workers

During the twentieth century, immigrants from Cyprus, Pakistan and Bangladesh have continued to boost the textile industry.

Italians

In the first half of the twentieth century, many Italians migrated to Britain. The Clerkenwell district of London became known as 'Little Italy'. Italians introduced street vending of ice cream and worked in the catering trade as waiters, chefs, bakers, confectioners and café owners. Later on, in the 1940s and 1950s, men and women from the south of Italy were recruited to work in factories in Luton and Bedford. Some went on to open Italian restaurants and pizzerias.

Other imported delicacies including curry and chow mein, smoked salmon and fried fish have all been introduced by people from overseas and are now part of everyone's diet.

After the Second World War

After the Second World War, there was a labour shortage. People forced to leave their homes (displaced) from Poland, Italy, the Ukraine and Germany were recruited to fill the gaps. Later, the National Health Service (NHS) and organisations like London Transport recruited men and women from the Caribbean to build up their labour force.

Immigrants have brought new musical sounds like reggae and calypso. Some have become sporting heroes and founders of many well-known businesses. Today, health and transport services continue to be supported by nurses, doctors and managers from overseas. In towns and cities, there are not only churches but also synagogues, mosques, gurdwaras, Hindu and Buddhist temples.

ACTIVITY

14 Using the information in this topic – and any other you have researched – create a presentation (music, drama or art can be used) that highlights the ways England has benefited from the immigration of people from other cultures over the past 500 years.

CAMPAIGN TO GET BRITAIN OUT OF EUROPE

NOW

The 'Get Britain out of Europe' campaign is a pressure group determined to change government policy on Europe. Throughout the history of this proud NATION, we have been independent. We have never had anything to do with Europe in the past and we do not intend to start now! What has Europe ever done for us? Nothing! In fact, we have often found ourselves fighting them. We, the British, have always led the world in technology and business.

We say it is time to stop the slide into Europe. We have a distinct British culture and we want to keep it that way.

Keep Britain out of Europe!

In 1533, Henry VIII of England broke away from the Roman Catholic Church and made himself head of the Church of England (Anglican). There were now two major groups of Christians in Britain: Anglicans, also known as Protestants, and Catholics. Henry had the powerbase of the Catholics, their monasteries and churches, destroyed and looted.

In 1553, Queen Mary, Henry's daughter and a Catholic, changed the country back to Catholicism and had many Protestants who would not change burned at the stake.

In 1558, Queen Elizabeth I, also Henry's daughter, but a Protestant, changed England back to Anglicanism. It has been the official religion of the UK ever since. After Charles I was executed at the end of the English Civil War (1649), Parliament ruled that a Catholic could never become king or queen. This rule remains in force today. Some believed the Anglicans did not go far enough in changing their form of worship and over the next centuries formed other Christian groups (or denominations) such as Puritans, Presbyterians, Quakers and Methodists.

ACTIVITY

15 a) Copy the leaflet above and highlight any inaccuracies.
b) Now write a letter to the campaign organisers to explain to them in what ways they are wrong.

Beliefs – the cornerstone of a culture?

Of course, it is likely you have already thought about this question when you studied the Amish in Topic 1.5 (pages 19–23).

The Amish have an organised set of beliefs – a religion that is very apparent in the way they live their lives. Does this case study prove, therefore, that everyone's behaviour is based on their beliefs, even if we do not follow a religion? How important is having a shared set of beliefs to any culture?

A quick history of religion in England

During Roman times, England became a Roman Catholic (Christian) country. The head of the whole Church was the Pope, based in Rome. Nearly the whole of Europe became Catholic.

ACTIVITY

16 Look at the following aspects of behaviour that are commonly observed in Britain. Each one is based on a belief or beliefs. What are they? Complete and add to the table. Some examples have been given.

Behaviour	Possible underlying beliefs
Wedding	1 You should make a lifetime commitment to the person you are marrying. 2 The marriage should be celebrated.
Working in an office with computers	Using modern technology is acceptable.
Drinking alcohol	It is not harmful.
Gambling (casino)	
Army training	
Building motorways	
Eating meat	It is not wrong to kill animals for food.
Keeping budgies in a cage	
Watching a DVD with an 18 certificate	
Cigarette advertising	

What religions are there in the UK in the twenty-first century?

The UK is a multi-faith society in which everyone has the right to religious freedom. This is now part of the European human rights law.

Although religious faith in the UK is mainly Christian, most of the world's religions are practised. Due to immigration in the last century there are important Hindu, Jewish, Muslim and Sikh communities, and also smaller communities of Bahá'í, Buddhists, Jains, and Zoroastrians, as well as followers of new religious movements.

There are beliefs underlying all our actions. They do not have to be religious. For example, a feature of culture in England is the payment of taxes to support the armed forces. This is done because the government believes it is right to do so and the majority of people accept it.

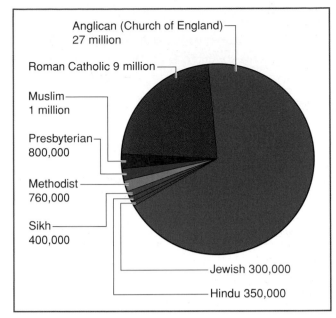

Approximate numbers of religious followers in the UK out of a total population of 60 million (2005).

ACTIVITIES

17 Divide into small groups and imagine that you are on the school council. Students from several ethnic groups attend your school but they do not really mix together. Draw up some proposals to put to the next council meeting to bring about more interaction and understanding in the school. Role-play the council meeting and vote for the most convincing proposals.

18 Working with a partner, use the spider diagram on page 3 and the one you did for the Amish (page 23) as models to draw a similar diagram of culture in England. What makes this diagram more complicated than the others?

19 a) The Amish's behaviour is based on their Christian beliefs. Which, if any, of the following words and phrases do you think are appropriate to use in describing the beliefs underlying culture in England? Are there others you would use?

> Non-violent; Calm/relaxed; Liberal; Multi-cultural; Caring; Tolerant; Traditional; Modern; Christian; Atheist; Family-based; Respectful; Freedom of choice; Success is measured by wealth; Competitive; Fashion-driven

b) With a partner, make a list of what you think are the top five of these words and phrases to describe the nature of culture in Britain, then have a class discussion to decide the top three.

20 Using your knowledge as well as the information on pages 26–30, would you say that England is a multi-cultural society?

21 Here is a poem written by Daniel Defoe in 1701 (he is probably most famous for his novel *Robinson Crusoe*). Take the last two lines as the title and discuss whether they are true *or* write an up-to-date version of his poem/rap including more modern references.

The True Born Englishman
In eager rapes, and furious lust begot,
Between a painted Briton and a Scot:
Whose gen'ring offspring quickly learnt to bow.
And yoke their heifers to the Roman plough:
From whence a mongrel half-bred race there came,
With neither name nor nation, speech or fame:
In whose hot veins now mixtures quickly ran,
Infus'd betwixt a Saxon and a Dane.
While their rank daughters, to their parents just,
Receiv'd all nations with promiscuous lust.
This nauseous brood directly did contain,
The well-extracted blood of Englishmen …
… A True Born Englishman's a contradiction!
In speech, an irony! In fact, a fiction!

Investigations

1 Study the table below. It has been completed using data collected from the social history page of the BBC website. Research whether there is an English culture. Consider:

- the role of the Celts/Romans/Normans/other ethnic groups in influencing culture in the UK
- further examples of Latin, Greek and French influences on English language

- the experiences and contributions of immigrants to England since the first century CE. See Channel 4 (Originations) and the museum-based website called 'movinghere' for an excellent start to this research. Seek guidance on the use of these large websites
- what the statistics in the table show. Overall, have more people migrated from or to Britain over the last 200 years?

The main phases in the growth of the population of Britain.

Time period (approx.) changes	Population (millions)	Ethnic groups involved	Emigration (E) or Immigration (I)	Comments on population and reasons
500BCE–43CE	1	Celtic tribes	I	Celtic tribes from North Europe settled in England, Scotland and Wales. Searching for good land.
43–410CE	1.5	Romans	I	There is still much evidence of the Roman occupation, which lasted nearly 400 years. There were over 125,000 Roman soldiers and their families living here. Tin and farming.
450–865	1.5	Anglo-Saxons	I	Came from northern Europe. Gradually took control of the whole of the area we call England today.
865–1000	1.5	Vikings	I	From Scandinavia. Took control of most of Scotland, Wales and Northern Ireland.
1066–1348	3.5	Normans	I	From North France. Eventually took control of all England and Wales.
1350–1642	6	English, Belgian, Dutch, French	Some E and I. Migration from towns began. Some emigration to the USA. Some immigrated from Europe to the UK.	It took until the end of the Tudor period for the population to recover from the effects of the Black Death. Many fled to avoid religious persecution.
1700–1850	21	English, Scottish, Irish	Mainly I. Migration from countryside to towns. Immigration from Ireland.	Massive growth of cities due to Industrial and Agricultural revolutions. Religious persecution.
1850–1910	37	English, Scottish, Welsh, Irish Lithuanian, Polish, Russian	E and I. Emigration to mainly USA, Canada. Some immigration from Europe.	Mainly to USA. Highland clearance, Irish potato famine.
1914–45	49	English, Scottish, Welsh, Irish, European	E and I. Migration within UK. Three million emigrated before the Second World War. Immigration of refugees.	Continuing Industrial Revolution. New start in colonies and USA. Religious persecution in Europe.
1945–99	58.6	English, Scottish, Welsh, Irish, European Caribbean, African countries, South East Asia	E and I. Migration within UK. Immigration from colonies. Emigration to Canada, USA, Australia and South Africa.	Sharp fall in UK city populations 1950–80. Active recruiting in colonies due to labour shortages in UK. UK citizens leave to start new life. More emigrate than immigrate during this period.

2 As a piece of advanced research, you could consider: is there a British culture? If so, how different is it from an English culture?

1.7 Why do people have different views on moral issues?

- Why are moral issues important to all cultures?
- How do we reach decisions about MORALITY?

Do you know what your own code of morals is and why? As this book shows, people have different beliefs about how to live. This includes beliefs about what is morally the 'right' and 'wrong' way to behave. This topic will help you to think about your own and others' morals.

We have the right to make our own moral decisions. This places upon us a responsibility to reflect on these decisions and be clear about how we reach them. This section on culture and beliefs ends with a study of morality and how a person's moral decisions are closely linked to other aspects of their culture.

What is a moral issue?

A moral issue concerns beliefs about whether an action is right or wrong in the sense of it being good or bad. We can use 'wrong' to mean immoral and 'right' to mean moral. The words 'right' and 'wrong', however, can be used in different contexts. Consider the following choices:

1 Which pair of shoes *should* I buy?
2 What answer *should* I give to this maths problem?
3 *Should* I take the £10 note that is sticking out of someone's pocket, or warn them they are about to lose it?

Each of these decisions is right or wrong in a different sense:

1 Which shoes represents the best value? Which looks the best?
2 Which answer can be proved?
3 Which action is the most honest?

Only the third is a moral decision. We *all* make moral decisions, even if we do not think about it.

ACTIVITY

1 A school secretary is collecting money as students arrive for a 'no uniform day', to support a local hospice. A 15-year-old student sees some of this money lying in a container unattended and pockets it whilst the secretary is distracted by an emergency phone call.

a) Which of the following statements do you agree with most?

- The student is stealing. I believe stealing is wrong because you have no right to take something that does not belong to you.

- The student is not exactly stealing. The money is not being taken from someone so there is no victim.

b) Attempt to explain the beliefs you hold that influence your decision. Give your reasons for rejecting the argument you do not agree with. Consider:

- your beliefs about fairness, justice, rights
- your beliefs about survival, looking out for yourself.

The moral issue in the activity is to do with stealing and whether we consider stealing 'wrong' or immoral. We are usually socialised to believe that stealing is immoral, but this is in turn based on other beliefs. There is no proof that stealing is immoral, as there is in, say, maths, that 2 + 2 = 4, or in history, that Henry VIII had six wives. Instead, we have to look for the most persuasive line of reasoning.

In a moral issue, this line of reasoning may relate to ideas about fairness, justice, the purpose of life and obeying a code of behaviour as set out in any religion.

Moral issues, then, are any issues requiring a decision based on beliefs about what is 'good' or 'bad' behaviour.

Norms of behaviour

Since human beings live in groups, norms of behaviour need to be established. As we showed earlier in this section, every culture has a set of norms that guides behaviour. Many of these norms are based on the beliefs of that culture.

For example, the Amish refuse to use violence in any situation (see Topic 1.5, pages 19–23). This is a norm of their culture. It is based on the belief that using violence is always wrong, which comes from their acceptance of what Jesus taught: that God wants us to love each other:

'Love thy neighbour'
'Blessed are the peacemakers'.

These are quotes from Jesus that the Amish interpret in their everyday lives. This excludes the use of violence at all times. To apply this belief, they refuse to participate in the US armed forces and forbid the use of any weapon in their communities. They will never hit another person. If someone breaks this norm they will use a sanction, such as shunning, to show their disapproval.

Decision making

Moral	A moral decision concerns what we consider permissible behaviour with regard to basic human values (for example, fairness, individual freedoms, respect for others). For instance, you may decide that giving money to help disaster victims is a moral act.
Immoral	An immoral decision is the exact opposite of a moral decision. For example, you might think that shoplifting is immoral.
Amoral	An amoral decision or action is taken in the absence of knowledge of morality. For example, a five-year-old child hits his brother in the eye and hurts him simply because he wants to see what will happen. He did not understand the consequences of his decision.
Non-moral	A non-moral decision does not concern the 'big questions'. A non-moral decision is more to do with everyday decisions. For example, deciding what to wear in the morning is a non-moral decision.

Adapted from the BBC Education website at www.bbc.co.uk/education/asguru/generalstudies/culture/02morality/morality01.shtml

ACTIVITIES

2 What would the Amish attitude to capital punishment be? Draw a diagram to show the links between their Christian beliefs and their attitude towards this moral issue.

3 a) 'It is always wrong to carry a weapon.' Write down in bullet points your thoughts on this view. State whether you agree or disagree, with reasons. How do your beliefs about violence affect your answer?

b) Interview another student to compare notes. Share your ideas in a class debate.

4 Do you believe it is better to be aware of your own morals? Explain, using the decision making table below.

5 In order to survive, cultures have to establish norms on a range of moral issues such as the taking of life, sexual relationships, use of violence and rights concerning private property. In small groups, discuss your beliefs about some of these issues. Attempt to make links between what your attitude is towards the moral issue and the deeper belief on which this attitude is based.

What are the different ways of reaching a moral decision?

There are two ways of arriving at moral decisions.

1 By applying your beliefs as *rules* for living, which may never be broken. These are principles. For those of us who have religious beliefs or who live in a culture based on a set of religious beliefs, we have to obey the teachings of that religion. These lay down rules for right and wrong behaviour. Christians and Muslims believe that Jesus and Muhammad both taught that life is sacred, that only God can create life and only God has the right to take it.

Therefore followers may argue that capital punishment, abortion and euthanasia are all, always, immoral.

> The technical term for this approach: deontological

2 By looking at the *outcome* of a decision and trying to achieve the outcome you believe to be desirable. For example, lying may be justified if it protects someone against an INJUSTICE. Humanists believe that human beings should be in control of their lives and that all actions should seek to have loving, caring outcomes. Therefore, they would argue, abortion can be justified if the

> The technical term for this approach: consequentialist

pregnant woman feels it would bring her peace of mind in a situation where she is distraught at being pregnant following a rape, or if she is very young.

There are difficulties with both approaches.

- In the first approach, does anyone have the right to decide that their rules or beliefs are more important than anyone else's?
- In the second approach, who decides which outcome is the most desirable? What is the timescale for deciding the 'final' outcome?

Very often, moral decisions involve choosing between options that are both undesirable. For example, if you are very poor and your child is hungry, you can face a choice between stealing some food, which you believe to be wrong, and letting your child suffer, which is also wrong.

ACTIVITIES

6 Why are followers of an organised religion unlikely to be consequentialists?

7 Which approach to reaching a moral decision would an atheist be more likely to adopt? Explain.

How do we learn right from wrong (our moral code)?

As with other norms of our culture, we learn what is right and wrong through the various agents of socialisation.

1 Initially, a child will learn from its parents and immediate family. This may be through the methods shown in the diagram below.

2 As we grow up, we are exposed to other agents of socialisation such as school, the mass media and peer groups. Often the messages about what is morally acceptable in that culture will tend to reinforce each other.

3 In multi-cultural societies, however, which are also multi-faith, people are exposed to conflicting messages. Cultural groups do not have the same unchallenged influence on their members.

4 PEER PRESSURE is a powerful force in all cultures. Peer pressure for teenagers is particularly strong. It is sometimes difficult to remember that the morality of an action is never decided by how many people approve of it.

Even if we are members of an organised religion with holy books to refer to, we still have to make moral decisions. This is particularly so in cases where only morally wrong alternatives seem available.

For example, you believe it is always wrong to tell lies and you also believe racism is wrong. What would you say to a violent racist who threatened you and asked you where a particular asylum seeker was hiding, if you knew where they were?

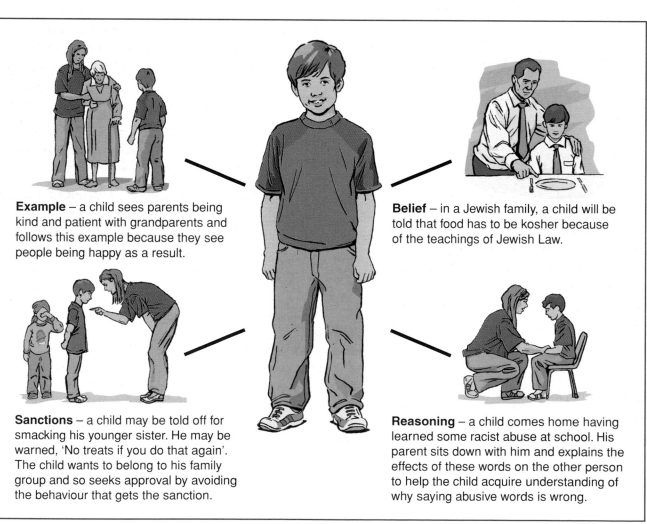

Example – a child sees parents being kind and patient with grandparents and follows this example because they see people being happy as a result.

Belief – in a Jewish family, a child will be told that food has to be kosher because of the teachings of Jewish Law.

Sanctions – a child may be told off for smacking his younger sister. He may be warned, 'No treats if you do that again'. The child wants to belong to his family group and so seeks approval by avoiding the behaviour that gets the sanction.

Reasoning – a child comes home having learned some racist abuse at school. His parent sits down with him and explains the effects of these words on the other person to help the child acquire understanding of why saying abusive words is wrong.

Four ways in which children may learn their 'moral code'.

How important is a shared moral code?

Our beliefs decide our morals and our morals decide our behaviour. If people in a culture develop widely different ETHICS, or moral codes, then even though they may share the same language and eat similar food, there will be little shared behaviour. So, a shared moral code is central to the survival of any culture because it underpins the behaviour of that culture. If behaviour is not shared then the people will not feel a common identity. The culture will break up and people will form into new groups that do share a moral code. There is a problem, however.

Why do we need to discuss moral issues?

We are living through a period of great cultural, technological and scientific change, both nationally and globally. This means we have to constantly rethink our ethics in new situations.

In other words, our cultures are under pressure to adapt. History teaches us what happens to cultures that fail to adapt. They die out. This means there is a need for discussion of different views. Many cultures have become democracies to allow these discussions to take place.

So cultures have both to allow for different views and try to keep their traditions. This is creating tensions within cultures around the world.

Until relatively recently, there was little interaction between people of different cultures. Armies were led by the rulers of one culture to fight the armies led by the rulers of another culture to sort out which culture controlled what. With few exceptions there was little contact apart from that. This allowed people to believe their ways were the only right ways. This is known as ETHNOCENTRISM.

Cultures were based on clear religious traditions and moral codes based on them were enforced ruthlessly by rulers and other leading figures who held power.

Cultural changes

Since then, there have been important cultural changes, which put more pressure on each one of us to think through our own moral decisions.

- The influence of the mass media has grown. This means there are more people and organisations influencing us.
- We are more aware of different, often conflicting, values in our own and others' cultures.
- Organised religions have a much more uneven influence on large sections of society (not just in the UK).

Technological and scientific changes

Human beings have not only developed the technology of the mass media, they have extended the scale on which we EXPLOIT NATURAL RESOURCES to the point where we are influencing the climate and ECOSYSTEMS of this planet.

Other technological and scientific advances enable human beings now to genetically modify crops, animals and humans, and extend life in ways that could not even be imagined 200 years ago.

These changes challenge us in two ways.

1 They place before us new moral questions: for example, should research into the cloning of human embryos be allowed?

2 They increasingly require internationally agreed decisions. A country can ban abortion but cannot prevent someone travelling to another country for an abortion where it is legal.

Can we rise to these challenges?

ACTIVITIES

8 Study page 34.
   a) Draw a diagram to show, with examples, the main ways you 'learned' your moral code.
   b) Were there any 'conflicting messages' abour right and wrong in your childhood?
   c) How did this affect you?

9 Why does a culture need a shared set of morals?

10 How has moral decision-making changed over the last 200 years?

Here is some guidance on researching the moral issue of euthanasia. The aim of the research is to:

- find out what arguments (or lines of reasoning) are used
- see how opponents of that view deal with each argument.

This is followed by a list of other moral issues that can be researched and debated in a similar way.

Possible research title

Why do people hold different views on whether euthanasia should be legalised?

Research this question and prepare to debate it formally according to your teacher's instructions.

Your research should:
- define key terms (for example, 'euthanasia', 'moral')
- explain what moral issue is raised by euthanasia (for example, sanctity of life, right to control own life)
- identify groups supporting different views
- explain the beliefs underlying the different views
- state and explain your conclusion.

Definitions

Those who argue in favour of the right to euthanasia have a different definition to those who argue against. Euthanasia has many definitions.

The Pro-Life Alliance defines it as:

'Any action or omission intended to end the life of a patient on the grounds that his or her life is not worth living.'

The Voluntary Euthanasia Society looks to the word's Greek origins – 'eu' and 'thanatos', which together mean 'a good death' – and says a modern definition is:

'A good death brought about by a doctor providing drugs or an injection to bring a peaceful end to the dying process.'

Different viewpoints

Some arguments used when discussing whether euthanasia is immoral include the following:

a) Patients can recover after being 'written off' by doctors.

b) It can quickly and humanely end a patient's suffering.

c) Life is a gift from God. It is sacrosanct. Only God can take it away.

d) Old people might feel they are a nuisance to others ('in the way') and so choose this course of action without really wanting to.

e) It can help reduce the grief and suffering of the patient's loved ones.

f) Everyone should have the right to decide when and how they should die.

g) It would change the role of a doctor.

h) A patient may not be able to make a rational decision, or might change their mind and not be able to communicate this.

i) It would help all concerned if a decision could be made before the individual entered the very last stage of suffering.

j) It would help others to face death if they realised they could die with dignity.

k) If it became legal in principle, it would be the thin end of the wedge.

l) There are now many painkilling drugs that can relieve suffering.

m) If the law were changed, doctors could legally act on a patient's desire to die without further suffering.

Investigation

1 a) Sort the arguments in the speech bubbles above into those supporting euthanasia and those against.

When sorting out the arguments, be aware that it is possible to argue that a person has the right to make a certain decision but not support the decision he/she actually makes.

b) Now carry out further research to find out more about these arguments and others for or against euthanasia.

Alongside each argument, note any key terms you find as a result of your research such as:

- sanctity of life,
- human rights,
- doctors' Hippocratic Oath,
- palliative care,
- suffering,
- right to dignity,
- humanist.

There are some very good books and websites to support this research. Seek guidance from your teacher. Keep an exact record of all the sources you have used: website addresses, authors, book titles.

c) Develop your research by identifying conflicting beliefs and attitudes. Find quotations from books, or speeches the various groups for and against use to back up their views. Websites for various religious groups can also be a useful source. Draw a flow diagram that links attitudes concerning the moral issue to the underlying beliefs and to the evidence/ quotes used to back this up.

d) Reflect on your research and consider possible conclusions. Make sure the conclusion you decide on follows logically from the evidence and analysis you have put forward.

Examples of other moral issues for research and debate

- **Abortion**: should women have the right to terminate a pregnancy?
- **Animal experiments**: can experimenting on animals be justified?
- **Arranged marriage**: should parents have the right to arrange a marriage for their children?
- **Asylum seekers**: is it immoral to turn away an asylum seeker?
- **Boxing**: can a fight industry be justified?
- **Bullfighting**: is killing bulls for entertainment morally acceptable?
- **Capital punishment**: is the taking of someone's life as a punishment morally justifiable?
- **Divorce**: should married couples have the right to separate?
- **Euthanasia**: should a person who is terminally ill have the right to help in ending their life?
- **Genetic medicine**: is genetic engineering wrong?
- **Global warming**: is it immoral of the USA not to sign up to the Kyoto Protocol?
- **Human cloning**: should research into the cloning of human embryos be allowed?
- **The law**: is breaking the law always wrong?
- **Lying**: is lying always wrong?
- **Plastic surgery**: is plastic surgery on the NHS morally justified?
- **Poverty**: is it immoral to allow millions to starve when there is more than enough food in the world to feed everyone?
- **Recreational drugs**: is the use of recreational drugs wrong?
- **School uniform**: is the requirement to wear school uniform a moral issue?
- **War**: can war be morally justified?
- **Xenotransplatation**: is the transplanting of a pig's liver into a human immoral?

2.1 What is conflict?

- What does 'CONFLICT' mean?
- Why does conflict occur?
- What are the effects of conflict?

This topic should help you understand what conflict is and that there are different types and a range of causes and effects of conflict.

ACTIVITY

1 Look at the picture above. List the different types of conflict it shows and, in groups, brainstorm the ideas and feelings you associate with conflict.

Conflict is the struggle between two or more opposing forces, ideas or interests. For many people, 'conflict' means 'violence'. In the activity above, the ideas and feelings you came up with may have been centred around images of violence – beatings, killings, guns, war, etc. However, although conflict is inevitable when people have different VALUES, ATTITUDES or BELIEFS, it is important to understand that not all conflict results in violence. Conflict only explodes into violence if it is not dealt with constructively.

Violence is a LEARNED RESPONSE to conflict, so, if violence can be learned, other responses are possible and can be learned as well.

At the root of all conflict is the attempt by people to achieve MUTUALLY EXCLUSIVE goals. A simple example would be a brother and sister arguing because they want to watch different TV programmes at the same time. How many ways of resolving this conflict can you think of?

Conflict affects everybody at some time in their lives. It may affect you in your FAMILY, at school, at work or in your social life. Man has been in conflict with his fellow man since time began. Competing for food was probably the cause of the earliest conflict between individuals. Soon after, when Early Man started living in groups (see Topic 1.2, pages 4–5), the conflict simply occurred on a larger scale.

Types of conflict

Conflict can occur at an individual or group level. Examples of this might be bullying (see Topic 2.3, pages 48–49), disputes between neighbours, and disputes over local issues. These can be referred to as SMALL-SCALE CONFLICTS because they do not affect a large number of people but cause conflict within the COMMUNITY.

Conflicts also occur at a national or international level. These can be referred to as large-scale conflicts as they affect a large number of people. Examples of conflict at a national level are the Civil Rights Movement in the USA (see Topic 2.4, pages 50–60) and the conflict in Northern Ireland.

Conflict at an international level involves disputes between different countries, so examples of this would be the two World Wars, the COLD WAR, the Vietnam War (see Topic 2.5, pages 61–69) and the Gulf Wars. The development of weapons of mass destruction (WMDs) has meant that human conflict on an international level, if not managed carefully, has the potential to destroy the world we live in.

Causes of conflict

Some causes of conflict are long-term (going back many years) and some short-term (more recent or immediate). These causes are often linked. For example, the long-term causes of the First World War (1914–18) can be traced back to the system of alliances set up in the nineteenth century. These alliances became suspicious of each other and so began to build up armaments. However, it needed a short-term cause, the assassination of the heir to the throne of the Austrian empire in Serbia, in 1914, to trigger Austria to declare war on Serbia, which caused the alliance system to kick in and bring Britain, France and Russia into war with Germany and Austria-Hungary.

Causes of small-scale conflict

Although not all conflicts have the same cause, the causes of small-scale or large-scale conflicts can be put into the same categories:

• Religious
• Political
• Economic
• Social
• MORAL

Some small-scale conflicts, such as divorce, might have more than one cause. Although few divorces will have all the causes described in Source A, many will have more than one of them.

Source A

Cause	Example: divorce
Religious	If partners are of different religions, it may cause tension on important decisions.
Political	Family 'politics' may mean one partner is overpowering.
Economic	Debt and financial worries can cause tension and are often a cause of divorce.
Social	Partners from different backgrounds – upbringing, class, culture – may have irreconcilable differences in their values.
Moral	One partner considers the other's behaviour wrong, e.g. adultery.

ACTIVITIES

A MUSLIM STUDENT IN DISPUTE WITH SCHOOL OVER RIGHT TO WEAR HIJAB

Firemen on strike over pay and conditions

PENSIONERS CLAIM THEY HAVE BEEN CHEATED OVER PENSIONS

Villagers up in arms about traveller camp – say crime and litter will increase

MOTHER TAKES HOSPITAL TO COURT TO ALLOW HER SICK BABY THE RIGHT TO LIFE

2 In pairs, using the causes listed in Source A, decide what was the cause of each of the conflicts described in the newspaper headlines above.

3 Choose another small-scale conflict – for example, someone taking their employer to court for unfair dismissal – and create a table similar to that in Source A. You may not be able to fill in all of the different causes, depending on what conflict you choose to use.

Causes of large-scale conflict

Causes of conflict at a national and international level can be split into the same categories as those for small-scale conflict. The following case study on the Palestine–Israeli conflict illustrates this.

Case Study
The Palestine–Israeli conflict

Over 2,000 years ago Jews and Arabs lived together in Palestine. However, when the Romans conquered the land they forced most of the Jews to flee to Europe and elsewhere. This was called the Diaspora. This meant that the Jewish people had no country to call their own. They were made to feel unwelcome in most of Europe, which had become Christian and hostile to Jews. Persecution continued into the nineteenth and twentieth centuries (see Topic 5.4, pages 143–47).

So, at the end of the nineteenth century, a campaign was launched in Europe to establish a homeland controlled and run by Jews. Supporters of a homeland were known as Zionists.

At the beginning of the twentieth century, some Jews began to return to Palestine, their original home. In 1948, the United Nations (UN) decided that Palestine should be divided into two states – one for Palestinians and one for the Jews (named Israel). The Palestinians could not accept the loss of their land and conflict has ensued since then. The diagram below suggests some causes of this conflict.

1. By the end of the nineteenth century we were fed up of being treated as outsiders. We suffered discrimination and persecution in Europe and, in the middle of the twentieth century, the Holocaust made it clear we had no future in Europe.

2. In 1916 the British Government made a clear commitment to support our cause: independence for us from the oppression of the Turks (the old Ottoman Empire). It was this commitment that won us over to support the British in the First World War.

3. The UN's proposal to partition Palestine in 1948 was not a perfect plan – but it was a start. We have simply built on this. We shall never give in to terrorists who are our enemy.

4. Jerusalem is our holy city. They have no right to take it from us.

10. We want to be independent so that we can create our own wealth.

9. The British government made a clear commitment in 1917 that it would help us establish our own country in our promised land.

8. In our holy book, the Torah, it makes it clear that we are God's chosen people and that this land is rightly our land – it is the 'promised land'.

7. We have a right to our country. We have lived here continuously for thousands of years. At first we had no problem with a few refugees. But when they came in larger numbers, intent on taking over our land, we had to resist.

6. The UN's proposal to partition Palestine was unfair. The US president, who depended on the Jewish vote in the US for his election, dictated it. We shall never surrender whilst our land is occupied and we live as refugees.

5. Jerusalem is our holy city. It belongs to us.

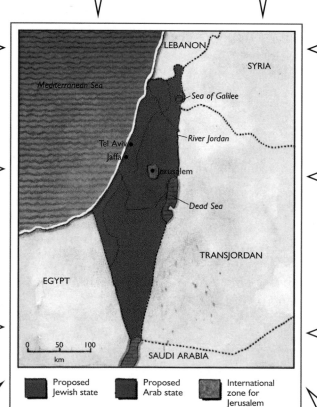

The UN partition plan. What problems might you expect in a state which is divided into three parts?

Effects of conflict

The consequences of conflict can also be short term or long term and can be classified in the same way as the causes. They can affect individuals, groups or states. A short-term effect of most wars is death and destruction, whilst a long-term effect might be growing hatred. Sometimes an effect of a conflict can also be a cause of prolonging that conflict or starting another one. For example, the Treaty of Versailles, which was the peace settlement following the First World War, caused resentment in Germany and became one of the long-term causes of the Second World War.

The conflict in Northern Ireland makes an excellent case study of the effects of national conflict.

Case Study
Conflict in Northern Ireland

In 1801, the Act of Union joined England and Ireland and led the Irish to demand Home Rule. This meant they wanted to run the home affairs of Ireland themselves. This was not granted, so at the beginning of the twentieth century many of the Irish began to demand independence. A COMPROMISE solution was reached in 1921. A Catholic REPUBLIC was established with its capital in Dublin, while Protestant Ulster (Northern Ireland) remained part of the UK.

In the 1960s, the Catholic minority in Ulster complained of DISCRIMINATION while an IRA bombing campaign started in support of a united Ireland. The Protestants feared being ruled by a Catholic majority so their MILITANT EXTREMISTS retaliated with violence. In 1998, the Good Friday agreement was signed. This has provided Northern Ireland's divided SOCIETY with a political framework to resolve its differences.

The conflict had a number of different effects – as can be seen in Source B.

Source B

Effect of conflict	Example: conflict in Northern Ireland
Religious	Some Roman Catholics and Protestants are reluctant to live and work together. Most schools remain segregated.
Political	Direct rule from England.
Economic	Lack of investment in Belfast because of bombing of businesses. Increase in taxation to pay for army in Northern Ireland.
Social	Communities destroyed by bombing, for example, in Enniskillen. Young people turning to drugs because of fear and disillusionment.
Moral	Condemnation of British government by other nations. Loss of support for IRA because of bombing campaigns on mainland Britain.

ACTIVITIES

4 Study the speech bubbles opposite.
  a) In groups decide what type of cause of the Palestine–Israeli conflict is suggested in each bubble. Some bubbles may suggest more than one cause. Record the results of your discussion in a table like the one below.

Cause of conflict	Example
Religious	Speech bubble 4
Political	
Economic	
Social	
Moral	

  b) Discuss which are Israeli and which are Palestinian supporters. Give reasons.

  c) Can one cause be said to be more important than another? Explain your views.

5 Copy and complete the table below about the effects of a small-scale conflict. Remember, effects can become causes of further conflict.

Effect of conflict	Example: divorce
Religious	'Until death us do part.' The difficulty of remarriage in some religions.
Political	
Economic	
Social	
Moral	

6 Choose one effect of divorce from Source A and suggest what this, in turn, might cause.

2.2 How can conflict be resolved?

- What is CO-OPERATION?
- How can individuals, groups, nations and international organisations play a ROLE in resolving conflict?

This topic looks at ways of resolving conflict to achieve co-operation and should help you realise that you have choices in the ways you respond to and manage conflict through developing negotiation and problem-solving skills.

Source A

'THE TWO MULES'

CO-OPERATION
IS BETTER THAN CONFLICT

ACTIVITIES

1 What do you think the message of Source A is?

2 Look at the six steps of problem solving. How might this method have worked in resolving one of the conflicts studied in Topic 2.1 (pages 38–41)?

The resolution of a conflict requires the underlying causes to be addressed. There has to be some form of co-operation. This means acting or working together with others to achieve a common goal. Talking to each other is a good starting point. A meeting allows both sides to put over their point of view and to NEGOTIATE. One way of resolving a conflict is the six-step solution.

Six-step problem solving
1 Identify each side's needs.
2 Define the problem.
3 Brainstorm solutions.
4 Evaluate solutions.
5 Decide on best solution and try it.
6 Check how things turn out.

Methods of resolving conflict

Sometimes it is necessary for an INTERMEDIARY or third party to become involved. For instance, a couple might try to save their marriage by going to a counsellor; a dispute at work could be taken to an INDUSTRIAL TRIBUNAL. The third party is, however, unlikely to succeed without some give and take on behalf of those involved in the conflict. In other words, MEDIATION has to lead to compromise.

In some disputes, there is no obvious third party to refer to, so it might be necessary to approach someone or some organisation that both sides respect, for example, the Church. In other instances, there are obvious places to go for ARBITRATION, for example, ACAS (Advisory, Conciliation and Arbitration Service). This is an organisation that hears both sides of an industrial dispute and decides the outcome, such as the 2003 fire officers' strike.

When all else fails, force or punishment might have to be used. For example, a student might have to be excluded, a worker might be sacked, or a persistent offender might be imprisoned.

Sometimes people on the same side in a conflict might have different views on how it should be resolved. Martin Luther King was a great believer in PACIFISM during the Civil Rights Movement in the USA, while Malcolm X preferred to resort to more direct and extreme methods (see Topic 2.4, pages 50–60).

Just like individuals or groups, nations also have to seek to end conflict, often using a variety of methods. The methods in Source B (opposite) can have negative as well as positive outcomes, illustrating the complexity of resolving conflict.

Methods	Examples and comments
Appeasement	In 1939, the British Prime Minister, Neville Chamberlain, thought that he had guaranteed 'peace in our time' at Munich by getting Hitler to make a written promise not to seize more land. But his policy of appeasement failed to prevent the Second World War.
Force	In Afghanistan, in 2002, and Iraq, in 2003/4, the US President, George Bush, preferred force as an instrument to ultimately end terrorism. This does not seem to have worked in the short term, but it might be too early to judge. Certainly, in the Second World War, the use of force was important in saving democracy from fascism.
Protest	Greenpeace activists scaled Big Ben as part of a non-violent protest against the war in Iraq. This protest was completely ignored by the governments involved. However, protest can work – for example, Gandhi's methods of peaceful demonstrations gained independence for India from the British Empire in 1947.
Sanctions	Sanctions against Iraq, Cuba and Libya by various Western governments have failed to make them change their ways. These sometimes make the country more determined while denying food and medicine to millions of innocent people. On the other hand, the use of sanctions against South Africa helped bring an end to apartheid.
Deterrent	Building up weapons as a deterrent is sometimes seen as making conflict less likely. For example, Pakistan and India have both developed nuclear weapons and know that if they went to war they could both completely destroy each other. This makes the decision to go to war less likely.
Improving links	In India and Pakistan, an agreement was made in 2004, after nearly 50 years of non-contact, to play test cricket against each other in an attempt to ease tension.
International co-operation	Undoubtedly the greatest attempt to resolve conflict in the last 50 years has been the setting up of the UN in 1945. The UN is an international organisation, which attempts to resolve conflict and problems throughout the world.

ACTIVITY

3 a) List the methods of resolving conflict in Source B and give each a rating out of 10 (with 10 being very effective and 1 being least effective).

b) Discuss your ratings and the strengths and weaknesses of each method in groups.

c) In your group, decide on which you think is the most and the least effective.

d) Feed back to the class with your reasons and listen to the other groups' reasons for their choice.

e) Take a class vote on which you think is the most effective and least effective.

Investigation

Carry out an investigation into how the UN or one of its agencies attempts to resolve conflict.

The UN

Formed after the Second World War, the UN aims to:

- maintain international peace and security
- develop friendly relations amongst nations
- achieve international CO-OPERATION
- encourage respect for human rights and fundamental freedoms.

As well as sending peacekeeping forces to troubled areas, it tries to get rid of the causes of conflict through the work of its many agencies like the WORLD HEALTH ORGANISATION (WHO), the UN Children's Fund (UNICEF), the UN Development Program (UNDP), the Commissioners for Refugees (UNHCR) and Human Rights (UNCFHR), and its Education Program (UNESCO).

2 CONFLICT AND CO-OPERATION

2.3 How are small-scale conflicts caused and resolved?

- Why is bullying a good example of small-scale conflict?
- What are the different causes and effects of bullying?
- How does bullying deny people their rights as an individual?
- What methods can be used to resolve bullying and how successful are they?

The next topic takes the case study of bullying to give you an understanding of the causes and effects of small-scale conflict and how they can be resolved. It starts by looking at how bullying is caused and how it results in denying the victims of bullying their basic rights and freedoms. It should help you understand that the effects of small-scale conflict can be harmful and that there are ways to resolve conflict that can be successful in achieving co-operation.

Case Study
Bullying

ACTIVITY

1 Look at the text message above and discuss in groups how bullying has changed in the twenty-first century. Has modern TECHNOLOGY made it easier to bully?

What is bullying?

Bullying is any BEHAVIOUR that deliberately upsets, threatens or hurts another person. It is a good example of conflict between individuals as well as conflict within the community where it is taking place, such as school or work. Like most small-scale conflicts it is caused by intolerance, INJUSTICE and CONFRONTATION (see Topic 2.1, page 39). It results in the basic rights and freedoms individuals have in society, such as peace, education and beliefs, being denied in some way.

There are different types of bullying. These are:

- physical – violence (for example, punching, kicking), stealing (for example, sweets or money)
- verbal – teasing, name-calling, racist or sexual remarks
- emotional – socially isolating people (for example, leaving people out, the 'silent treatment'), spreading rumours, dirty looks.

Types of bullying change with age: playground bullying, sexual HARASSMENT, gang attacks, date violence, assault, marital violence, child abuse, workplace harassment and abuse in care homes are all examples of bullying that can take place throughout different stages of life and in different communities.

Reasons for bullying

People become bullies for a variety of reasons. These can include:

- poor discipline at home – children are not taught what is right or wrong
- abuse or lack of love at home – bullies have often been bullied themselves
- a sense of failure at school or work – bullies take out their frustration on others
- a sense of power and success – bullies are often good at what they do and so do not want to stop
- PEER PRESSURE – some people simply join in because their friends do it or because they are afraid if they do not they will be bullied themselves.

Anyone can be bullied, but some are more likely victims than others:

- those who are different (in race, RELIGION, size or shape, ability)
- those who lack friends or are shy
- those who come from an over-protective family ENVIRONMENT.

Source A

Source A

Holes

This source is an extract from a novel called *Holes* by Louis Sachar.

Stanley didn't have any friends at home. He was overweight and the kids often teased him about his size. Even his teachers sometimes made cruel comments without realising it. On his last day of school, his maths teacher, Mrs Bell, taught ratios. As an example, she chose the heaviest kid in the class and the lightest, and had them weigh themselves. Stanley weighed three times as much as the other boy. Mrs Bell wrote the ratio on the board, 3:1, unaware of how much embarrassment she had caused them both.

A bully named Derrick Dunne also used to torment Stanley. The teachers never took Stanley's complaints seriously because Derrick was so much smaller than Stanley. Some teachers even seemed to find it amusing that a little kid like Derrick could pick on somebody as big as Stanley.

Source B

Confessions of a victim

At first I was called nicknames. After the nicknames came laughter – not particularly disruptive – when I answered questions in class. Small things, but relentless enough to be classified as PERSECUTION. I never told my parents I was bullied because it would have upset them, and they might have changed my school. And I had a feeling that it was me, not the school, at fault, and that it would be the same wherever I went … I started to have my back spat on, and became used to finding globules of spit in my hair if the aim was bad.

Sunday Telegraph, 1999

Source C

'Bully genes'

A recent study suggests that people who bully others are likely to have children who are also bullies. The aggression of a bully is likely to be inherited from 'bully GENES'. The findings suggest that a tendency to bully is about 60 per cent influenced by genes and 40 per cent by upbringing and environment.

Daily Telegraph, 1999

ACTIVITIES

2 What two surprising facts can you learn about bullies from Source A?

3 What do you think is meant by the following statements? How do they explain why some children become bullies?

- Bullying is a way of refusing to become invisible.
- Children fear, despise and refuse to tolerate non-conformity.
- Power is the ability to make other people suffer.

4 Look at Source C and discuss with your group whether children are more likely to inherit aggression than to acquire it from their upbringing and environment.

5 Look at Source B. What types of bullying does the victim experience? Discuss what she could have done differently in response to being bullied.

2 CONFLICT AND CO-OPERATION

Effects of bullying

ACTIVITY

6 One of the main effects of conflict is that it denies certain rights and freedoms that all individuals are entitled to under the HUMAN RIGHTS ACT. This applies to small-scale conflict such as bullying, as well as to large-scale conflict. Look at the list below of some basic rights and freedoms for children, as outlined in the UN CONVENTION ON THE RIGHTS OF THE CHILD. Discuss which rights you think bullying denies and how it does this.

- Life
- Privacy
- Protection from being hurt, violence, abuse and neglect
- The best health possible and access to medical care
- Help from the government if you are poor or in need
- A good enough standard of living to develop properly
- Education
- Use your own language and practise your own CULTURE and religion
- Play and free time
- Protection from work that is bad for your health or education.

Bullying should be challenged because it has a harmful effect on its victims. Some of the main effects on victims are:

- safety – they can be injured and property destroyed
- well-being – their lives are made miserable; they can lose their SELF-ESTEEM and self-confidence; some blame themselves; some cannot sleep and become depressed; some commit suicide
- educational progress – they cannot concentrate on their work and so their learning suffers; many are afraid to go to school and so play truant.

Bullying also affects the reputation of the community in which it takes place. For example, a school or workplace needs to be seen as effective and caring through policy and action. If it is not dealt with, bullying can provide a model for bad behaviour – if bullies are allowed to get away with it, others are encouraged to bully. Not doing anything can be taken as condoning bullying. It is therefore important that something should be done to stop bullying, wherever it occurs.

Bullying does not only have a profound effect on its victims but also on those who care for them. Some of the sources below and opposite illustrate this.

Source D

I'm the King of the Castle

In the novel *I'm the King of the Castle*, by Susan Hill, Charles Kingshaw and his mother are forced to move to live in an ugly, isolated Victorian house with Joseph Hooper and his son Edmund. To young Edmund, Charles is an intruder, a boy to be persecuted. On his arrival at his new home, Edmund passes him a note – 'I didn't want you to come here.' The rest of the novel concentrates on the bullying of Charles. This extract describes the tragic end to the story.

Kingshaw took all his clothes off by the stream and folded them in a pile. He shivered and the water was very cold, silky, against his body. For a second, he hesitated, part of his mind starting to come awake. And then he thought of everything, of what else would happen, he thought of the things that Hooper had done and what he was going to do ... and the wedding of his mother. He began to splash and stumble forwards, into the middle of the stream, where the water was deepest. When it had reached up to his thighs, he lay down slowly and put his face into it and breathed in a long careful breath.

It was Hooper who found him ... When he saw Kingshaw's body upside down in the water, he thought suddenly, it was because of me, and a spurt of triumph went through him.

Source E

Report of a court case in 2002

A schoolgirl broke into the house of an alleged bully and repeatedly stabbed her in the head. The victim, 14, woke up and screamed out to her mother, who rushed into the bedroom to see a figure standing over the bed, screaming, 'You have ruined my life.'

The mother intervened and pushed her daughter's attacker to the floor. The victim needed 14 stitches for wounds to her head.

Adapted from *The Times*, 2002

Source F

Suicide

A 13-year-old schoolgirl from South Wales took a fatal overdose to escape being bullied at her comprehensive school. Her treatment made her feel 'ugly and worthless'. She left a note saying that she wanted to die rather than walk through the school gates.

The Times, 2004

Source G

Confessions of a victim

My bullying went on for four years non-stop. I practically lost the faculty of speech and put on weight. My shyness became so severe it was almost a medical condition.

Sunday Telegraph, 1999

Source H

Crime statistics

Five deaths have occurred as a result of fights in school in just over a decade:

- a 16-year-old boy who suffered brain damage during a playground fight in a Gateshead comprehensive in 1998
- a 15-year-old boy knifed in London in a lunch-break row
- a 12-year-old boy who died in another London playground fight
- a 14-year-old boy who was stabbed in the corridor of a Lincolnshire school.

Source I

Bully Cycle from *A Study in Child Development*

1 Students who are bullied frequently are more likely to develop depression or antisocial behaviour, which in turn makes them more likely to attract further bullying.

2 People who bully others are likely to have children who are also bullies.

ACTIVITIES

7 Study Source D. What effect did the events described have on the bully? How might this explain why bullying takes place?

8 How does the reaction of the victim of bullying in Source E differ from that in Sources F and G?

9 Write a letter to a newspaper explaining why it is important to stop bullying from happening using the sources and the information above and opposite.

10 Draw a poster for your school to help prevent bullying.

Bullying – resolving conflict

Source J

Janet Clare was in her kitchen when she overheard her daughter and friends saying unpleasant things and telling stories, which showed they had been needling a particular girl. When the others had gone, she confronted her daughter. She said, 'I would feel horrible if people were saying those things about me. How would you feel?' Her daughter said nothing, just looked down at the table. But then, a few months later, she announced suddenly, 'I used to be a bully. But I stopped doing it because you said something.'

The Times, 2004

ACTIVITY

11 Look at Source J. This shows how a parent can help stop bullying. In groups, discuss how you as students can help stop bullying.

Not all scenarios are so easily resolved as in Source J, but both at school and at work attempts have been made to deal with the problem of bullying. The diagram will help you understand different methods that could be used to resolve small-scale conflict.

Bullying in school

Most schools now have an official policy on bullying, although many do not like to admit that the problem exists. There is also the danger that highlighting or talking about bullying might encourage it.

1. Exclusion
Bullies are removed to special centres for problem children. Such centres are not popular with local residents.

2. Assertiveness training
Teaching students how to leave a bullying situation and get support from bystanders. Attempting to boost their SELF-ESTEEM.

3. Quality circles (qc)
This idea comes from industry where discussion circles are used. This encourages students to discuss and come up with their own solutions to bullying by:

• Identifying the problem.
• Analysing the problem – considering possible causes and establishing the extent of the problem by collecting data through surveys, interviews or observations.
• Developing a solution – such as improved supervision, a playground development plan to get rid of danger areas, drama to raise awareness, activities at lunchtime to avoid boredom (a known cause of bullying).
• Presenting the solution to the school management.
• Reviewing the solution – the solution is tried and evaluation takes place to see if it worked.

4. Student mediators
Training students in basic MEDIATION TECHNIQUES, such as listening to both sides, showing no bias, and asking the warring students to come up with their own solution to their argument. The 'peacemakers' then mediate, rather formally, over a school desk. The idea is that peer pressure can be used to reduce conflict and bullying rather than persuading bullied students to go to the teachers for help, as this risks further harassment for 'telling tales'.

7. Surveillance
The use of CCTV to catch and deter bullies.

6. Behaviour management
Students are taught to understand and control their emotions. Disruptive students are helped to channel their anger and aggression into positive relationships and more effective learning. Schools that teach this claim that students are less stressed, achieve better results, possess better INTERPERSONAL SKILLS and can 'manage conflicts'.

5. 'No blame' approach
Under this system no one is blamed or punished. Instead, with their teachers' help, the children work out solutions. This approach works on the idea that bullying is normal human behaviour. The bully is not labelled as a bully, but seen as simply a person whose behaviour needs to be changed. KIDSCAPE, the anti-bullying charity, believes that the method will produce a generation of violent louts which takes no responsibility for the consequences of its actions.

Some of the methods used by schools to resolve the problem of bullying. Which of the methods listed here do you think would be most effective?

Luke Walmsley was stabbed and killed by a school bully in November 2003.

Bullying at work

In the past, victims of bullying at work have gone to industrial tribunals or court. But this involves asking people to go through a legal process that could be damaging to them emotionally. Recently, some firms have set up harassment advice services. Staff are invited to ring a hotline if they feel they are being bullied. An adviser then organises a face-to-face meeting. Some trade unions are also promoting the idea of independent OMBUDSMEN to handle unresolved complaints.

Source K

Code of advice

The website Bully OnLine has the following advice for someone being bullied at work.

- Recognise that you are being bullied.
- Realise that it is not your fault.
- Tell the bully that his/her actions are unacceptable.
- Inform your manager/personnel department.
- Keep a diary of what happens.
- Keep copies of letters, memos, emails.
- Build a support network (friends, family).
- See your doctor if the bullying causes you stress.
- Record a formal grievance.

ACTIVITIES

12 List all the methods 1–7 given in the diagram opposite in rank order according to how you think they would work. Give a mark out of 10 for each method.

13 Choose one of the methods 1–7 and list all its advantages and disadvantages.

14 Develop a code of advice, like the one in Source K, for a victim of bullying at school.

15 Design your own website for victims of bullying.

16 Having looked at all the evidence in this topic (pages 44–49), explain why you think it is difficult to find a perfect solution to the problem of bullying.

2.4 *What are the causes and effects of national conflict?*

- How can the causes and effects of conflict affect individuals, groups and societies?
- What were the causes and effects of the struggle for civil rights in the USA?

In this topic, the case study of the struggle for civil rights in the USA is used to investigate the different causes of national conflict – both long term and short term.

It then goes on to look at the variety of effects this conflict had on the individuals involved as well as society as a whole.

Case Study
The struggle for civil rights in the USA in the 1950s and 1960s

1 Causes of the struggle

Source A

Extract from the American Declaration of Independence, 1776
All men are created equal. God gave all men life, freedom and the right to be happy.

ACTIVITIES

1 The UK CONSTITUTION holds the same values as those in Source A. In groups, discuss:
   - the ways in which we are all equal and free
   - the ways in which we are not all equal and free.

2 Read Sources A and B and the information on pages 50–51. List the causes of the conflict that developed between black and white Americans in the 1950s. Try to arrange these into long-term and short-term causes. What was the spark that ignited the conflict?

Source B

From a speech by Martin Luther King, Washington DC, 1963
I have a dream that one day this nation will rise up and live out the true meaning of its creed … that all men are created equal.

When we let freedom ring … we will be able to speed up that day when all of God's children, black men and white men, Jews and Gentiles, Protestants and Catholics, will be able to join hands and sing in the words of the old Negro spiritual, 'Free at last! Free at last! Thank God Almighty, we are free at last!'

Martin Luther King's speech in Source B was delivered only about 40 years ago. His campaign for civil rights helped make life much better for black Americans.

More than 200 years of discrimination was behind this campaign. In spite of the abolition of slavery in 1863 and amendments to the Constitution granting equal status, blacks in the southern states of the USA were deprived of their rights in the following ways:

- *politically* – STATE LAWS devised 'qualifications' for voting, which were carefully designed to exclude blacks. For example, they had to own property or be able to write
- *economically* – blacks were given the worst jobs with poor pay, or were unemployed. This inevitably meant they lived in the worst houses in the worst areas
- *socially* – some STATE GOVERNMENTS in the 1890s imposed complete racial segregation through the so-called 'Jim Crow' laws (see photo opposite), covering every area of life. For example, black people had their own schools, entrances to cinemas, waiting rooms at stations.

Source C

Michael Howard, Conservative politician

In 1963 I toured the USA. There was no official segregation on the buses but it was taken for granted that white people sat at the front and blacks at the back. In Mississippi, I deliberately sat at the back next to a black teacher. When the bus stopped for a break, I suggested we got out for a cup of coffee. The teacher said, 'We can't have a cup of coffee together.' I said, 'That's ridiculous! If you can't come and have a coffee in a place reserved for whites, I'll come and have a coffee in a place where you can go!' He said, 'They'll put you in jail.' I couldn't believe that that happened in my lifetime.

The Times, 2001

The government in Washington allowed this to happen, as it was reluctant to confront the southern politicians who strongly argued for individual states to govern themselves rather than central FEDERAL GOVERNMENT to impose laws to say how states should be run. The complex system of government and laws in the USA made intervention by central government difficult.

ACTIVITY

3 Read Source C and the information on pages 50–52.

a) What is segregation? Make a list of the ways blacks and whites were SEGREGATED.

b) Apart from segregation, in what other ways were black Americans deprived of their civil rights?

Jim Crow was a musical character in the theatre in the 1870s who dressed in rags and blacked up his face and made fun of black people. He came to represent the white view of blacks and his name was given to the segregation laws.

The Real History of Jim Crow.

"Him so werry scientific
Him go down to L below
And ebbery one who hear him
Dance & jump Jim Crow."

(Moncrieff's Comic Songs)

Discrimination continues

Blacks in the northern states of the USA were also discriminated against. They were forced to live in GHETTOES, suffered segregation and persecution. In 1919, a black teenager was stoned to death in Chicago for swimming in a 'whites only' part of a lake. This incident set off a race riot that lasted a week.

During the Second World War (1939–45), many blacks joined the US forces and played a significant part in the Allied victory. After the war they expected change – they had been fighting for freedom abroad and so were no longer prepared to remain second-class citizens in their own country. Many left the south and moved to the industrial towns of the north. They hoped to share in the economic boom of the 1950s, but many failed to get jobs and were living below the poverty line. The unemployment rate for non-whites was always almost double the national rate. They were becoming disenchanted and impatient.

In December 1955, Rosa Parks was arrested for refusing to give up her seat on a bus in Montgomery, Alabama. Martin Luther King, a local Baptist preacher, organised a protest that involved a bus boycott by black people. This demand for integration (mixing) of the races on public transport was the beginning of the campaign for equal civil rights in the USA.

Civil right activist Rosa Parks.

Rosa Parks got on a bus after work in a department store. Feeling tired she sat down in the black section. A few stops later when the bus was full, the driver told her to give up her seat to a white man. Her feet were hurting and feeling humiliated once too often she refused to get up. The police were called and she was arrested for defying the local bus segregation law. She was later fined $14.

Source D

A graph showing illiteracy as a percentage of the American population

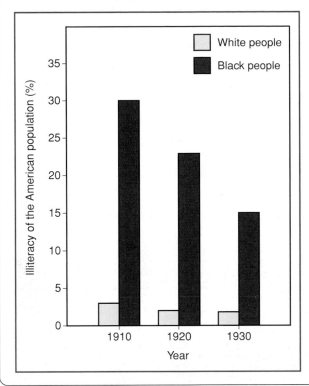

Source E

Extract from the KKK 'bible'

Are you a native born, white, gentile American? Do you believe in and will you faithfully strive for the eternal maintenance of white supremacy?

Ku Klux Klan members. What influence might they have had on the child's socialisation?

ACTIVITIES

4 Look at the graph in Source D. It shows that many more blacks than whites were illiterate. Discuss how this contributed to maintaining segregation.

5 Use Source E and the information box and photo on page 51 to answer the following questions.
  a) Why did so many people join the KKK?
  b) What appeal would the uniform and ceremonial aspect have to these people?
  c) Why did the federal government fail to stop the KKK?

6 Imagine you are a black teenager in Montgomery in 1955. Write a diary for one week describing your experiences. (You could mention cases of discrimination, segregation and persecution and explain how you might feel towards white Americans there.)

The Ku Klux Klan (KKK)

The original KKK was set up in 1866 to persecute black Americans recently freed from slavery. In the 1920s, WASP Americans (white, Anglo-Saxon, Protestants) felt threatened by non-WASP immigration. This led to a revival of the Klan. They not only attacked blacks but also Roman Catholics, Jews and all foreigners. By 1924 there were four million members, including judges, local officials, politicians, police officers and business people. Most supporters were ignorant, southern whites, who believed that they were defending the American way of life against all kinds of enemies. The rituals and uniform brought a sense of purpose and excitement to their lives. Some of their actions included LYNCHING blacks, burning crosses and firebombing homes and churches.

2 Effects of the struggle

Supreme Court rulings

The Civil Rights Movement took off in the 1950s, but long before Martin Luther King there had been a campaign for equality for blacks. The National Association for the Advancement of Coloured People (NAACP) had been set up in 1905. Unfortunately, it had very little success until 1954, when the SUPREME COURT finally accepted that segregated schools were UNCONSTITUTIONAL and directed local authorities to desegregate them. In 1956, following Martin Luther King's bus boycott, the Supreme Court decided that the Alabama bus laws were illegal. In the same year, King was elected president of NAACP.

Many southern whites ignored these rulings. In September 1957, the State Governor used the NATIONAL GUARD to prevent nine black students from enrolling for the Central High School in Little Rock, Arkansas. The president had to send 1000 federal paratroopers to ensure they got in. There was violence on a large scale as the white community fought to preserve its way of life.

It was obvious that the decisions of the Supreme Court were not enough. A civil rights law needed to be passed to ensure those decisions were carried out, and so in 1959 Martin Luther King decided to sacrifice his career as a preacher to concentrate on his work as a civil rights leader.

ACTIVITY

7 What do the events at Little Rock suggest about the strength of white opposition to the Civil Rights Movement? How do you think Elizabeth Eckford felt about white people? Use Source A in your answer.

Source A

Elizabeth Eckford at Little Rock Central High School, 1957. Elizabeth was one of the nine black students who were turned away by the National Guard.

Peaceful protest

Martin Luther King believed in peaceful protest as the main way of resolving the conflict. Both his religious background and his admiration for the pacifist Indian leader Mahatma Gandhi made him opposed to violence. He set up a training centre, which provided workshops for his followers, teaching them how to deal with the expected threats against them. Early action concentrated on sit-ins. Black students all over the south began to enter 'whites-only' lunch-counters. They would ask politely to be served and would not leave until served in an effort to end segregation. King often joined in and, like others, suffered attack by white on-lookers, arrest and imprisonment. The King HOUSEHOLD received threatening phone calls, 30–40 hate letters a day, and was even bombed.

Source B

The words of Martin Luther King, 1955

We will not resort to violence. We will return hate with love. If we are arrested every day, if we are EXPLOITED every day, if we are trampled over every day, don't let anyone pull you so low as to hate them.

In our protest, there will be no cross burnings. No white person will be taken from his home by a hooded Negro mob and brutally murdered. There will be no threats and intimidation. We will be guided by the highest principle of law and order.

Our cause is right. If we are wrong, the Supreme Court is wrong, the Constitution of the USA is wrong, God Almighty is wrong.

Martin Luther King (1929–68) was the son of a Baptist minister who, after a good education, became a minister himself. He was convinced that non-violent resistance was the most powerful weapon available to oppressed people in their struggle for freedom. His part in the Montgomery bus boycott made him a national hero. He often suffered for his beliefs. In 1968, he moved to Chicago to concentrate on helping the poor. He remained committed to non-violence but became less hopeful of peaceful change after his experience of violence there. He was shot dead on the balcony of a Memphis hotel by a white racist, James Earl Ray. This set off riots in cities across the USA.

In 1961, freedom rides were introduced to take the students on buses to wherever there was segregation. They met such violence and intimidation that federal troops were sent in to protect them. One bus was stopped and set on fire, while the KKK, carrying lead pipes, bats and bicycle chains, attacked another.

Birmingham, Alabama

Source C

Children participating in a civil rights protest wait for a police van to take them to jail in Birmingham, Alabama.

In 1963, the Movement focused on Birmingham, Alabama, the most segregated city in the USA. A Children's Crusade was organised – where thousands of children marched in the hope that they would grow up in a country where blacks and whites were equal. Millions of Americans saw on TV pictures of police brutality against the protestors. Powerful fire hoses were used to throw marchers against buildings and dogs were unleashed amongst them.

Newspapers also stirred the people's conscience. This created a backlash. Public opinion polls showed Americans increasingly sympathetic to the civil rights cause. President Kennedy commented, 'I can well understand why the Negroes of Birmingham are tired of being patient.'

March to Washington

In August 1963, a quarter of a million people, both black and white, took part in a march to Washington. It was there that King delivered his famous speech: 'I have a dream …' It was 100 years after the end of slavery in America. He told

the crowd, 'We seek the freedom in 1963 promised us in 1863 … I have a dream that one day sons of slaves and sons of slave owners will be able to sit down together at the table of brotherhood.'

His words echoed around the world and a year later he was given the NOBEL PEACE PRIZE. His faith in non-violent resistance was partly rewarded. The black people had found their pride and a way to use it effectively. 'We got our heads up now,' one of them said, 'we won't bow down again, except before God.'

ACTIVITY

8 Read Source B (page 55) and look at Sources A (page 54) and C (above). How might newspaper and TV pictures of events at Little Rock and Birmingham have helped the Civil Rights Movement? In your answer, think about how the aim of the protestors contrasts to the reaction to them.

The Black Muslims

However, by this time, many blacks were becoming increasingly disillusioned with the slow pace of progress. Civil rights still seemed a long way off.

A new movement called the Black Muslims came to the forefront of the struggle. They broke away from King and challenged his policy of non-violence and the help of whites to achieve his aims. They wanted a blacks-only protest; some wanted blacks-only communities. In other words, they wanted separation. They believed in BLACK POWER and were led by Malcolm X.

They believed in BLACK POWER and their SEPARATIST attitudes and aggressive speeches led the media to portray them as dangerous black racists in contrast to the peace-loving Martin Luther King. One of their most prominent members was Malcolm X.

Malcolm X (1925–65) was born Malcolm Little, the son of a preacher. Both of his parents were involved in the fight for black rights. He did well at school but on leaving turned to crime. He was jailed and there joined the Black Muslims and changed his name. When released, he became a Muslim preacher.

Later he broke with the Black Muslims and was converted to integration. He realised after visits to Mecca how many white Muslim 'brothers' he had and so became more forgiving towards whites. His home was bombed in 1965 and he was assassinated in 1968 by a Black Muslim.

Source D

Martin Luther King, 1963

We have waited more than 340 years for our constitutional and God-given rights. The nations of Asia and Africa are moving with jet-like speed towards gaining political independence, but we still creep at horse-and-buggy pace toward gaining a cup of coffee at a lunch-counter.

Source E

The words of Malcolm X

When a person places the proper value on freedom, there is nothing under the sun that he will not do to acquire that freedom … A man who believes in freedom will do anything under the sun to acquire … or preserve his freedom.

Source F

Malcolm X speaking in New York City, December 1964

I believe in the brotherhood of man, all men, but I don't believe in brotherhood with anybody who doesn't want brotherhood with me …
I'm not going to waste my time trying to treat somebody right who doesn't know how to return the treatment.

ACTIVITIES

9 In groups, discuss how the struggle for civil rights might have affected:
   a) a black student protester
   b) a white southern racist
   c) a white liberal (someone who believes in civil rights for all).

10 Read sources D, E and F, and the short biographies of Martin Luther King (page 55) and Malcolm X (left).
   a) How were their views of the conflict and how to resolve it similar?
   b) How were they different?
   c) Which views most closely fit the six-step 'model' for conflict resolution on page 42? Give reasons.

3 Results of the struggle

PRESIDENT	DATE	ACTION
Harry S. Truman	1945–53	Wanted to end segregation but could not get his plans passed by a conservative CONGRESS.
Dwight D. Eisenhower	1953–61	Keen not to make an issue of civil rights because he knew it would upset many important people. Despite his lack of action, the Supreme Court declared separate schools and public facilities unconstitutional.
John F. Kennedy	1961–63	Promised a 'New Frontier' – a policy of social reform, which included equality and eliminating poverty for black people. But foreign affairs took up most of his time and little progress was made before his assassination in 1963.
Lyndon B. Johnson	1963–69	Introduced a programme called 'The Great Society' to help the disadvantaged, most of whom were black people. He did pass some important reforms, but the cost and distraction of the Vietnam War meant he could not increase spending on welfare and could not deal directly with the conditions in the black ghettoes.

The peaceful campaigning of black leaders like Martin Luther King in the 1950s and 1960s did produce some notable victories for the Civil Rights Movement and had political, economic and social effects on the lives of black people. However, progress was painfully slow because the presidents of the time found it difficult to act. The table above shows the complexity of resolving the conflict as most of the presidents were sympathetic but were not free to act as they might have wished.

Johnson did, however, introduce the following acts that addressed the inequalities the Civil Rights Movement had been fighting against.

- The 1964 Civil Rights Act made illegal all segregation and discrimination on grounds of race.
- In 1965, the Voting Rights Act ended intimidation of voters. The number of black voters rose dramatically, especially in the Deep South.
- In 1968, another Civil Rights Act made discrimination in housing illegal.

There was by now a marked improvement in the poverty statistics as non-whites moved into jobs formerly closed to them.

They also made great progress in government and politics. By 1975, over 3,000 black Americans held office; they occupied 18 seats in Congress and 278 in state governments; while 120 large towns and cities were run by non-white mayors.

Unfortunately, this progress was not maintained. Inner city ghettoes still remain one of the biggest problems facing the US government, while many black people say that although they might be equal in law, in reality these laws are not always upheld and they are still discriminated against in employment and education.

Sources A–D on pages 59–60 provide some more information on the results of the Civil Rights Movement.

ACTIVITIES

11 Give two reasons why the US presidents in the 1950s and 1960s found it difficult to give the black Americans their civil rights.

12 What can be learned from the table above about achieving conflict resolution on a national scale?

Source A

Three different black people looking back on life in the 1950s

Segregation wasn't such a bad thing. You went to school, shopped and worked with black people. It was better than going into an integrated place and feeling all of those white people hating you.

Segregation wore you down. You felt you were worth less than the white man. You always got the worst schools, homes and jobs.

Over 30,000 black teachers lost their jobs when segregation ended. Many black-owned businesses and shops had to close. They could not compete with the fancy places run by whites that now had to let black people in.

ACTIVITIES

13 Study Source A and answer the following questions.
  a) Why did some people think that segregation was a good thing?
  b) Why would black people have such different views about segregation?

14 Study Source B. What part was played in resolving the conflict between blacks and whites by:
  a) the American Constitution
  b) the Supreme Court
  c) US presidents?

15 Imagine a non-racist and a racist are arguing about segregation:

  Non-racist: 'Segregation is a cause and effect of the segregation.'
  Racist: 'Segregation is a way of resolving the conflict.'

  Explain these differences of opinion.

Source B

1954	Supreme Court declared segregated schools unconstitutional
1956	Alabama bus laws declared unconstitutional
1957	A sheriff in Mississippi beat a black man to death with a truncheon for no apparent reason. He was freed after 20 minutes of interrogation even though there were four witnesses to the murder
1959	Alabama still did not have a single integrated school
1961	Police in Jackson arrested a black woman for attempting to enter a toilet marked 'White Women'
1961	Whites tried to ban black music from local radio stations in Alabama
1964	George Wallace elected Governor of Alabama. He campaigned strongly as a firm believer in segregation
1964	The town of Selma, Alabama still kept blacks off the voting register for the most trivial reasons, for example, not dotting an 'i' on registration forms. The sheriff and two deputies beat up a black woman who tried to register
1964	Civil Rights Act
1965	Voting Rights Act
1968	Civil Rights Act
1981	A black teenager was lynched by a couple of white thugs in Mobile, Alabama. They chose the innocent victim at random
2002	In Belle Glade a black unemployed handy man was apparently hanged for dating a white neighbour. The police (90 per cent white) insisted it was suicide even though the man was hanging 3 m (10 feet) up a tree. The president of the local branch of the NAACP commented 'They have not told us how he got up in that tree. They have shown no bark under his fingernails or on the souls of his shoes. It's as if he flew up there.'

Source C

Martin Luther King talking at the time of the Vietnam War, 1965

We were taking the black young men who had been crippled by our society and sending them to guard the liberties in South East Asia, which they had not found in South West Georgia and in East Harlem … We can watch Negro and white boys on TV screens as they kill and die together for a nation that has been unable to seat them together in the same schools.

Source D

Stokely Carmichael, one of the leaders of Black Power, speaking in 1969

Institutional racism keeps black people in dilapidated slum tenements, subject to the daily prey of exploitative landlords, merchants, loan sharks, etc.

International effects

In spite of disappointments at home, the Civil Rights Movement in the USA influenced similar movements elsewhere.

In South Africa, it inspired Nelson Mandela's stand against apartheid, which denied CITIZENSHIP to a vast majority of the population.

In Northern Ireland, Roman Catholic protestors copied the idea of peaceful marches in their struggle for civil rights in the 1960s. They, too, were often met by violence.

It could even be claimed that the struggle for equality for blacks has naturally developed into a struggle for equality for all persecuted minorities, including women. The WOMEN'S LIBERATION MOVEMENT sprang to life in the 1960s.

A civil rights protest in South Africa.

ACTIVITIES

16 Copy and complete the table below on the effects of the civil rights struggle. Indicate the ways the black people have benefited (+) and how things have remained the same or changed for the worse (–). Some examples have been done for you.

Effects	Short term	Long term
Political	+ Black people allowed to vote	+
	–	–
Economic	+	+
	– 30,000 teachers lost their job	–
Social	+	+
	–	– Ghettoes still remain

17 Study Sources B (page 59), C and D. Discuss in groups whether you think the reforms of the 1950s and 1960s created a just and equal society in the USA.

18 Design the front page of a newspaper for 5 April 1968 – the day Martin Luther King was shot. It should contain mention of the assassination, his involvement in the Civil Rights Movement and the effect his death is likely to have on race relations in the USA.

19 What has been the significance of the Civil Rights Movement in the USA to the rest of the world?

2.5 What are the causes and effects of international conflict?

- How do long-term and short-term causes interact to produce conflict?
- What were the causes of the Vietnam War, 1963–75?

The Vietnam War is an ideal case study to show the different causes of international conflict. It demonstrates how the causes of conflict are a result of different parties and countries having ideas and demands that are incompatible. It also shows how a national conflict involving the people of one country can develop into an international conflict affecting countries all over the world.

Case Study
The Vietnam War, 1963–75

1 Causes of the conflict

Background

In 1939, Vietnam, Laos and Cambodia were part of French Indo-China. They had been COLONISED by France in the nineteenth century. During the Second World War (1939–45), Japan occupied the area to gain control of valuable NATURAL RESOURCES such as rice, coal and rubber. The Japanese treated the people badly – millions starved to death. In response, organised RESISTANCE GROUPS were formed. One of them was the League for the Independence of Vietnam (or Vietminh). It was mainly communist and led by Ho Chi Minh. It carried out a GUERRILLA CAMPAIGN against the Japanese.

In August 1945, Japan surrendered. The Second World War was over, but the twentieth century's longest war soon began. It was to decide who should now rule Vietnam – the French or the Vietminh. The French tried to re-take Vietnam, but Ho Chi Minh would not let them. War broke out.

This was the era of the Cold War. The USA was determined to stop the spread of communism throughout South East Asia. They believed in the

Source A

Source B

US President Eisenhower, 1954

You have a row of dominoes … You knock over the first one. What will happen to the last one is the certainty that it will go over very quickly. Asia has already lost some 450 million of its people to communist dictatorships. We simply can't afford greater losses.

'domino theory' – the idea that countries were closely linked together and if one fell to communism, the others would follow (see Sources A and B).

The USA gave nearly $3 million to help the French oppose the spread of communism. China, which had become communist in 1949, gave military supplies to the Vietminh. In 1954, the war came to an end with the decisive communist victory at Dien Bien Phu.

ACTIVITY

1 Study Sources A and B above. How did the domino theory help to bring about America's involvement in the Vietnam War?

Peace talks

Peace talks were held at Geneva. It was agreed that Vietnam would be split temporarily along the line of the 17th parallel. The North became a communist republic under Ho Chi Minh and the South a democratic republic under Ngo Dinh Diem. An election was to be held for the whole country in two years so that it could be united again.

The election was never held. Diem knew that many in the South were supporters of Ho Chi Minh and an election would turn all of Vietnam into a communist country. The USA also feared this and so supported Diem's government of South Vietnam despite the fact that it was corrupt and unpopular.

Civil war breaks out

In 1959, Ho Chi Minh issued orders to the communists in the South to rebel against Diem's government. They became known as the 'Vietcong' (Vietnamese communists). Civil war soon started with most of the peasants on the communist side.

US involvement increases

In 1961, John F. Kennedy became US president. He wanted to be seen as tough on communism. He realised American money and arms had not saved Diem, so he decided to send more advisers and military experts. In the meantime, Diem's government was becoming more and more unpopular. In November 1963, it was overthrown and Diem was shot dead. A few weeks later, Kennedy was also shot dead.

The next president, Lyndon B. Johnson decided to get even more involved. The US navy patrolled the coast of Vietnam. In August 1964, the North Vietnamese attacked a US destroyer in the Gulf of Tonkin. This gave Johnson the excuse to escalate the war.

Congress passed a law to allow the army to fight a full-scale war against the North (the Tonkin Resolution). It has been recently accepted that the Johnson government manipulated intelligence in this incident to go to war, that is, they made up the story of the attack on the US destroyer.

Ho Chi Minh was the son of a peasant. He came to Europe as a young man. He was first and foremost a nationalist who wanted to get rid of the French from his country. He became a communist because the USSR promised to help all peoples struggling for independence from foreign rule.

Source C

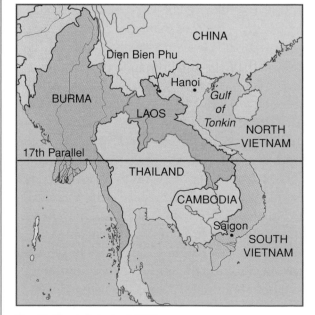

South East Asia in 1954.

Source D

The Tonkin Resolution, Johnson's message to US Congress, August 1964

- North Vietnam has broken the Geneva Agreement of 1954.
- The USA will continue to help all nations of South East Asia to defend their freedom from communism.
- The USA will promote the maintenance of international peace and security in South East Asia.

Investigation

The Tonkin incident never happened – the US government misled its people to provide an excuse for intervention in Vietnam. The British government has been accused of similar deception regarding Saddam Hussein's possession of WMDs as the reason for invading Iraq in 2003 (Operation Iraqi Freedom). Research Operation Iraqi Freedom to find similarities between this and the Gulf of Tonkin incident as a cause of an international conflict.

ACTIVITIES

2 What were the strengths and weaknesses of the Geneva Agreement (1954) as a means of resolving conflict?

3 Look at all of the sources (pages 61–63) and explain why the USA was ready to get involved in Vietnam.

4 List three stages of US involvement, showing how it escalated.

5 'The USA were right to support the corrupt government of South Vietnam.' Discuss this statement.

6 Different countries had different reasons to become involved in the conflict in Vietnam. Copy the table below and fill in reasons why they wanted to become involved. Some examples have been done for you.

Reasons for going to war in Vietnam

	France	Japan	USA	Government South Vietnam	Government North Vietnam
Political		To build an empire			
Economic	To gain resources				
Social					To bring equality to the peasants
Moral			To maintain freedom		

2 Effects of the conflict

- What were the political, social and economic effects on the people involved in Vietnam?
- What were the effects on the people in the USA?

This topic goes on to illustrate how an international conflict can have a range of effects that often interacts. It looks at the short-term effects of both US and Vietcong tactics during the war – showing how the USA was 'sinking into quicksand' by being drawn into a war it could not possibly win and which most of the people did not want. It also looks at the longer term effects of the war.

One hundred and fifty thousand US marines arrived in Vietnam in early 1965. By 1969, there were half a million. During the war, 200,000 South Vietnamese soldiers, one million North Vietnamese soldiers, over 50,000 US soldiers and 500,000 civilians were killed. The war destroyed 50 per cent of the country's forest cover and 20 per cent of agricultural land.

Vietcong tactics

1 Booby-traps – the Vietcong hid in a network of tunnels which ran for 320 km (200 miles) in South Vietnam. These tunnels were often heavily booby-trapped to avoid capture. Sharpened bamboo stakes were camouflaged in shallow pits. Trip wires tied to grenades were strung along paths or in shallow water.

2 Guerilla warfare – the Vietcong had no aircraft, no tanks and no artillery, but they were

South Vietnamese civilians training to be guerrillas.

experienced guerrilla fighters. They avoided open battle in which US equipment and weaponry would be decisive. Instead, they attacked the enemy when they least expected it and then ran away to hide amongst the peasants. Many peasants actually helped them – working in the fields by day and joining in raids at night. In the photo (below left), South Vietnamese civilians are training to be guerrillas.

3 The Tet Offensive – in January 1968, during the Vietnamese New Year or Tet holiday, 70,000 Vietcong attacked 100 towns and cities in South Vietnam in a dramatic departure from the usual guerrilla warfare. They fought conventional battles in urban areas. The objective was to break the deadlock in Vietnam and convince the USA that they could not win the war. But the tactic failed – although the offensive only lasted a month, the Vietcong suffered heavy losses (45,000 killed). However, it did have the effect of turning the US media against the war. The photo below shows the bombing of Saigon.

The bombing of Saigon, 1968.

US tactics

The USA had a variety of tactics in Vietnam to win the war. Rather than convincing the peasants not to support the Vietcong, these tactics made them even more determined to do so.

1 'Operation Rolling Thunder' – a bombing campaign over North Vietnam to destroy supply routes along the Ho Chi Minh Trail, which ran through Laos and Cambodia. The USSR and China sent up to 6,000 tonnes of supplies along this route each day. Three times more bombs

were dropped here by the US air force than were dropped in the whole of the Second World War. The worst bombs were cluster bombs, which exploded in the air and released up to 600 smaller bombs, which exploded into thousands of metal pellets on hitting the ground, causing terrible wounds.

2 Search and destroy – the aim was to flush out the Vietcong hiding in the jungle. This was impossible as it was very difficult to distinguish between a member of the Vietcong and an ordinary peasant.

3 Strategic hamlets – they turned the peasants out of their homes and put them in squalid camps surrounded by barbed wire to prevent them helping the Vietcong.

4 'Winning hearts and minds' (WHAM) – the Americans hoped that the people of South Vietnam would join them in the war against the Vietcong. They were given farming advice and support, schools were built and children were inoculated. However, this tactic failed as the US army was accused of trying to tell the people how to run their own country.

5 Chemical warfare – as the enemy could not be seen, the Americans sprayed Agent Orange to defoliate the trees and destroy crops. Traces of it contaminated the water and caused cancer. Napalm (a bomb which exploded and showered victims with a petroleum jelly that burnt at 800°C) was used to clear undergrowth.

ACTIVITIES

7 a) What advantages did the Americans have in pitched battles against the Vietcong?
  b) What advantages did guerrilla warfare offer the Vietcong?

8 Why do you think the Americans failed to win over the 'hearts and minds' of the people of South Vietnam even though they fought on their side?

9 What impact did foreign intervention have on the Vietnam War?

Effects on views about war

The Vietnam War convinced the people involved and observers of the futility of war. It was a lesson that the use of modern weaponry and the intervention of superpowers is no guarantee of resolving conflict. Robert McNamara, the US Defence Secretary at the time and the man responsible for escalating the war has recently admitted that they were wrong. He said that the toughest issues relating to Vietnam had not been foreseen and believed that the same was true of the war in Iraq.

Effects on morale

American soldiers

At the end of the conflict, the morale of US troops was at an all time low. Most of them were DRAFTED and only served a year in Vietnam, which meant they were not professional soldiers and were inexperienced. They were not committed to the cause and could not see what the war had to do with them. There was tension between black and white soldiers. The blacks did not want to fight the white man's war (this was the time of the Civil Rights Movement dealt with in Topic 2.4, pages 50–60). The officers were regular soldiers and so were more committed. Three per cent were killed by their own troops for putting their lives at risk (this was known as 'fragging' as fragmented grenades were used).

The constant heat, rain and mosquitoes depressed many soldiers. They tried to escape the horrors of war by taking drugs such as marijuana or took 'speed' to keep them alert in the jungle. They became very racist towards the Vietnamese, calling them 'gooks'. Between 1966–73 there were over half a million incidents of desertion.

Vietcong soldiers

Their morale was better as they were fighting for two causes (communism and NATIONALISM) and were backed by the peasants. But even they suffered as they lacked supplies and weapons, and spent a great deal of time in hiding underground.

At home in the USA

By 1967, US opinion began to turn against the war as horrifying images on TV shocked many people. They realised that the cost was too high in terms of men and money ($20 billion a year). The media took on an anti-war attitude and said that it was illegal and immoral. They informed the people that they had been misled and were not being told the truth about casualties.

Dramatic images such as the shooting of a Vietcong prisoner in the head (see photo below) made Americans feel ashamed. Revelations of torture under the supervision of the CIA, the mutilation of bodies and the collection of body parts as trophies were evidence of serious war crimes.

The final straw was a press report of the My Lai massacre of between 300–500 civilians by a US platoon led by Lieutenant Calley (March 1968). Calley was convicted of murder in 1971 and was sentenced to life imprisonment, but only served three and a half years.

These events illustrated the deterioration taking place in the behaviour of US troops and undermined the arguments about the need to save Vietnam from 'the evils of communism'. As one mother of an accused soldier said, 'I sent them [US army] a good boy, and they made him a murderer.'

The Saigon Chief of Police shoots a Vietcong prisoner during the Tet Offensive (see page 64).

Opposition to the war

Opposition came from many quarters: pacifists were against the war on moral and religious grounds; LIBERALS felt the people of Vietnam were fighting for freedom and their own country; while the great majority thought the war was not the USA's concern. Protests included DRAFT-DODGING and the burning of draft cards. Mohammad Ali was the most famous to refuse to fight – he explained, 'No Vietnamese called me a nigger.' Students went on protest marches (half a million marched to Washington in 1971). Martin Luther King denounced the sending of blacks to fight for a country that treated them so badly at home (see page 60). The film star Jane Fonda became known as 'Hanoi Jane' for her involvement in demonstrations. Ex-soldiers formed 'Vietnam Veterans Against the War'. Below are some anti-war slogans and extracts from anti-war songs.

ACTIVITIES

10 Work in a group of three. Each person in the group must take the part of one of the following:
   a) A US soldier.
   b) A communist soldier.
   c) A member of the American public.
   Prepare a short play for the class as a discussion between these three people about why the USA should withdraw from the Vietnam War.

11 Design an anti-war poster for the Vietnam War – you could use the slogans in the picture or make up your own slogan.

12 What part did the US media play in spreading opposition to the war?

Summary of the effects of the war

	SHORT-TERM EFFECTS	LONG-TERM EFFECTS
Political	The US had lost its first war.	The Vietnam War played its part in ending the Cold War. The superpowers realised the danger of war and moved towards *DÉTENTE*. President Nixon visited China and the USSR, and the superpowers agreed to limit how many nuclear missiles they built.
	Vietnam turned Johnson into the most unpopular US President in history. He did not stand for re-election.	
	The domino theory was proved wrong. Vietnam, Laos and Cambodia became communist but not the rest of South East Asia, which remained unstable.	
Social	2 million people were killed. Millions more were injured or lost their homes.	Many mines and booby-traps are still in Vietnam, while the people continue to suffer from the effects of chemicals and defoliants.
		Two million people fled from Vietnam to escape famine and communism. These included 1 million 'boat people', who tried to sail away (many drowned).
		Many American GIs found it difficult to readjust to civilian life. They felt betrayed because they were often treated as war criminals rather than heroes.
		Half a million suffered from 'post-traumatic stress disorder'. This often led to alcoholism, drug addiction and divorce. Many found it difficult to find work. More have committed suicide since the war than were killed in the fighting.
Economic	The fighting cost the US $120 billion, which meant that the US government was unable to spend money on much needed welfare reform so that poverty and racial inequalities continued.	Vietnam was united as a communist country, but a devastated one with its economy in ruins.
		From being a major exporter of rice, Vietnam was reduced to a country unable to feed itself.

ACTIVITY

13 Choose any two of the following and write about 300 words in a letter to a friend describing the social and economic effects of the war on:
   a) the Vietcong
   b) a South Vietnamese peasant
   c) a US marine.

Investigation

Carry out research about:

* mistreatment of prisoners at Abu Ghraib prison during the 2003/4 Iraq war
* protests against the war in Iraq in London.

Compare what you have found out with what you have learned about similar events relating to the Vietnam War.

3 Resolving the conflict

- Why was it so difficult to end the war in Vietnam?
- How far did the Treaty of Paris go in resolving the conflict?

This section will show how individuals, groups, nations and international organisations can play a role in resolving conflict. It will also show how attempts to resolve conflict can use a range of approaches.

There are many ways of resolving international conflict as we have seen in Topic 2.2 (pages 42–43). Not all of these methods were used in Vietnam. APPEASEMENT and SANCTIONS, for instance, were never considered as they were not practical. Negotiation was difficult because:

- communism and CAPITALISM represent very different ideals
- the strong nationalism of the Vietnamese meant they were completely against the division of their country
- the interference of outside powers, each with their own agenda, complicated matters.

Nevertheless, listed on the right are some of the methods that were tried.

By 1968, a large number of Americans were against the war and politicians began to look for a way out. This photo shows a student anti-Vietnam rally in Iowa, 5 November 1968. The demonstration was staged on the steps of the Iowa capitol building after a 5-km (3-mile) march under police supervision.

1 Force
Both sides used force – initially in the hope of a quick end to the conflict, but then as a means of continuing the conflict in the hope that the enemy would give in. All force achieved was an escalation of the war. The ensuing suffering also meant there was less likelihood of either side compromising with each other.

2 Deterrent
The possession of nuclear weapons by both the USA and the USSR prevented a full-scale war, but it also meant that both the USA and the USSR could only fight or support a limited war, which gave both sides less chance of winning.

3 Protest
The peace movement with its anti-war demonstrations played a major role in ending the conflict. When the American public turned against the war, the politicians were forced to negotiate.

4 International co-operation
In 1968, President Johnson decided to seek an end to the fighting and started peace talks. Each time the US government tried to involve the UN in talks the North Vietnamese refused to co-operate. They insisted that the US forces leave Vietnam first. Johnson's successor, Richard Nixon began the policy of Vietnamisation, which meant pulling troops out and leaving South Vietnam to defend itself.

Talks now began but it took five years of negotiations in Paris before an agreement was finally reached (January, 1973). The South Vietnamese had objected to the Vietcong being present while the USA and the North Vietnamese were reluctant to make any concessions. When a settlement was finally agreed, the US representative, Dr Henry Kissinger, and the Vietnamese delegate were awarded the Nobel Peace Prize between them. This was indeed a tremendous achievement when seen in the context of the Cold War. However, relations between East and West had been improving because of *détente*. Neither side had wished to jeopardise this.

The war still dragged on for a further two years because the government of South Vietnam would not give up. They finally surrendered and in 1976 North and South Vietnam were united at last as an independent nation.

Vietnam is now a popular tourist destination and has begun to recover from the war.

ACTIVITIES

14 Look at the table below. Was the USA right or wrong to get involved in the war in Vietnam? For each argument in column 1, put a tick in column 2 if you think it is an argument for US involvement. Put a tick in column 3 if you think it is an argument against.

Argument	For	Against
Use of force by North Vietnam against terms of 1954 Geneva Agreement.		
Only use of force can stop communism taking over in South Vietnam.		
Might lead to Third World War.		
Doing nothing will encourage the USSR and China elsewhere.		
Action will encourage the USSR and China to get involved.		
Talking is the only sensible way to resolve conflict.		
A democracy should not support an undemocratic government.		
Stability in South East Asia is vital to the West.		
If South Vietnam falls, other Asian states will follow (domino theory).		
The war is a civil war: foreign countries should not interfere.		

15 Do you think the countries involved in the Vietnam War acted to make a better world or acted in their best interests? Support your argument.

16 Explain why the causes and effects of the Vietnam War made it difficult to resolve.

17 In groups, imagine that you are members of the UN trying to end the conflict in Vietnam in 1968. Use the six-step problem solving method outlined in Topic 2.2, page 42. Write down what action you would take for each step.

18 Draw a spider diagram showing how the results of the war not only affected Vietnam but also other countries. Show how some results lead on to others.

19 The twentieth century was the bloodiest in all of history – 160 million human beings were killed in conflict. As a class, discuss how we can avoid similar bloodshed in this century.

20 Choose any national or international conflict you have studied and copy and fill in the boxes below to show how it had a range of causes and effects. It may not be possible to fill in all of the boxes.

A political cause	A political effect	An effect that is also a cause
A religious cause	A religious effect	An attempt to resolve conflict
An economic cause	An economic effect	A reason for failing to resolve the conflict
A moral cause	A moral effect	How the conflict ended
A social cause	A social effect	

3.1 *What are environmental issues?*

- Why is the ENVIRONMENT important?
- Why have we become more aware of environmental problems in recent years?

Concerns, problems and worries about the NATURAL ENVIRONMENT are called environmental issues. The natural environment is the part of the planet that is already there (such as land, sea, rivers, atmosphere, vegetation) – not made by people. This topic examines the question: why have environmental issues become a major concern now? The rest of the section is going to explore some of these environmental issues and look at:

- *what are the problems (issues)?*
- *how did they come about?*
- *what are the possible effects?*
- *what has been (or could be) done about them?*

ACTIVITY

1. **a)** Make a list of at least six environmental issues that you have heard about.
   b) Put your issues in rank order showing which you think are the greatest threats to the planet (the most serious first, the least serious last).
   c) Give explanations for your choices of the most and least serious.

No one wants to destroy or damage their environment. The environment is where we live, our homeland. It is where we find the things we need to survive like food, materials for shelter, tools to make things, fuel for heat, light and power. It is where we take our rest and leisure, and enjoy our lives. Only a fool or a mad person would deliberately destroy their environment.

The human species has lived in and used the natural environment for many thousands of years. In that time, they have chopped and burned down trees, mined and quarried rocks, and dumped rubbish in rivers and the sea. Until recently, more than 99 per cent of the natural environment was unaffected and unchanged. People moved away to new, untouched territory and the damaged environment adapted to the changes or REGENERATED and recovered.

But now, at the beginning of the twenty-first century, there are many people who believe that the natural environment is being changed so rapidly that it cannot regenerate or recover. We have nearly exhausted (completely used up) some NATURAL RESOURCES. We are destroying species of plant and animal life that may never be seen again. We are polluting the air, the land, the sea and fresh water supplies. Some people worry that we are doing so much damage to the environment of the planet that it will become more and more difficult to live healthy and happy lives, and in the future we may not be able to survive here at all.

The first question we should ask is: why are these environmental problems happening now?

There are three main reasons.

Reason 1

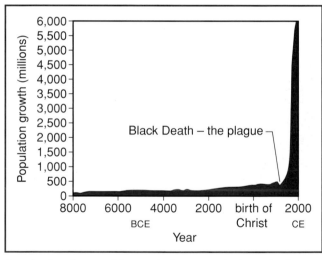

Graph showing world population growth through time (the figures are estimates).

There has been a massive increase in the world population over the last 200 years. In 1800, the world population was about 800 million. Two hundred years later, the world population was six billion (nearly eight times larger). At the moment, over 75 million more people are added to the world population each year. By 2050, the world population is expected to be nine billion.

Reason 2

Our scientific understanding and advanced technical skills have resulted in most of the world using a lot more TECHNOLOGY in their daily lives. This has meant that we use more and more natural resources on a daily basis. Natural resources are the raw materials (such as coal, oil and wood) we take from the environment and use to make things or use to make energy (like electricity). When these resources are used, they change the environment and create by-products such as carbon dioxide and toxic chemicals.

Eighteenth-century rural life. What technology is being used by the farmers?

Reason 3

Many people's desires and expectations for their lives have changed. Simply, people want more material things. This is because the more economically developed countries (MEDCS) (such as the UK, Japan, North America, Germany) have become much richer. Most people in these places have enough food and good housing, and have come to expect a comfortable lifestyle with lots of luxuries. Other people who live in less economically developed countries (LEDCS), for example, in Zaire or Indonesia, want the same lifestyle as people in MEDCs.

Modern city life (Tokyo).

Thing we want	Materials needed	Resources used
Car	Steel, rubber, plastic, glass, leather, petrol	Iron ore, oil, animal skin, trees, sand
Plasma screen TV	Glass, plastic, metal, rubber, copper, electronic equipment, electricity	Copper, silicone, trees, sand, either coal or oil or nuclear power

3.2 *How do people interact differently with the environment?*

- How do different CULTURES and individuals view the environment?
- Why do they EXPLOIT the natural resources in different ways?
- What is the effect of this exploitation of natural resources?

This topic uses the exploitation of tropical rainforests as a case study to explore different ATTITUDES to the environment and the different ways natural resources are exploited. The topic looks at:

- *the rainforest as an ECOSYSTEM*
- *the process of DEFORESTATION*
- *the ways different groups relate to the rainforest*
- *the problems caused by deforestation and possible ways forward in the future.*

If everyone had the same caring attitude to the environment, and they could agree how to treat it, it could be quite easy to protect it from lasting damage. However, this clearly is not the way things are. In Section 1 on culture and BELIEFS, you will have learned that cultures across the world are different. They have different goals, beliefs, technology and lifestyles. As a result, groups with different cultures and different VALUES have very different attitudes towards the environment, and different ways of exploiting it.

An ecosystem

Tropical rainforests are a very important ecosystem for the planet. A third of the world's trees grow there. Half of the world's species of plants and animals exist there; many of them can be found nowhere else. They contain a largely unexplored BIO-DIVERSITY, which could provide the world with new medicines, foods and knowledge, and which could benefit all the world's population.

If an ecosystem is disturbed by plants or animals being removed or damaged, there will be knock-on effects on all other parts of the ecosystem. For example, if a certain type of plant disappears from an area, all the living organisms that relied on that plant to survive will die out or move from the area. This will have further knock-on effects on other living organisms.

Rainforests play a central role in influencing the world's climate and in producing and modifying the atmosphere we breathe. Trees absorb carbon dioxide and produce oxygen. This process cleanses and purifies the atmosphere. Trees also absorb solar radiation. Without the forests, more radiation bounces back into the atmosphere, raising atmospheric temperature. This could alter global patterns of air circulation, CONVECTION and wind. Rainforests also play a role in recycling the earth's water, as moisture is absorbed by the trees and evaporated into the atmosphere to return as rainfall in other parts of the world. Without the forests to store water, streams can disappear during the dry season and deprive human populations of water. This is already happening in parts of Africa.

What is happening to rainforests?

Rainforests are being cut down at a furious rate. This is called deforestation. There are no accurate figures for the loss of trees, and estimates vary, but 15,000 km² (5,800 square miles) of rainforest lost per year is a commonly quoted figure. This amounts to two football pitches disappearing each second, an area larger than New York City each day, and an area larger than Poland each year.

In some places, the tropical rainforest has almost gone, such as Nigeria and Cote d'Ivoire; in many places, forests are down to 20 per cent of the size they were in 1960, such as Thailand, the Philippines, Mexico and Vietnam. In the last 40 years, the value of the rainforest has been recognised and exploited by many different people and groups. This has meant that for many different reasons people have been cutting down the trees and about one-third has been destroyed.

The case study we will look at is the world's largest, the Brazilian (Amazonian) rainforest, but the reasons for the loss of rainforests around the world are much the same.

Rainforest uses

Most of the uses for the rainforest described and shown in the photos below and on page 74 are connected with ECONOMIC DEVELOPMENT of the countries where the rainforest grows.

Logging: Deforestation in the Amazon Basin Rainforest – trees are being converted into timber to sell abroad, especially hardwoods (mahogany, sapele, ebony), which are in demand in MEDCs. The big trees are transported and sold, but smaller trees and plants are ripped up and left to die.

Extraction of minerals: Minerals are extracted from the land beneath the trees (these might include iron ore, diamonds, precious metals – this photo is of a gold mine near Pocone in Brazil). This involves the removal of trees to mine/quarry and to build transport systems. This creates wealth, as well as environmental destruction.

1 Use the photographs and captions on this page and page 73 to answer these questions:
  a) What advantages does the exploitation of the rainforest bring to different groups of people?

b) What problems has this exploitation brought to the survival of the rainforest and the health of the planet?

Small-scale farming: The clearance of the rainforest has provided plots of land for the rapidly growing population who need food and jobs. For many local people, farming land cleared from the rainforest has changed their lives for the better. This photo shows a typical settlement with turtle-breeding pens at the water side.

Cattle ranching: The first stage is clearing the land by burning (as in photo). Then grass grows over the burnt land, but often only lasts a year or two before the land is worn out and the cattle have to be moved to another area where the forest has been cleared.

Major engineering projects: Such as dams for hydroelectric power, building roads, building settlements for farmers, loggers, miners and others living in the forest. These projects bring great advantages to local people, opening up territory for farming, or bringing electricity to the area, but at the same time, they destroy the rainforest. This photo shows the Samuel Dam on the Jamari River in Brazil. 654 km^2 (253 square miles) of forest were drowned when the lake formed, but the dam provides electricity for Porto Velho, which has a population of over 650,000.

There are several different groups with interests in the rainforest.

1 Scientists, environmental researchers, meteorologists, medical researchers

They want to discover what effects deforestation will have on local and global living conditions. Some will want to continue doing research on plants and animal life, often for medical purposes. Others will be very concerned about weather and climate change. They will be trying to assess how the ecosystem is changing, and how this will affect the environment in the future.

2 The Brazilian government

They are trying to cope with a big increase in population and to develop a growing economy. They are hoping to reduce the national debt. They wish to provide work, and to do this they need money for investment, raw materials and electrical power. They are in favour of some logging and mining because this will provide WEALTH to be invested. They want to build roads to open up the land for farming and settlements for the Brazilian people, and want to produce electricity to allow modernisation.

3 Commercial companies involved in logging, mining, road building, etc.

They want to make profits from the raw materials and expand their businesses. This is part of helping an economy to grow and provides jobs and wealth. To get logs out roads need to be built, and large areas of the forest are destroyed.

4 The original inhabitants of the forest

They have lived in the rainforest and learned how to use its resources without damaging the forest or overusing its materials. The native Amazonians live by a process called 'shifting cultivation': they live in one area and farm it, moving on when the land is no longer cultivable. This does not harm the forest, which quickly recovers. When the NUTRIENTS in the soil have been depleted by growing the crops, that area will no longer grow enough food and the farmers have to move on. They see the rainforest as home, often as part of their family.

Now they are seeing their land and way of life disappearing as the forest is changed by outsiders with new technology, who are taking away the trees and other resources.

Amazonian tribes, such as the Kayapo people still try to follow a traditional way of life.

5 The growing population of poor people from the surrounding countryside

They are hoping for a better life with more room to live and a means of providing for their families. In order to make land suitable for farming, they often burn the trees and scrub to clear the land so that crops can be grown and cattle can be raised. Despite this wasteful destruction of plant life, the ability to farm and be more self-sufficient has been a massive benefit to the growing populations of Brazil, Venezuela, Indonesia and other countries where rainforests grow.

ACTIVITY

2 Get into teams of five. Each person in the team plays the part of one of the five groups of rainforest users described on this page and prepares a presentation for the rest of the team, which has the following elements:
- describe how you are using the rainforest
- explain why you think it is right to use it in this way
- say what you think of the other groups' attitudes to the forest.

At the end of the session, make a summary of the attitudes of each group.

What are the environmental effects of rainforest depletion?

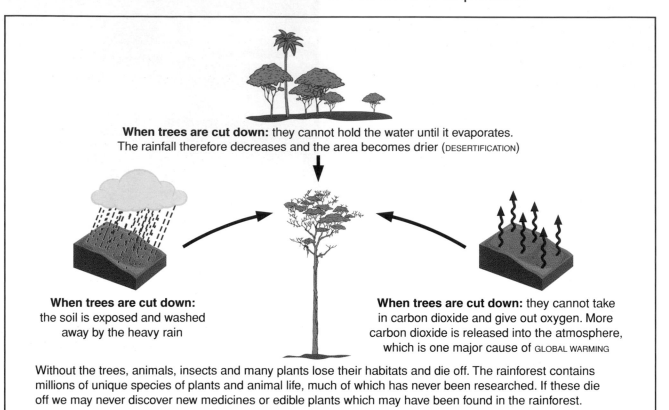

When trees are cut down: they cannot hold the water until it evaporates. The rainfall therefore decreases and the area becomes drier (DESERTIFICATION)

When trees are cut down: the soil is exposed and washed away by the heavy rain

When trees are cut down: they cannot take in carbon dioxide and give out oxygen. More carbon dioxide is released into the atmosphere, which is one major cause of GLOBAL WARMING

Without the trees, animals, insects and many plants lose their habitats and die off. The rainforest contains millions of unique species of plants and animal life, much of which has never been researched. If these die off we may never discover new medicines or edible plants which may have been found in the rainforest.

What can be done about disappearing rainforests?

1 Stewardship

The original inhabitants of the rainforests (such as the Yanomani) may have shown the way. They were able to live in the forest, use its resources and keep it healthy and thriving. This approach is sometimes called 'stewardship', where the people using the land understand what it needs to survive and treat it with respect and concern for the future.

Here is one approach to stewardship:

'In what might be considered the most significant progress to date in protecting the Amazon, WWF, the World Bank, the Global Environmental Facility (GEF) and the Government of Brazil, in 2002 launched the largest, most ambitious effort ever made to safeguard tropical forests. The initiative, known as the Amazon Region Protected Area (ARPA), creates a system of approximately 80 reserves and parks, preserving intact an area roughly the size of California.'

World Wildlife Fund (WWF)

However, major changes will not be easily achieved in the present circumstances. It is not just commercial greed that is causing deforestation; much of the pressure comes from local people struggling to survive and the governments of rainforest countries who need to trade to build their economies.

Investigations
1 Investigate ARPA on the Internet and find out what exactly they have done in the Amazon region.
2 Use the Internet to discover other approaches to 'stewardship'. Try using a search engine to look for: 'environmental stewardship' or 'environmental protection schemes'. As a result of your research, describe two other methods or projects designed to maintain the environment.

2 Sustainable development

What does 'SUSTAINABLE DEVELOPMENT' mean? Sustainable means something that can be kept going in the future. Development means making changes that improve a situation.

In terms of the rainforest, sustainable development means making use of its resources, but in a way that does not eventually destroy it and which reduces the waste.

What would have to be done to bring about 'sustainable development' of the rainforest?

- **Protect and manage the remaining forests:** Make some areas protected and untouchable, and make sure that any logging, farming, quarrying, or building that goes on does minimal damage.

- **Help people improve their quality of life without damaging more of the forest:** Look for alternative, efficient ways of farming. To make land suitable for farming, some trees will have to be cut, and the land cleared, but at the moment, timber is taken and land is cleared in the cheapest way possible using bulldozers and fire. Much of the forest is wasted because it is more expensive to do this carefully. But in the long term, careful clearing will leave the forest healthy and provide timber and land that can be used to produce cocoa, coffee, rubber, plants for medicine, crops that produce a better income than cattle and cereals.

- **Get governments and international groups to agree to work to conserve the rainforest:** If no one controls what is going on, people will still cut mahogany down and sell it to be made into conservatories and toilet seats, for example. Set limits to the amount of timber that can be felled and increase research to find ways of helping the forest survive.

Summary of the Brazilian rainforest case study

1 The rainforests are vital ecosystems for the whole world, providing unique resources and controlling world climate and weather patterns.

2 Rainforests across the world are being cut down at an enormous rate. Hardwood and minerals beneath the forest soil are valuable commodities for world trade.

3 Many people such as medical researchers, ecologists, METEOROLOGISTS, climatologists and ENVIRONMENTALISTS think this process and the methods used to get the timber and minerals is wasteful and extremely hazardous for the future of the world.

4 Other people think that exploiting the wealth of the rainforest is the only way of supporting a rising population and developing weak economies to improve the quality of life for people in countries where the rainforest grows.

5 The loss of rainforest is already causing problems to the world, and further destruction will have wide-reaching effects on our climate and our need for new materials for medicine and human development.

6 The answer to these problems, or at least a way of dealing with them, involves everyone across the world learning to protect the rainforest by acting as 'stewards of the forest' and adopting methods of development that are 'sustainable'.

7 This new approach may be difficult to organise on a worldwide basis. Many people have different ways of interacting with the environment.

ACTIVITY

3 Use the information in this case study (pages 73–76) to explain why sustainable development of the rainforest might be difficult to achieve.

3.3 How are natural resources exploited?

- What do we mean by 'the exploitation of natural resources'?
- Why do problems arise from the different ways people want to exploit the environment?

In Topic 3.2 (pages 72–77), we saw that people have different ways of perceiving and exploiting natural resources. From the example of the rainforest, we can see that these differences in attitude and interests result in problems for other people and the natural environment. This next case study on the Aral Sea shows how changing the natural environment by exploiting resources will have far-reaching effects. It shows that unless the environment and the resources it contains are understood fully, attempts to change it may cause greater problems than existed before.

ACTIVITY

1 Make a list of natural resources that humans exploit. Draw a table like the one below and, in it, show how humans exploit these resources.

Natural resource	How is it exploited?
Fossil fuels	Burned to provide heat and light, used as fuel for vehicles

The word 'exploit' means to make use of something for the benefit of individuals or groups. The word can also mean 'use to make a profit'. Exploiting resources is not in itself bad. All living things survive by making use of the environment to provide what they need, for example, food and materials for shelter.

The rainforest, timber, metal ores, minerals and land are not the only resources that we exploit. We also exploit:

- the sea and sea life
- fresh water supplies
- FOSSIL FUELS such as coal, oil and natural gas.

Case Study
The story of the Aral Sea

The Aral Sea was once the fourth biggest inland sea in the world. Fishing and a busy shipping trade provided a healthy livelihood for several hundred thousand people. The Aral Sea surface was 66,100 km² (25,520 square miles). Salt content was one per cent.

Then, in the 1960s, the flow of water into the sea began to drop alarmingly. The Soviet government had set up a major irrigation scheme in order to grow huge amounts of rice and cotton to help the Russian economy.

This scheme involved diverting water from the rivers that flowed into the Aral Sea to areas where the rice and cotton were planted. This irrigation scheme sucked out more than 90 per cent of the natural flow of water into the sea. As a result, 27,000 km² (10,425 square miles) of former sea bottom became dry surface.

About 60 per cent of water volume was lost. The sea level fell 14 metres. The water became twice as salty. Every year, about 200,000 tonnes of salt and sand are being carried away by wind.

The effects of the changes to the Aral Sea

Climate

Because of the draining of the sea, important climatic changes have taken place. The water of the sea used to moderate the temperature. It made winters warmer and summers cooler. Now winters are colder and summers hotter. Rainfall has declined because there is less water to evaporate and the area is much dryer. The area is always dusty because the wind has increased.

Desertification

The salt in the air damages the farming area, destroying pastures and creating a shortage of food for domestic animals. Deserted and sandy areas are extended by the dust being carried further by the wind. As the desertification increases, there is more toxic dust in the air from the wind blowing over the exposed seabed.

Work

The cotton and rice industries are failing. The fishing industry has collapsed. The harbours are

A fishing boat which is now stranded 7 km (11 miles) from the nearest seawater. The man on the boat is its former captain.

now miles from the sea, and the fish could not survive in the over-salted polluted water. Other businesses such as boat building and papermaking have closed down completely, or work half days only. All these issues are destroying the traditional social life of the region. Many people are unemployed, there is widespread poverty, and many of the old workforce are leaving the area.

Water supply

The water the people need to drink, wash, and use for SANITATION is in very short supply. The water that is available is polluted. The Soviet government had not worked out in advance what might happen to the local ECOLOGY. The impact of the irrigation system on the local communities was never considered. Poor planning and management left the local people in desperate conditions.

Health

The drying-up of the sea, the reduction in the quality and quantity of water, and the salt and dust laden air, has had a damaging effect on the health of the people, and the animal and plant life as well. Diseases like anaemia, cancer, tuberculosis, and allergies are frequent.

> ### Summary of the Aral Sea case study
> 1 There is rarely agreement about how the environment should be perceived and exploited.
>
> 2 There are usually two forces at work. The desire to:
>   - exploit the natural environment to produce resources that people want to use or consume to improve the quality of their lives
>   - conserve the natural environment and to limit damage to the ecosystem.
>
> 3 Some parts of an ecosystem may be damaged as a result of commercial pressures, where the desire to get and trade a specific resource overrides other concerns.

ACTIVITIES

2 Explain or draw a diagram to show what happened to the Aral Sea.

3 What effect did the Aral Sea crisis have on the people living in the area? Organise your answers into long- and short-term effects.

4 What mistakes did the Soviet government make in exploiting the Aral Sea? What should they have thought about and planned for to avoid making these mistakes?

3.4 How do some species become endangered?

- Why are there concerns about life in the oceans?
- How can ENDANGERED SPECIES be protected and conserved?

This topic examines the problems we encounter when we exploit natural resources to such an extent that we endanger the survival of whole species of living creatures. It examines the problems this causes through looking at a case study of the oceans – examining the threats to many fish species and other sea life, and various attempts to control or limit the damage.

ACTIVITY

1 Make a list of species that you believe are endangered and give reasons why they are under threat of extinction.

The oceans and marine life

Seawater covers 71 per cent of the planet's surface. It is teeming with life, ranging from microscopic PLANKTON to massive whales. It is a crucial part of the ecology of the planet. It provides food, minerals and plant life, which are vital for human needs.

It also plays a central part in weather control by:

- absorbing or retaining heat
- absorbing carbon dioxide
- providing rainfall from water, which evaporates from its surface.

The following case study looks at what is happening to one of the greatest resources the oceans provide: fish and marine life.

At the end of this topic, you will be able to answer the question: 'Why should this concern me?'

Case Study
Fish and marine life

Fish is an important part of the human diet in many parts of the world. It provides protein and essential vitamins and minerals. It is particularly valuable as food in developing countries such as Bangladesh, Ghana, North Korea and Indonesia, where it provides half the protein consumed. In the DEVELOPED WORLD, the demand for fish has grown, and consumption of fish by the rising populations of Asia has increased ten-fold since 1970.

The chart below shows how the total world sea fish catch has increased steadily since 1950. By the year 2000, the world's fishing fleets were catching five times the amount of fish they had taken 50 years ago.

However, in the twenty-first century, the total harvest of fish has stopped increasing. Overall it has dropped a little. This is because the world's fish stocks have been almost FULLY EXPLOITED.

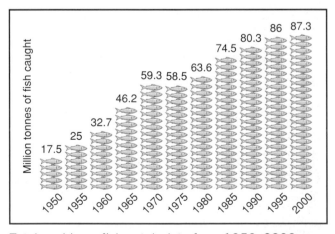

Total world sea fish catch data from 1950–2000.

What does fully exploited mean?

This means that the fish numbers have dropped to a level where the species might die out.

Look at the chart opposite to see how the current level of fishing is a threat to the survival of many species of fish.

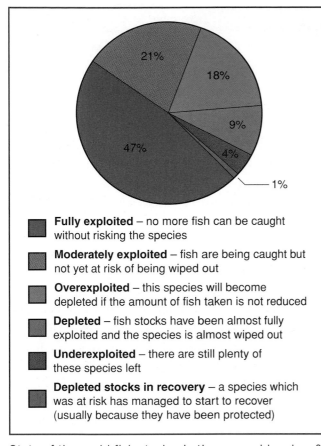

■ **Fully exploited** – no more fish can be caught without risking the species

■ **Moderately exploited** – fish are being caught but not yet at risk of being wiped out

■ **Overexploited** – this species will become depleted if the amount of fish taken is not reduced

■ **Depleted** – fish stocks have been almost fully exploited and the species is almost wiped out

■ **Underexploited** – there are still plenty of these species left

■ **Depleted stocks in recovery** – a species which was at risk has managed to start to recover (usually because they have been protected)

State of the world fish stocks. Is there a problem here?

ACTIVITY

2 Use the information in the charts (left and opposite) to write a newspaper article to explain why it is important to cut down the amount of fish taken from world oceans.

Fishing methods

Fishing has changed since the 1950s. Until then, boats with small nets sailed out and hoped to catch a few tonnes of fish, then get back to sell the fish while it was still fresh. Their nets were quite small, and the mesh was set to catch good-sized fish and let the rest escape. When the net was hauled in, small or unwanted fish were thrown back. There was some waste, but not much.

By the mid-twentieth century, fishing boats were huge factory ships. They caught thousands of tonnes of fish, which they froze, and continued fishing. The nets were much bigger – sometimes four km (2.5 miles) long – and the fish were detected electronically with great accuracy. These ships could catch everything in the area, including the young fish which had not yet started to breed.

A huge catch of pollock on the deck of a factory trawler.

3 ENVIRONMENTAL ISSUES

What is 'by-catch'?

The growing demand for fish has created a dangerous form of fishing, an approach which results in lots of fish being killed needlessly. This is the problem of 'BY-CATCH'.

Fishing on a big scale is not careful. Bottom trawlers pull a huge weighted net along the seabed. Sometimes two boats work together to pull a net five km (three miles) long between them, catching everything in a wide area. Other nets scrape the seabed and scoop up fish eggs and young sea creatures indiscriminately. These are dumped as they are not useful, but it means millions of sea inhabitants never mature and breed.

Other fishing methods, such as nets, traps and hooked lines, also catch a wide variety of fish. This means that as well as the 'target' species of fish it catches, any number of 'non-target' species may also be hauled in. This accidental catch of other species is referred to as 'by-catch'.

By-catch is not limited to fish species. All types of marine life including whales, dolphins, porpoises, fur seals, albatrosses and turtles are killed as by-catch.

ACTIVITIES

3 Give two reasons why people want to catch more fish.

4 Explain how this huge increase in fish catches has been made possible.

5 Why is it a problem for future fish stocks if many young fish are caught?

6 Explain in your own words what 'overexploitation' of species means.

The picture below shows a porpoise, which was killed by being trapped in a fishing net.

The fisheries with the highest levels of by-catch are shrimp fisheries – often over 80 per cent of a catch comprises marine species other than shrimp.

Globally, it is estimated that a quarter of what is caught is merely killed and dumped. That means about 20 million tonnes of unwanted fish are thrown back into the sea every year. Most of these will be dead or will die.

A porpoise killed by fishing, washed up in South Devon, January 2004.

Why should we be concerned?

Fishing has a huge impact on the marine (sea) FOOD CHAIN. Fishing is like hunting, and we already understand that if you kill off the animals that breed, the whole species will die out. For example, the buffalo and wild boars have been killed off in many parts of the world by hunting and killing the animals capable of breeding.

Over-fishing has meant that there are so few fish of some species that they cannot breed enough to renew themselves. So one result is that fish like cod, which used to be plentiful and cheap, are now rare and expensive. The species becomes depleted and finally, unsustainable.

But the problem does not end with some fish disappearing or becoming more expensive for customers.

The marine ecosystem

The fish we take out in huge numbers is also the food for other species (see food chain below).

In order to survive, these marine creatures have to move away or change their eating habits. This in turn affects the whole balance of the marine ecology in ways that are still not understood by scientists.

What ecologists fear is that once this food chain is broken, the health of all the ocean's life, fish, plants and animals may be permanently damaged, and the ocean itself may not perform its other vital role: as the most effective mechanism for cleaning and purifying the planet. This will be examined in the next case study: POLLUTION of the oceans (pages 85–90).

What can be done to stop the depletion of fish stocks?

It is generally agreed that there should be some way of controlling the amount of fish and marine life taken from the sea to ensure that the species can be replenished (sustained). This means that somehow, the whole of the world's fishing industries must be regulated. This will need international laws to be agreed and enforced.

The UN Convention on the Law of the Seas (UNCLOS) has tried to set out rules to conserve fish and to settle disputes. But these laws and rules are extremely difficult to enforce.

Here are some of the problems of depleted fish stocks:

- Oceans are huge, far too big to patrol and observe.
- Countries regard their coastal waters as their territory under their control. The fish in these waters is seen as their property. Sometimes countries claim that their culture depends on being able to take various kinds of marine life (for example, Iceland and whaling).
- Most of the oceans are international waters, which means that there are no legal controls of this water, and no one has clear legal responsibility for what goes on.
- The growing populations of LEDCs and the rising wealth of MEDC mean that the demand for products of the seas is rising year on year.
- The whole scheme depends on fishermen being honest about sticking to their QUOTA.

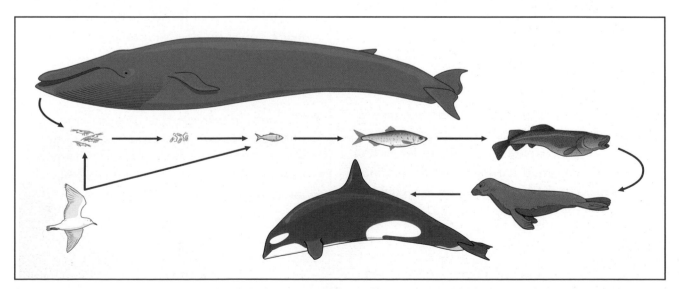

Once any one of these parts of the food chain gets smaller or disappears, everything else in the chain is affected.

However, there is an optimistic side to this problem:

- ✓ Most governments recognise that unless they protect fish stocks, their own country will suffer.
- ✓ Fishermen also recognise that they risk losing their jobs in the future if they do not follow their quotas.
- ✓ Satellite technology and tracking devices make it easier to identify and punish 'rogue' fishing vessels.
- ✓ More people are becoming aware of endangered marine species, especially whales, thanks to the 'Save the Whale' campaign. This campaign was started by Greenpeace in 1975 and won massive support from the public. A ban on commercial whaling took effect in 1986 and succeeded in protecting thousands of whales. Many people now support maritime laws and restrictions on many types of fishing, notably fishing that endangers dolphins and sharks. The publicity has also encouraged some people to adjust their lifestyle and eating habits.
- ✓ Some commercial organisations have environmental policies that limit and control the species and origins of the seafood they sell.
- ✓ Fish farming (AQUACULTURE) is on the increase, which may replace depleted stocks of some marine species.

Despite these efforts, over-fishing and marine species depletion are continuing. International bodies such as the International Whaling Commission (IWC), the Food and Agriculture Organisation of the UNITED NATIONS (FAO) and many others are still very worried that many oceans and their inhabitants are in crisis.

Investigation
Use the Internet to identify three marine species that have been brought close to extinction. Explain how this situation came about for each of the species. Suggested starting point: the decline of cod stocks in the North Atlantic. You could start by looking at www.greenpeace.org.uk/oceans

ACTIVITIES

7 Devise a publicity campaign to make people aware of the risks to marine species and to encourage them to do something about it.

8 In groups, try to work out a way of controlling international fishing. Describe what should be done and assess the chances of your scheme working. What problems would have to be overcome?

Summary of fish and marine life case study

1 Life in the sea is an important source of food across the world. In some countries, it is the main source of protein.

2 Fish stocks across the world are falling; in some places, the seas are almost empty of life. Some species have become extinct and others are close to extinction.

3 The main cause of this depletion is a growing world population and the rise of technologies that are able to locate fish accurately and scoop them up in vast quantities.

4 Despite dwindling amounts of fish, much sea life is wasted as a result of by-catch.

5 When the number of a fish species falls below a certain figure, the whole species may become unsustainable, as it cannot breed fast enough to replace losses.

6 The loss of part of the food chain will have major knock-on effects on other species of plant and animal life in the area. These effects are unpredictable and may have massive repercussions on linked ecologies.

7 The only answer seems to be some kind of international control of fishing around the world, but multi-national CO-OPERATION is difficult to achieve, and many people have interests in continuing to catch as much as they can.

3.5 Why is pollution a problem?

- What causes pollution?
- How does pollution affect the environment?
- How can pollution be controlled?

Pollution covers a very wide range of environmental problems. This topic uses the pollution of the oceans as a case study, continuing the theme from Topic 3.4, but later in the section other forms of pollution are examined.

ACTIVITY

1 A definition of pollution is:

'Any substance in water, soil or air which damages the natural quality of the environment. It may offend people's sight, taste, hearing, or smell, and/or may cause a health hazard. The usefulness of a natural resource is usually reduced by being polluted.'

Use the information above to create five statements beginning: 'Pollution is …'.

Pollution takes place in virtually every part of the world. It affects the land, the air and water. As mentioned in Topic 3.1 (page 70), human beings have always created waste and usually left it in the natural environment to decay naturally or to be dispersed by natural forces such as wind, rain and tides. With a small population, this was not a big problem for the planet.

However, today, the various forms of pollution created by people in a crowded, heavily industrialised world are one of the biggest problems we have to face.

Case Study
Pollution of the oceans

What does the sea do for us apart from providing food?

For years, because the sea is so vast, people have assumed that our bits of waste and rubbish would be literally 'a drop in the ocean', easily carried away and cleaned up magically by the action of seawater. '*The solution to pollution is dilution*' was the theory.

This was the human attitude for most of our history. But now we know that even the sea can be damaged and unable to repair itself.

This case study will look at:

- what we are putting into the oceans
- what effect this is having on the water, animals, plants and humans
- whether we can put it right.

What are we putting into the oceans?

We treat the oceans like an open sewer, dumping huge amounts of waste in them every day. We use drains and outflow pipes, and often rivers to dispose of this waste, and much of it eventually ends up in the sea.

This pollution includes human sewage and domestic wastewater, factory outflows of acids and poisonous metals, engine oil from roadside drains and garages, farm chemicals leaking from the land, nuclear waste from power plants, and oil from wells, refineries and tankers.

The daily flow of materials into the sea also includes a million plastic items such as bags, nets, and bits of packaging. Some of this pollution is accidental, but many factories and sewage systems still legally dump waste in the sea.

The oceans break up, disperse, or dissolve large quantities of waste. But there are limits, and we have reached them in many areas of the oceans.

In recent years, the sheer volume and the toxicity (the degree to which a substance is poisonous to an environment) of the waste we are dumpling into the sea has increased so much that we know it is causing damage to the oceans. Some of this damage may be irreparable.

The table below lists the main types of marine pollution.

TYPE OF MARINE POLLUTION	% OF TOTAL	EXAMPLES	PICTURE
Run-off from land, industry, domestic waste	44	• Sewage • Agricultural waste (fertilisers, dung, etc.) • Industrial waste (acids, oil, chemicals, etc.) • Food and drink (brewing waste, bad meat and vegetables)	 Industrial pollution pouring into the sea.
Atmosphere	33	• Windblown dust and gases from factories, fires and vehicles	 Forest fires not only kill trees and wildlife, they also produce carbon dioxide and acid rain – threatening pollution of the atmosphere for wide areas of the world.
Marine transport	12	• Oil leaks • Other cargo spills (chemicals, containers of food) • Pleasure boating (fuel spills, dumping rubbish)	 An oil tanker in the Gulf of Mexico. Note the oil spill around the tanker.
Dumping at sea	10	• Sewage sludge • Ships' rubbish thrown overboard • Dredging • Bilge water discharges • Rubbish disposal by barges	 Barge in the Thames loaded with rubbish heading out to sea.
Off-shore production	1	Waste from oil and gas extraction	 Oil rig burning off gas.

The UK as a polluter

TYPE OF POLLUTION	HOW DOES THE UK DO?
Disposing of hazardous waste at sea	The UK is the only country in the world that continues to burn hazardous waste at sea – on average, 90,000 tonnes of PESTICIDES, solvents, metals and plastics are incinerated at sea by the UK every year.
Disposing of radioactive waste at sea	Since the 1950s, radioactive waste from Sellafield nuclear plant has been discharged into the Irish sea, which is now thought to be one of the most radioactive stretches of water in the world. Spray from the Irish Sea turns into radioactive dust and can be found on beaches and in people's homes. Increased rates of cancer have been reported on the east coast of Ireland and west coast of England.
Discharging raw sewage into the sea	A staggering 3.8 billion litres of sewage is produced every day in the UK, of which 24 per cent is discharged untreated, compared to West Germany and Denmark, which have no untreated sewage discharges. Many beaches, particularly on the south and west coasts of England, are regarded as unfit for safe bathing, and marine life from such areas is often contaminated.

The pollution of the sea is a worldwide problem, and most countries contribute to it in one way or another. Many countries have no other affordable way to dispose of sewage and other waste. Industries that have not modernised remain major polluters of land, sea and air. Many industries in LEDCs and the developing world are still at this stage.

However, Britain is a wealthy country, but it is still is a major polluter of the seas around the UK.

ACTIVITIES

2 From the information on pages 85–87, draw a diagram or picture that shows how the oceans are being polluted. Indicate which are the heaviest forms of pollution.

3 Read the newspaper article (right). Look at an atlas and explain why you think the North Atlantic is the 'most acidic' ocean.

4 Answer the question at the beginning of this case study: 'What does the sea do for us apart from providing food?'

Oceans turn to acid

The world's oceans are sacrificing themselves to try to stave off GLOBAL WARMING. Their waters have absorbed about half of the CO_2 produced by humans over the past two centuries. Without this moderating effect, climate change would have been much more severe and rapid. But in the process, the seas have become more acidic, which threatens their very life. Research warns that this could kill off their coral reefs, shellfish and plankton, on which all marine life depends.

As the water absorbs carbon dioxide it forms carbonic acid. And the acid then mops up calcium carbonate, which sea creatures use to make the protective shells they need to survive. The results are incalculable because shelled creatures ranging from clams and corals to plankton form the base of the entire food chain of the oceans.

Adapted from The Independent,
1 August 2004

What effect do different types of marine pollution have?

- *Agricultural waste*
  Some agricultural waste (manure from animals and rotting vegetation) contains nutrients (nitrates and phosphates) from FERTILISERS. Too much of this causes algae to grow rapidly, which destroys other marine life. These are sometimes called red, brown or green tides. One effect of this is the death of coral around the world.

- *Sewage*
  Human excrement, which contains both nutrients and toxic material, is often dumped in the sea in huge quantities (for example, nine million tonnes dumped off the coast of New York and New Jersey every year). This kills nearly every living thing for miles. In Europe, things are no better, and along with untreated sewage other materials flushed down the toilet end up in the sea or on beaches. This does harm to marine life, but also causes health problems to humans. Surfers are particularly at risk because they breathe in a fine spray from the surface water – the most toxic part of the sea.

- *Oil spills and discharges*
  Although oil spills from tanker accidents do damage sea life and birds, the evidence is that the sea can cope with crude oil quite well over time. Ships, however, are responsible for more dangerous discharges into the sea, from pumping out BALLAST, which may contain toxins, or just dumping rubbish into the sea such as food waste and sewage.

- *Chemicals and airborne gases and particles*
  Many new chemicals such as DDTA and PCBs end up in the fat of many sea predators such as bears, seals, whales and sharks. These chemicals are known to be harmful to marine life and are believed to be a threat to human health. They seem to affect the hormones of animals so they cannot breed. If these effects are widespread, the marine ecosystem will be permanently changed and a major food source will disappear or be contaminated.

Many beaches across the world are polluted by sewage and urban wastewater.

- *Other dumped waste*
  Until recently, most waste material that ended up in the sea disintegrated or decomposed. But most plastic waste stays intact. Bottles, polystyrene packing, ropes and nets, plastic bags and toys all end up floating around for years. This debris has the additional effect of making many coastal areas unattractive and unhealthy for human beings.

ACTIVITY

5 Work in a group to devise and create a display that explains why pollution of the seas is bad for all living things including human beings. The display should tell the story in pictures and be understood without the use of words, or with no more than twenty words.

How pollution affects both wealth and health.

Can we put it right?

It will not be easy to stop the pollution of the oceans for the following reasons:

- The human race has grown used to the idea that the sea can be used to clean the world. It will be hard to change people's habits of living, and in many parts of the world, wealth and resources are not available to replace the sea with a purer system of waste disposal.
- Even in richer countries, many sewage systems would have to be redesigned and replaced, at enormous cost, which taxpayers and local authorities would object to paying.
- Similarly, industries and shipping companies argue that using any method of waste disposal, other than pouring into waterways and so, eventually, into the sea, would be so expensive that the companies would be bankrupted and have to close down.

- As with fishing, the seas are so huge it is impossible to police them. Apart from coastal waters, most of the ocean is open access (nobody owns or controls it). Pollution spreads around the world, pushed by tides, currents and wind.
- And, as always, growing populations and the process of industrialisation across the world create yet more pollution year on year.

Despite these difficulties, pressure is growing across the world to clean up the seas.

The most powerful pressure comes from people who live around the affected coasts. Their motives are often based on self-interest (their livelihood is at stake), but the end result could be cleaner seas. The cartoon above illustrates some important concerns for people in coastal areas.

Action by governments and environmental pressure groups is having some impact across the world. The UN has set up laws governing marine activities, including legislation on what and how much pollution ships can dump (this includes oil, chemicals and rubbish). This can result in hefty fines for ships caught breaking the rules.

Government action

Other areas like beaches and inland estuaries (the Thames estuary is an example) are monitored, and dumping is controlled by local authorities and the EU. Polluters are fined or the area is defined as being unsafe or even toxic, which destroys tourism and property values. Currently, the Irish, Norwegian, and French governments are making serious protests about the dumping of radioactive waste in the North Sea by Sellafield and Dounreay nuclear plants.

Pressure group action

• Greenpeace occupied the Brent Spar oil rig to prevent it being sunk and polluting the surrounding area. They succeeded in preventing this by arousing public feeling against it. However, some environmentalists said the pollution created by towing it away to be dismantled was greater than if it had been sunk. Nonetheless, their actions made more people aware of the problem of marine pollution, and this may help persuade people to pay money to clean up the seas.

• Surfers Against Sewage, a group of surfers based in Cornwall, has gained fame by protesting and demonstrating. They have joined with other local groups to restrict sewage outflows on the south coast of Britain.

• In California, members of a surfing club have sued paper companies for polluting the ocean. The companies paid $6 million in fines and $50 million for treatment plants.

ACTIVITIES

6 a) What does 'The solution to pollution is dilution' mean?

b) What evidence in this topic shows that this is not true?

7 Use the information on pages 85–90 to describe one form of marine pollution and explain:
• why it is difficult to stop
• why it is worth the effort and expense to stop.

Summary of pollution of the oceans case study

1 Humans have used the sea as a place to dump waste for thousands of years. For a long time, the small population and limited technology meant that it was not an environmental problem except in very localised coastal areas.

2 Nowadays, the volume and toxicity of the waste being dumped in the sea is causing problems across the world. These are threatening sea life and creating an ecological crisis.

3 There are many different ways in which pollution enters the oceans, but the greatest threats are from industrial, agricultural and human waste pouring into the sea from the land, and pollution that is airborne such as gases and solid particles.

4 This pollution is damaging to both marine life and humans. Even more so, the increase or decrease of species and micro-organisms is changing the whole marine ecosystem in ways that scientists cannot predict.

5 The outcome of these changes will adversely affect both the food supply and human health across the world.

6 This situation is hard to change, as human beings are used to using the sea as a waste disposal unit, and any changes to domestic or industrial waste disposal will be expensive and require massive changes in the way people live and work. It is difficult to police the oceans.

7 However, there are many groups who are aware of these dangers, both governmental and voluntary organisations, and there is a growing awareness that this problem needs to be controlled. Laws restricting pollution have been passed and are being enforced across the world.

3.6 How can the natural environment be exploited sustainably?

- What are renewable and NON-RENEWABLE RESOURCES?
- What problems does using non-renewable resources create?
- How can renewable resources bring about sustainable development?
- Why are renewable resources not used more?

This topic focuses on the production of energy and the need to provide increasing amounts of it as the world population grows and societies become more industrialised. It will look at:

- *different sources of energy, both non-renewable and renewable*
- *the problems associated with these sources of energy*
- *how sustainable development could be achieved in the future.*

What are non-renewable natural resources?

Non-renewable natural resources are simply described by saying that once we have used up this type of resource, there will be no more created. The best-known examples of these are fossil fuels: coal, oil and natural gas. For most of our history, since the Industrial Revolution, our energy needs have been supplied by non-renewable fossil fuels.

These non-renewable sources of energy were responsible for the great advances in industry, transport and domestic living that took place over the last 200 years. Over the last 100 years, the use of these non-renewable resources has increased seventeen-fold. MEDCs use them most. The USA uses six times as much as the average usage across the world.

These sources of energy are cheap to use, flexible, and are reasonably efficient in producing the power needed to keep industry and transport growing.

But there are problems …

- *Wood is in very short supply*
  Wood is still the most widely used fuel in many LEDCs. It is not a very efficient source of power. It is a renewable resource (new trees can be grown) but big trees are being cut down a lot more quickly than they can be grown (see Topic 3.2, pages 72–77).

- *Fossil fuels (coal, oil and gas) are running out*
  These took a very long time to be created. Each year we use a huge amount of fossil fuels that took about a million years to be made. There is still about 200 years' supply of coal, but oil and gas are close to being used up. Estimates vary, but most say 60–70 years before we run out. This figure does not take into account increases in demand for oil or gas.

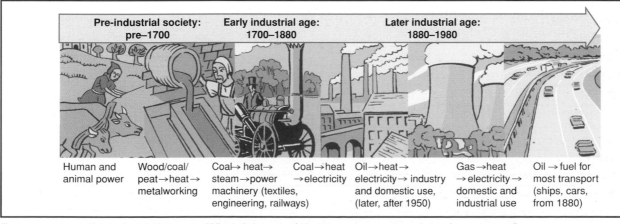

Pre-industrial society: pre–1700		Early industrial age: 1700–1880		Later industrial age: 1880–1980		
Human and animal power	Wood/coal/ peat→heat→ metalworking	Coal→ heat → steam→power machinery (textiles, engineering, railways)	Coal→heat →electricity	Oil→heat→ electricity→ industry and domestic use, (later, after 1950)	Gas →heat →electricity → domestic and industrial use	Oil → fuel for most transport (ships, cars, from 1880)

Energy sources throughout the ages. What do most of these energy sources have in common?

- *Fossil fuels cause pollution*

  Widely used fuels such as coal and oil/petroleum contain carbon, hydrogen, sulphur and nitrogen, which form carbon dioxide, sulphur oxides and nitrogen oxides when burned. These gases cause climate change (see Topic 3.8, pages 101–106). They also produce ACID RAIN. Petrol and diesel fuels produce many chemical by-products, which create PHOTOCHEMICAL SMOG. In big cities this smog is a major health risk to people in the area. Natural gas is cleaner, but produces much carbon dioxide.

  Fossil fuels still provide almost 80 per cent of the word's total energy needs and more than six billion tonnes of carbon emissions are produced annually from burning these fuels.

- *Nuclear power could be a severe threat to the environment and human life*

  Nuclear power provides 28 per cent of the UK's power needs, but many people worry about the threats to the environment caused by nuclear waste, or the risk of an accident like Chernobyl, where the area around the exploded reactor is now contaminated with radiation. The Irish Sea is polluted by waste from Sellafield (see Topic 3.5, pages 85–90). It is difficult and expensive to dispose of nuclear waste safely, and there are no methods that are completely effective. Uranium and other radioactive raw materials are also a non-renewable resource. However, there is enough uranium and other radioactive materials to keep nuclear power stations going for many years.

Solutions to the problems

The main two problems are that:

1 These resources are going to run out soon, especially because countries that are becoming more industrialised will need more of these fossil fuels as they develop.

2 Fossil fuel resources are the major source of air pollution. We know this is doing damage to the land, the oceans and the atmosphere, all of which affect humans, animals and marine life, and the climate.

But:

Fossil fuels have two very big advantages as power sources today.

1 Despite recent rises in cost, fossil fuels are still very cheap.

2 Most of our technology in industry, transport and in producing electricity is based on these fuels, and our investment in this technology is massive. To scrap power stations and our methods of transport (which include ships and aircraft as well as road vehicles) would cost an almost unthinkable amount of money.

However, we know we have to do something soon, and renewable energy is the only viable alternative. The answer that most environmental researchers and many governments have agreed on is that there is a need to develop new energy sources to add to, and eventually replace, fossil fuel use. These sources should minimise pollution and use energy efficiently.

ACTIVITY

1 Copy out the chart below and fill in the advantages and disadvantages of these non-renewable sources of energy.

Non-renewable source of energy	Advantages	Disadvantages
Coal		
Oil		
Gas		
Uranium (nuclear power)		

What are renewable energy sources?

They are sources of energy that occur naturally and are always available. They do not run out with use.

So the question is: if fossil fuels pollute the world and are running out, and renewable energy is so much cleaner and will not run out, why do we not use renewable sources for all our power needs?

All of the RENEWABLE ENERGY SOURCES are being used today across the world. But all of them create difficulties that need to be resolved before they can be used to replace fossil fuels. Below and on pages 94–95 is a list of the major sources of energy we can tap into and some of the problems associated with them.

1 Water power from rivers

HYDROPOWER makes use of the movement of fresh water in rivers, using the flow of water to generate electricity by passing the water through a turbine. The diagram below shows how a hydropower plant works.

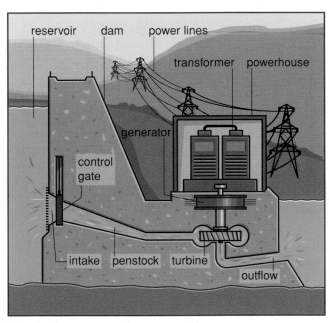

How hydropower works.

Hydropower does not cause much pollution and water is a renewable resource, but there are some problems in using it.

- The cost of building dams is enormous. It would be years before the cost was covered by the cheap electricity produced. However, they can produce a lot of electricity.
- They can be built in a limited number of places.

- To build them, lots of land has to be flooded, farms and towns disappear, and many people have to be displaced. One very big dam built in China recently, the Three Gorges Dam, displaced 1.2 million people when the area behind the dam was flooded.
- The local ecosystem is damaged (both plants and animals) and the environmental impact is widespread. Think of the fish that cannot get to breeding grounds or get killed by turbine blades.
- Water in huge reservoirs is lost through evaporation, especially in hot countries.

2 Water power from the sea

- Tidal power uses tidal movement of the sea in a similar way to the river power: water flowing in and out of a basin moving a wheel or turbine.
- Wave power uses the movement of waves to produce energy and converting this movement into electricity.

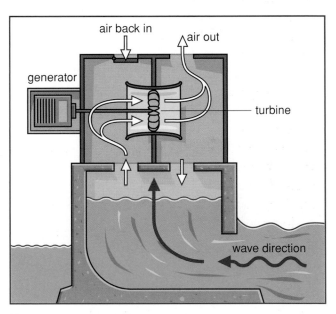

How wave power works.

In theory, the vast energy of the sea should be a major source of power, but attempts to use tides and waves to drive turbines have not produced very good results. It is expensive to build anything in the sea, and the problem of linking turbines with rising and sinking levels of water or the movement of waves has not been effectively solved except at enormous expense.

Where it has been tried, there was large-scale disruption to the ocean ecosystem and relatively little energy was produced.

3 Power from the sun

SOLAR ENERGY makes use of the heat and light of the sun. Photovoltaic cells (solar panels) can convert light to electricity. They can be placed on buildings or large numbers can be set up in sunny areas. The sunlight strikes a photovoltaic cell and is converted into electricity. Other simpler solar panels run water between panes of glass, which provide hot water for a building.

Unlike hydropower and wind power, solar energy is not used to provide much power. In theory, the sun could provide us with thousands of times our energy needs, but it is difficult to capture this resource to produce energy on a large scale.

For solar cells, the fuel is free, they cost virtually nothing to maintain, they create no pollution, but they are expensive to make, and they are not very efficient in converting sunlight to energy (about 15 per cent efficient).

- Some houses in sunny areas can produce enough power to heat water and provide lighting, but large-scale solar power is very expensive to produce.
- Although they can work in a British type of climate, at the moment, photovoltaic cells can only work on a small scale and are very expensive to produce. However, in Denmark, buildings using special designs to collect solar energy and retain heat have been made to be self-sufficient and show that even in the north solar power has a chance of working.

4 Power from the atmosphere

A wind farm in California. Wind farms have a dramatic effect on the countryside. Some people think they are very ugly, but others think they add interest to a boring landscape.

Wind energy makes use of wind to power electrical generators. These act like windmills. The wind turns large vanes that provide power for a turbine, which produces electricity.

The use of wind power is growing. It does not cause pollution through waste or gas emissions; it does not need fuel or cooling liquids. It is the British government's favoured alternative to fossil fuelled power generation.

But there are practical problems:

- wind turbines are expensive to build
- to produce a fair amount of electricity, many wind turbines are needed, which take up a lot space
- the wind does not blow all the time, so there will not be a consistent supply of electricity. Wind generation of electricity has to be backed up by other methods of producing electricity.

And there are other objections to wind farms as the newspaper headlines opposite show.

The size of this installation in the Mojave Desert gives some idea of how much space and expensive technology is needed to produce a useable quantity of power for industry. This plant produces enough energy to power over 50,000 homes.

Low-frequency noise causes migraines and insomnia

TURBINE BLADES RESPONSIBLE FOR DEATH OF RED KITE

Property prices slump as wind farm built

Blight on our landscape – the residents fight back

5 Power from plants

BIOMASS is an energy resource derived from organic matter. It creates less pollution than conventional fuels and is a renewable resource. The energy from biomass (organic/living materials) is called 'bioenergy'.

Bioenergy can be used to provide heat, make fuels and generate electricity. Wood, which people have used to cook and keep warm for thousands of years, continues to be the largest biomass resource. Today, there are also many other types of biomass we can use to produce energy. These biomass resources include waste from agricultural and forest industries, landfill gas, aquatic plants and waste produced by cities and factories.

Today, biomass provides about three to four per cent of energy used in the USA and 12 per cent across the world. We are learning how to produce materials and chemicals from biomass, which could replace petrol or diesel oil. In fact, everything we get from fossil fuels could be made from biomass.

But there are problems:

- an enormous amount of land is needed to grow crops to support energy plants
- the planting, harvesting, producing and transporting of these crops produces air pollution and adds to global warming. The burning of these crops releases CO_2 and other greenhouse gases into the atmosphere.

ACTIVITIES

2 Copy the table below and explain the advantages and disadvantages of these sources of energy.

3 As a group, discuss the question asked in this topic (page 93): 'If fossil fuels pollute the world and are running out, and renewable energy is so much cleaner and will not run out, why do we not use renewable sources for all our power needs?'

Source of energy	Advantages	Disadvantages
Hydroelectric power		
Wind power		
Solar power		
Tidal and wave power		
Biomass		

3.7 What impact does leisure and tourism have on the environment?

- How important is leisure and tourism to the world economy?
- Why is leisure and tourism an environmental issue?
- How can the effects of tourism and leisure activities on the environment be controlled?

Leisure and tourism are not exactly the same thing, but the two worlds overlap. Tourism is the movement of people around the world for pleasure, and involves travel and temporary accommodation. Leisure activities include tourism, but also include sports like golf and football, going out locally to pubs, clubs, restaurants, cinemas and so on.

ACTIVITY

1 Make a list of all the jobs in a popular holiday resort that are a result of tourism.

From this activity, you can see that leisure and tourism is a big business. In fact, it is the world's biggest industry. It is impossible to get an accurate figure, but the annual turnover is heading towards $4 trillion ($4 thousand billion).

- This is about eight per cent of total world trade.

- In Britain, ten per cent of the population is involved directly or indirectly in the tourist and leisure industry.
- The Caribbean islands get 50 per cent of their income from tourism. Some countries are almost entirely dependent on tourism, for example, the Maldives.

Tourism is growing rapidly. Most tourists are from rich countries such as the USA, western European countries and Japan. As other countries grow richer, their people join the tourist population because people in richer countries have more leisure time, more disposable income, and because travel costs, particularly air travel, have become relatively cheap.

Many poor countries (LEDCs) see tourism as the quickest way of improving their economy so that they will be able to modernise their SOCIETY and bring advantages to their people.

ACTIVITY

2 Using the diagram below as a starting point, explain the advantages that travel and tourism can bring to an area or a COMMUNITY.
Use examples from your own experience or research examples to illustrate your points.

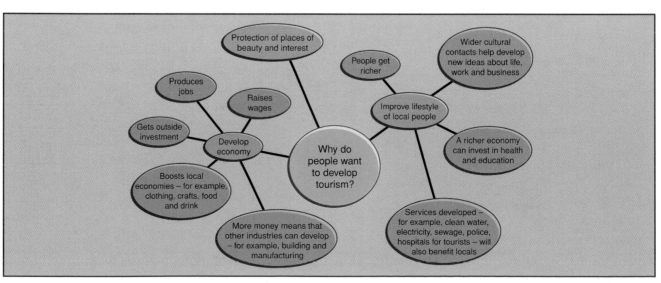

The benefits of tourism.

Why is tourism an environmental issue?

A large number of people moving around the world and staying away from home for a while brings about many environmental changes. The reasons for these changes can be broken down into these factors:

1 Transport (air travel, traffic and roads, parking).

2 Accommodation (hotels, food and drink supplies, sewage disposal) and use of resources (water supplies, use of electrical power).

3 Leisure activities (swimming pools, shops, eating and drinking facilities) and changes in land use (golf courses, safari parks, skiing, amusement parks, marinas).

4 Changes in lifestyle of local people.

1 Transport

Tourism means transport is essential. Airports, roads, docks and rail terminals have to be built or extended. A growth in traffic, especially road and air, means more air pollution. Aircraft and increases in road transport produce carbon dioxide and microscopic carbon and other particles in huge quantities. Roads and airports take up land and change the ecology of an area (see Topic 3.8, pages 101–106).

2 Accommodation and use of resources

Much tourism is centred in coastal areas. The classic desirable holiday image is a tropical beach scene, idyllic and peaceful. Many tourists want to go to areas such as the Caribbean, Goa, Thailand and the Seychelle Islands, which are new to mass tourism and were undeveloped until very recently.

Tourists usually want attractive, clean, comfortable places to stay. This involves building modern hotels and resorts, usually in the most attractive areas. Often the local people have to move out. The building work itself often creates pollution from cement dust and machinery.

Tourists want water for showers, pools and golf courses. They want electricity for lifts, air conditioning and DVD players. They want modern plumbing and waste disposal.

To provide this, power and water has to go to the tourists as a priority, but it may leave local people short of electricity, or it may drain limited water supplies.

- A large hotel in Egypt uses as much electricity as 3,600 families.
- A tourist in Spain uses 880 litres (194 gallons) of water a day, compared with 250 (55 gallons) by a local.
- Sewage disposal is a complex thing and the simplest way of disposing of a large increase in sewage is dumping dangerous waste into the sea a few miles from the tourist area.

3 Leisure activities and changes in land use

Mountains and countryside

Second only to beaches and coastlines, mountains are the most popular of tourist destinations, accounting for fifteen to twenty per cent of world tourism. People walk over them, climb them and ski on them.

Some examples are given below.

- The number of trekkers visiting the Everest region of Nepal has risen from none in 1960 to 17,000 in 1996. There were almost 2,000 ascents of Everest in 2003. Four out of five local HOUSEHOLDS derive some income from tourism. Twelve per cent of the trail network is damaged and there is an estimated 17 tonnes of rubbish per kilometre (0.6 miles) of trail.
- Up to 700,000 skiers use Switzerland's mountain slopes on any one day during peak season. Ecological damage inflicted by the ski industry includes:
  - changing the environment by the removal of forests, levelling of land and carving of pathways
  - the production of artificial snow, which uses up vast quantities of water and energy, and can deposit artificial additives in snow.
- As a result of this, many mountains have become unstable and avalanches are much more likely, which means artificial barriers have to be built. Most wildlife has left the area.
- In Britain, the most popular area for walkers is the Peak District National Park. There has been a steady increase in visits over the last 40 years as the area becomes more accessible to cars and coaches. The resulting traffic during holiday periods means that the air in some areas of the

park is more polluted than the air in central London. The people who walk or ride bikes or horses have eroded footpaths.

Lower lands and plains

- *Golf courses*
  There are 25,000 golf courses across the world, which use large areas of land and need millions of litres of water. Some, in dry areas such as Dubai, need 2.5 million litres (0.55 million gallons) a day, as well as fertilisers and pesticides.

- *Safari parks and national parks*
  In Kenya and Tanzania, the big attraction to tourists are the wildlife reserves of East Africa. Preserving an area and its wildlife seems a good thing for the environment, and in many ways it is. The species are protected from poachers and the land is left to renew itself.

But there are downsides:

- The Masai, the original inhabitants of the area, were forced off the land by the governments of Tanzania so that the land could become a 'protected area'. This is destroying their life and culture. Their only hope of work is in the tourist industry.
- Roads and hotels have been built. Heavy four-wheel drive trucks churn up the land as they carry tourists around to look at wild animals.
- Studies in Kenya's Masai Mara National Park found that cheetahs were so disturbed by the volume of tourists that they frequently failed to mate, feed or raise their young. The animals do not seem to have been protected. A 2001 report by Kenya's Regional Centre for Mapping of Resources for Development said wildlife in the park had declined by over 58 per cent in the past twenty years.

A golf course in Dubai. In a dry area such as this, the major expense is for water to keep the course green.

African safari buses. Wildlife find these daily intrusions very stressful. This is not the best way to see wildlife.

4 Changes in lifestyle of local people

Tourism not only changes the environment, it changes the way people live. Tourism brings jobs, and these jobs are very different from the traditional work such as farming and fishing, which used to be the way of life in the area. People often give up the traditional work to take on new jobs, possibly because the pay is better, or the work is more exciting because it is new and involves meeting new people. This can have the good effect of helping people widen their horizons, and learn new skills and develop new ambitions.

So, farming and fishing decline, and cooking and service jobs become the new life. As an area grows, local people are displaced by hotels, shops, restaurants and bars built where they used to live. The peaceful beauty of the place, which originally attracted the tourists, may be lost, and instead the area becomes a 'resort', which tries to provide the tourists with their 'home comforts'.

ACTIVITY

3 With a partner, make a list of the 'home comforts' you think a resort may have in order to provide for English tourists.

Natural beauty – the clear sea in Corfu.

New cultures replace the old

When the wealth of tourism comes to a country, its landscape changes and the people have to adapt. Some of the effects are good: more wealth, better INFRASTRUCTURE, new opportunities for the people, the land and sites of interest and beauty are protected and developed.

Some of the effects are bad: beaches and tourist areas are closed to locals, hotels and roads destroy the beauty of the natural environment, and the area is polluted by sewage and traffic fumes.

Moreover, the culture is changed and the people are influenced by affluent cultures that bring with them bars, drugs and the lure of easy money. Thailand has become a centre for sex tourism; some Masai tribesmen have ended up as dancers in hotel cabarets; crime, especially theft, has increased in countries where it was almost unknown. It is not hard to see why. The contrast between the lifestyles of the tourists and the locals is often extreme. In a community where earning enough to provide food and shelter is the goal of most people, the temptation of money, expensive clothing and technology, casually lying around on beaches and loungers beside swimming pools must be hard to resist.

These changes in culture and values change social life, which has an impact on the environment. For example, increasing crime may lead to the separation of tourists from the local population by gates and fences. Money from tourism may mean that the priority for land use is hotels, roads, airports and areas for tourist recreation rather than for agriculture and the local community.

The new Corfu, Kavos, 2003.

Can the effects of tourism on the environment be controlled?

This is a difficult question. In many ways, tourism is what many people want. It is one of the most effective ways of boosting an economy. It provides jobs and helps economies develop. People in more affluent countries see 'leisure' and 'holidays' as being a reward and a break from the stresses of working.

At the same time, tourism is responsible for many environmental problems, from pollution of the sea and air to the destruction of wildlife and areas of natural beauty.

What is being done?

Many tourists and people living in tourist areas want to see some limits to the damage to the environment. Already, many tourist areas have learned to their cost that over-development turns people away. More and more people see over-commercialised tourist destinations as unattractive.

There are many local, national and international organisations working to reduce the environmental impact of tourism. Their ideas and actions are described in various phrases: SUSTAINABLE TOURISM, eco-tourism, nature tourism, green travel and environmentally responsible tourism.

These groups, and examples of what they are doing, are shown in the table below.

ACTIVITIES

4 Draw a diagram like the one on page 96 where the central theme is: 'Why might people **not** want to develop tourism?'

5 Explain how tourism can cause both environmental and social problems in tourist destinations. Give examples from the material in this topic, from work you have done in class, and from your own experiences as a tourist.

TYPES OF ORGANISATION	EXAMPLES OF ACTION
Local council or community groups working to protect their home and the local environment	1 The local leaders in the Annapurna region of Nepal have created the Himalayan Code for Tourism, which has set up directives to limit the use of local resources and reduce the rubbish left behind. There is now a local organisation that controls the number of visitors, monitors them and uses some of the money paid for guides and 'sherpas' for local conservation and development.
	2 The local government in Malaga has demolished several high-rise apartments on the coast to open up the sea front, and ensured that new buildings are attractive and in keeping with the character of the old town.
Independent organisations and pressure groups that work to protect aspects of the environment which are under threat	The WWF (the World Wildlife Fund), the Nature Conservancy and Conservation International have put funding into projects that attempt to protect wildlife, and to ensure that essential local resources such as water, timber and areas of natural beauty are not damaged by commercial developments.
The travel industry	The travel industry has woken up to the concerns for the environment. The World Travel and Tourism Council (WTTC) has created an eco-travel association called 'Green Globe'. The idea is that joining this organisation will help travel companies become aware of environmental issues and change their approaches to make tourism more sustainable.

ACTIVITIES

6 What factors will encourage tourists, the travel industry and local communities to continue to expand tourism?

7 Explain why it may be difficult to develop 'sustainable' or 'eco-' tourism across the world.

3.8 Is climate change the world's biggest environmental problem?

- What is meant by 'global warming' and 'climate change'?
- What evidence is there that global warming and climate change is taking place?
- What will be the effects of global warming and climate change?
- Can we do anything to stop global warming and climate change taking place?

If you have been working through this section, you have probably realised that environmental issues are all linked to each other. The way we make use of the environment changes it, and by consuming raw materials and producing waste, we create problems of pollution and depletion. Human beings have always changed the environment by living in it, and so it will continue to change. The case studies in this section have given examples of how the ways people use the environment affect others. They have also shown why it is difficult to reach agreements to solve the problems.

In this topic we look at climate change. Many people describe it as the biggest problem the world faces. We examine why people think it is happening, what the likely effects of these changes are, and what we may be able to do about it.

'Climate change is the single most important issue we face as a global community.'

Tony Blair, Prime Minister of the UK, April 2004

ACTIVITY

In small groups:

1 a) Make a list of any changes or extremes of weather you have experienced or heard of in the last few years (such as floods, gales, heatwaves).
   b) Discuss the effects these weather events have had on people's lives.

What does 'climate change' mean?

Climate change is the result of global warming. The Intergovernmental Panel on Climate Change (IPCC) predicts that average global temperatures will rise by somewhere between 1.4 to 5.8°C during the twenty-first century. This may not seem to be much, but when this happens, weather patterns will change drastically. This in turn will affect animal and plant life.

Changes in global temperatures have taken place for millions of years, and some scientists argue that the current changes are just part of this pattern. However, most scientists are alarmed by how quickly this is happening and predict that these changes will cause global problems in the near future. They say this warming is taking place partly because of the increase in emissions of greenhouse gases.

Temperature figures from the past, using estimates from ancient arctic ice, and more recent records show that the global temperature is rising. The chart below gives an indication of this sudden rise.

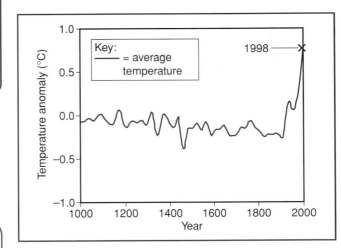

Reconstruction of temperatures for the past millennium averaged over the northern hemisphere.

The greenhouse effect shown in the diagram on page 102 explains how this temperature rise comes about.

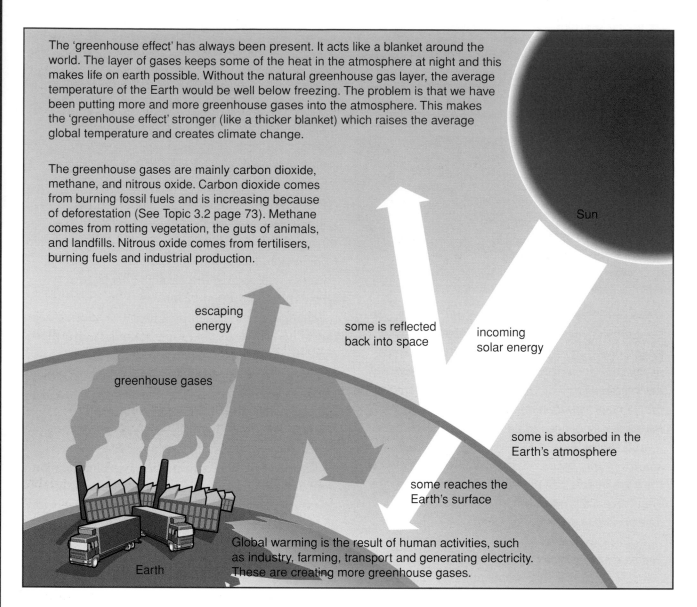

The 'greenhouse effect' has always been present. It acts like a blanket around the world. The layer of gases keeps some of the heat in the atmosphere at night and this makes life on earth possible. Without the natural greenhouse gas layer, the average temperature of the Earth would be well below freezing. The problem is that we have been putting more and more greenhouse gases into the atmosphere. This makes the 'greenhouse effect' stronger (like a thicker blanket) which raises the average global temperature and creates climate change.

The greenhouse gases are mainly carbon dioxide, methane, and nitrous oxide. Carbon dioxide comes from burning fossil fuels and is increasing because of deforestation (See Topic 3.2 page 73). Methane comes from rotting vegetation, the guts of animals, and landfills. Nitrous oxide comes from fertilisers, burning fuels and industrial production.

Sun

escaping energy

some is reflected back into space

incoming solar energy

greenhouse gases

some is absorbed in the Earth's atmosphere

some reaches the Earth's surface

Earth

Global warming is the result of human activities, such as industry, farming, transport and generating electricity. These are creating more greenhouse gases.

The ozone layer acts as a barrier to harmful ultraviolet (UV) radiation. UV can cause skin cancers and mutations in plants. Chemicals called CFCs have made holes in this layer and it is letting in more UV radiation. This is not, as some people think, a major cause of global warming. The hole in the ozone layer does not let more heat in but it is a threat to the health of people and animals.

Climate change

The result of these changes in the world temperature does not mean simply that everywhere is getting hotter. This will happen in some places, but it could also result in some places getting colder, wetter, drier, and more likely to experience extreme weather such as hurricanes and droughts. In other words, the effects of global warming on weather are unpredictable.

Does everyone think that climate change is taking place?

Most scientists accept that the climate is changing, that we produce more greenhouse gases than we used to, that global warming is taking place.

But not all scientists believe that this situation is a serious threat to the planet. They argue that:

- climate changes have taken place before and people have adapted
- heat will create water vapour and clouds which will cool the planet down
- more carbon dioxide will encourage plant growth, and these will absorb the excess CO_2
- the oceans are able to absorb more CO_2 (they already absorb a huge amount)
- climate change does not have to be bad; many people will benefit from warmer weather and more or less rainfall.

So why should we worry?

The vast majority of scientists *do* think this change in climate is a serious problem. Why?

1 Increasing CO_2

The most developed countries produce the most CO_2 and the USA is the world's largest producer. Other countries, such as India and China, have growing populations and are becoming industrialised rapidly. Despite attempts to use alternative sources of energy, the burning of fossil fuels is increasing. As a result, emissions of CO_2 and other greenhouse gases such as methane are also increasing.

China is industrialising rapidly.

2 Evidence of changes in climate

- Arctic sea ice is on average 1.8 m (6 ft) thick now, compared to 3 m (10 ft) thick in the 1970s. NASA satellite imagery suggests that arctic sea ice is shrinking at the edges by 2.9 per cent per decade.
- Two small islets in the Pacific Ocean have already disappeared in Kiribati and many low-lying islands are losing coastal land at a rate of up to 25 m (82 ft) each year from rising sea levels.
- In May 2003, a record heatwave in India, with the temperature reaching 49°C (117° Fahrenheit), claimed more than 1600 lives. In societies without air conditioning, there is no ready escape from the dangerous heat. But any society unaccustomed to high temperatures can be disrupted by a heatwave. In August 2003, record high temperatures across Europe claimed a startling 35,000 lives.
- Scientists now report ice and glaciers melting in all the world's major mountain ranges, including the Rocky Mountains, the Andes, the Alps and the Himalayas. Ski resorts in Europe have recently had to reduce the ski season by five weeks. In Scotland, two ski areas have closed because of limited snow in the last five years.
- Crop yields have fallen as temperatures have climbed in key food-producing countries such as the USA and India. Depressed world grain harvests over the last three years have left the world with a grain shortfall of some 92 million tonnes.
- Occasional droughts are common in southern Africa, but since the 1980s there has been an increase in the number of serious droughts – two or three during the early 1990s alone.
- In 2004, the Caribbean Islands and Florida experienced four major hurricanes over a two-month period. Two of these hurricanes were the most powerful for 30 years, and four major hurricanes in one year is double the average for the area.
- Bangladesh has suffered from floods for many years, but over the last decade, rainfall has been heavier and these floods have been more severe, lasted longer and extended over more land.
- Changing climate has resulted in some insects and diseases managing to survive and spread further across the world. Malaria, dengue ('breakbone') fever, yellow fever, cholera and rodent-borne viruses are also appearing with increased frequency. These diseases are transmitted by animals or water.

ACTIVITY

2 Take three of the examples listed above and explain what the short- and long-term effects could have been to the people and the environment in the area affected.

Investigation
Research other examples of climate change or unusual weather that could give support to the idea that global warming is causing changes. Prepare a short presentation of your findings.

Why is climate change seen as a major problem for the world?

1 Unpredictable effects
Climate changes will take place, but no one is sure what they will be.

Some people predict that the UK will have a climate similar to that of the south of France. But other people say that as sea currents may change, it is possible that the UK will become colder. Changing sea currents could make countries warmer or colder.

Sea levels are going to rise as ice melts at the poles. This could mean that many major cities near the sea (as many of them are) will be flooded. London, New York and Hong Kong are all at risk.

2 Uneven impact across the world
Some places will get less rain, and some will get more. Extreme weather such as floods, droughts and hurricanes will become more common.

Many countries that already have water shortages will be even drier – Africa is already worst hit by this. Europe is likely to get wetter.

In a crisis like a flood or a hurricane, the countries that are poorer will suffer most because they do not have the resources to cope with a large-scale problem.

Rising sea levels will affect many low-lying landmasses, wiping out coastal areas. Again, countries with wealth will be able to prepare for this but poor countries can do little.

3 Effects on plant and animal life
Changes in climate will obviously affect plant life, which will affect food production. In some areas, crops will fail; in others, new crops will thrive and provide a bonus for some people.

Animals, birds, fish and insects will all be affected, either dying out, or moving to new areas, or thriving and becoming a threat to food crops. Already, mosquitoes are spreading to countries where there are no predators to control them, which could lead to the spread of diseases in places where people have no immunity.

The future
Global warming and climate change is taking place. How much hotter the world becomes depends on the amount of greenhouse gases we continue to produce and whether the process of global warming can be reversed. Scientists disagree about how much the climate will change, but changes in climate and in the ecology of the natural environment are taking place right now and we should expect more changes in the future.

A satellite image of Hurricane Charley over Cuba. Scientists are monitoring climate change using images like this.

What can be done?

There are two approaches:

1 Try to control global warming by reducing the amount of greenhouse gases we produce. This may slow down or halt climate change.

2 Accept that climate change will continue to take place and start to prepare to adapt the way we live to cope with the changes.

Option 1: Control global warming

International agreement: The Kyoto Protocols (1977)

A start was made at Kyoto (in Japan) where the developed countries agreed a protocol (a set of rules) that sets out the amount of greenhouse gases each country would be allowed to produce. This meant that by 2010 they had to reduce gas emissions to be five per cent less than they were in 1990.

One hundred and thirty countries including the UK agreed to do this, but the biggest producer of CO_2, the USA, would not sign up because they said they were not convinced that the problem was so great, and their economy would suffer.

This is still a major problem. If the USA do not agree, then other countries' reductions of gas emissions will not make much difference. Developing countries who are starting to industrialise will add to the CO_2, and if the USA do not accept the Kyoto Agreement, they will not see why they should limit their own gas emissions.

National governments' policies

The UK government set itself a target of a 20 per cent reduction in CO_2 emissions over 20 years. The UK has made progress as a result of cutting down on coal burning and making laws to encourage cleaner energy production, but recent figures suggest the target will be missed.

However, more efficient transport, cleaner industry, good farming and forestry methods, and careful waste disposal (methane) can all contribute to reducing greenhouse gas emissions.

Other national governments are using some less-polluting energy production methods (for example, wind power in Denmark, nuclear power in France, geothermal power in Iceland, solar power in Mexico) and have reduced CO_2 emissions.

Individual changes of lifestyle

By changing our individual lifestyles, people can reduce greenhouse gas emissions:

- Use less energy – turning out lights, turning down heating.
- Use public transport more, cut down on personal travel, stop using cars for short journeys.
- Recycle materials such as paper, glass, aluminium and plastic so we use less raw materials and power.

Of course, to do these things well, governments need to change their policies too.

ACTIVITIES

3 In groups, design a poster showing ways in which you as individuals could reduce greenhouse gas emissions. The examples in this topic are not the only ways.

4 Take three of your ideas and explain how these approaches will reduce greenhouse gas emissions.

5 Give two examples of what a government could do to make sure that greenhouse gas emissions are reduced.

Option 2: Prepare for climate change

Extreme weather

Hurricanes, floods, droughts, high winds and hot weather will become more common. These can be predicted to some extent, for example hurricanes have a season in the Caribbean (August–October). They follow a similar path, so it would be possible to build houses that can resist the power of the wind and rain. Evacuation to safe places can be planned, even rehearsed.

Hurricane damage can be limited by good building design.

After the flood in Boscastle, Cornwall, 2004.

We know which places might flood, so we can prepare flood defences and build in order to hold out water. Once an area has flooded, we know it could happen again. The flood in Cornwall in 2004 was the result of heavy rainfall over-filling a river valley that usually runs gently through the village to the sea.

ACTIVITY

6 Discuss what precautions Boscastle village could take to prevent this happening again.

Prepare for changes in the environment

Some of these things are already happening, but the work needs to be extensive and worldwide. If countries simply look after their own interests, global inequality could lead to massive CONFLICTS. Measures need to be taken immediately to prepare for changes in the environment. Possible measures include:

- Begin to plan how to introduce new species of plants that can thrive in warmer/wetter/drier weather in different zones of the world.
- Make preparations to combat diseases that may come into an area after climate change, for example, malaria in the UK. Have anti-malaria medication.
- Prepare people for environmental changes before they happen through the media and education. Allow people time to adjust.
- Give experts time and money to research and find responses to predictable changes.
- Ensure that emergency water and food supplies and disaster relief are prepared, and that the delivery and distribution is planned.
- Set up worldwide organisations and funds to identify and help areas and countries in distress.

Unless these measures are taken on a worldwide basis, these outcomes will be a disaster for some if not all the people on the planet.

The devastation caused by the tsunami (tidal wave) in the Indian Ocean on 26 December 2004 to Indonesia, Thailand, Sri Lanka and other countries was not the result of climate change. However, many scientists believe that environmental disasters on this level are likely to become more common as climate change develops. The aid that was sent was extensive and generous, but it was not available when it was most needed to the people who needed it (immediately after the tsunami struck). This underlines the importance of planning to cope with the unexpected events that are likely to happen in the future.

3.9 What can we do about environmental problems?

- Why should we be concerned about environmental issues?
- Which groups have an influence on our attitudes?
- What methods have been used to influence people's behaviour, attitudes and values?
- How effective have these methods been?

This section on environmental issues has set out several case studies, illustrating some aspects of the struggle to maintain a healthy sustainable environment. These are not the only environmental issues, you can probably think of others. The important outcome of this section is to make you aware that we cannot assume that somehow everything will work out well.

This topic looks at the ways in which various groups have attempted to make people aware of the environmental problems we face. They have tried to show the risks for the future and to promote sustainable approaches to the environment.

We will examine their methods and assess how successful they have been so far.

Why should we be concerned?

Most scientists believe that the planet will survive, but there is no guarantee that human beings will. If we damage our environment seriously enough, we will not survive.

At the moment, this seems a remote possibility – populations are growing, many people live longer than ever before, and some of the world's population live in great comfort. But the case studies have shown us that we still face some problems, and each described how something could be done to improve or solve the situation.

For example:

- The loss of the rainforest (Topic 3.2, pages 72–77): protect and manage the use of the forest so it can regenerate.
- The pollution of the oceans (Topic 3.5, pages 85–90): governments have tried to limit both fishing and pollution by legislation.

- The pollution from burning fossil fuels for energy (Topic 3.6, pages 91–95): reduce pollution by adopting alternative energy sources developed by scientists and engineers, backed by governments.
- Tourism (Topic 3.7, pages 96–100): may become less damaging to the environment as both tourist and the tourist industry recognise that they must behave differently.

Each of these solutions has something in common. They all have three steps to taking action.

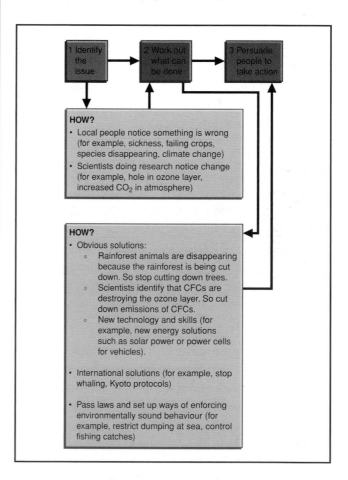

How can attitudes, behaviour and values be changed?

Some of this work is done by governments, large organisations, small groups and individuals. But it can only be successful if the public can be persuaded that it matters. The media play a big part in this process.

The government

When scientists, environmentalists, medical researchers, the voting public and usually the media are able to convince the government that there is a problem, the government may act and bring in laws to deal with the problem. For example, in the UK, the government has:

- set up an initiative called Local Agenda 21 (LA21). All local authorities are required to encourage local partnerships between communities, businesses and the local authority in order to do something about the global issues of climate change and sustainable development. This has resulted in recycling schemes, reductions in town centre traffic pollution and more efficient cleaning and waste disposal
- stopped the sale of leaded petrol to protect people's health
- set up inspections of industrial sites to reduce pollution and toxic waste
- tried to educate the public about environmental issues such as global warming through the media and their education policies.

The Green Party

The Green Party is a political party in the UK and in the European Parliament. Basically, they all see the main political issue as sustainability of the environment and societies across the world. Their policies are in support of protecting the environment, reducing conflict and sharing the world's resources more fairly. They have some voters' support and the opportunity to promote green policies.

- They campaign for election using 'green' issues as their policy: more public transport, restricting the growth of air travel, recycling, alternative energy production and urban restoration.
- They get people involved by standing for election and getting their ideas across in the media and through political rallies.
- They produce informative posters and pamphlets, and seek to educate people and exert political power.

Investigation

Find out:

- three more examples of actions and laws that the UK government or local authorities have introduced to protect the environment.
- two examples of ways the UK government has tried to educate people about environmental issues.

ACTIVITY

1 You are in charge of a government department who have responsibility for protecting the environment. You have been given the funding to improve the environment in one of the following areas:

- reducing air pollution
- cutting down congestion
- clearing up the coastline and the sea around Britain.

Choose one of these projects and draw up a series of measures which will bring about an improvement in the areas you have chosen. Measures could be:

- education (schools, media, publicity)
- legislation to prevent environmental abuse
- encouraging good practice by industry and people
- taxation to change peoples' attitudes to waste, pollution and abuse of the environment.

Design a political manifesto which explains what you will do.

Pressure groups

Environmental pressure groups are made up of people who do know and understand the issues. These groups are usually more forceful than the government because the issue is their main concern.

These groups have basically the same objectives:

- To inform the public about environmental issues.
- To make individuals concerned enough to do something about the issues.
- To try to get governments to do something about the issues.

'Global climate change is the single biggest environmental problem facing the planet.' This image vividly portrays the potential chaos ahead.

However, they use different methods to achieve these aims. For example:

• *The Union of Concerned Scientists*
This organisation operates in the USA and produce publications full of scientific data. This information is used by journalists in the media often to challenge the US government's policies. They are influential because their expertise makes it hard to challenge them. They encourage the public to use the Internet to tell the government what they think.

• *Friends of the Earth*
The first environmental pressure group in the UK to start campaigns to protect whales, endangered species and tropical rainforests. They were early campaigners against acid rain, ozone depletion and climate change. Their methods include:

• running campaigns to raise awareness of the issues
• advertising in the press
• collecting funds by appealing to people's sympathies through posters that describe or show environmental problems dramatically
• producing materials for schools and for local organisations that are fighting for an environmental issue
• taking part in demonstrations that relate to environmental concerns and keeping their name in the public's eye

• appearing in the media, producing materials for them and concentrating on getting publicity for their ideas, presenting well-thought out arguments that might influence the government.

Junked cars. Friends of the Earth use powerful images to show how 'our throw-away culture is risking people's health and squandering the world's natural resources.'

• *Greenpeace*
Greenpeace is the best-known environmental pressure group in the UK, and probably across the globe. They operate all over the world and they tend to get headlines for much of their campaigns.

They campaign about all the issues mentioned in this chapter and many others. In 2004, their environmental campaigns included: ocean pollution and over-fishing, deforestation, nuclear safety, climate change, toxic chemicals, waste disposal and genetically modified crops.

They are focused on environmental issues, but are also involved in campaigns to bring about global equality, fair trade and world peace.

Why is Greenpeace so well known?

The short answer is that their methods of getting publicity (and through this, getting attention from the public) are very effective. They have realised that to get ordinary people involved in these issues, they need spectacular publicity. So, rather than write articles, they carry out actions that will attract press attention. This means things that are unusual, possibly risky, and which can be photographed and filmed. This is sometimes called 'direct action'. The media themselves want dramatic stories, and Greenpeace provide them. The press, in describing these events, will have to discuss the issue, and this is what Greenpeace want.

For example, in recent years, Greenpeace activists have tried to stop whaling by sailing dangerously close to whaling ships and filming horrific sights of whales being killed. In this way, they got good pictures and videos, which the media used, and which reflected badly on the whalers, whilst the activists gained some support from admirers.

Greenpeace are well known because they have caught the public's imagination with their activities and made the issues seem urgent and real.

Their publicity operates on all levels: a very detailed website gives accessible information; their posters are distinctive and attractive; they provide schools and other institutions with materials that explain the issues clearly, and they concentrate on gaining support, particularly from young people.

Greenpeace activists being thrown off a Lithuanian trawler during a protest to stop bottom trawling (see Topic 3.5, page 81, on 'by-catch').

Investigation

Use the Internet to find information to make a presentation about a campaign by any pressure group.

• What methods were used to try to influence people's behaviour, attitudes and values?
• Did the campaign bring about changes in attitude or behaviour (either individual or other organisations)?

What can ordinary people do?

The government and pressure groups are not the only ways that change can be effected. Many environmental issues are dealt with on a local or individual level.

1 Local single interest groups

An environmental issue may be local, such as a canal filled with rubbish, or a factory near houses that is producing pollution and smells bad. There may be plans to build a by-pass through a rural beauty spot, or to extend an airport. In situations like these, the people who live locally can become the pressure group for this one single issue.

An example of the success of this approach is the story of Reef Relief, an organisation based in Key West, Florida. In 1987, a local group of fishing and charter-boat captains realised that the reefs around Key West were suffering damage from visitors who were diving and fishing there. They got together and installed a system of mooring buoys just away from the living coral to prevent anchor damage to the reef. They also developed a code for divers to follow, which stopped them accidentally damaging and polluting the reef and killing the coral.

One of the skippers, Craig Quirolo, and his wife DeeVon, set up a grassroots organisation called Reef Relief to protect the reef and to educate people about the importance of the reefs as a vital marine ecosystem, and the threats to reefs from pollution and careless tourism. Since then, Craig and Reef Relief have become international experts in the threats to reefs.

The mooring buoy program has been taken up by local groups to protect reefs around Jamaica, Puerto Rico, Mexico, Cuba, and other Caribbean islands. Over the years, Reef Relief has widened its range of influence. It works now to promote cleaner seas. It has campaigned successfully against oil-drilling near the Keys. It has supported environmental causes such as boater no-discharge zones, the Florida Keys National Marine Sanctuary Water Quality Protection Program, reduced cruise ship pollution, and an Everglades Restoration Plan. Reef relief has become a major local and national political influence and has taught thousands of boaters and divers to be environmentally friendly.

2 Individuals

In the UK, environmental issues can only be resolved if individuals are prepared to change the way they live. Governments have a lot of control over individual behaviour, but in a democracy, they usually act in a way that people accept and want. So, if we are concerned about climate change, we will:

- burn less fossil fuels
- use cars less
- recycle raw materials
- produce less waste
- buy 'environmentally friendly' goods
- insist on alternative energy sources for our power needs.

In the UK, many individuals have started to change their behaviour. Recycling has become common. Some people try to produce less waste and litter. People are encouraged by government action, for example smaller cars are cheaper to run, so fuel economy is not just good for the environment, it is good for our pockets.

Investigation

Research a local environmental issue that has resulted in some kind of protest.
a) Explain what the issue was (what was happening and why did people object?).
b) Describe what action was taken.
c) Describe the outcome.
d) Explain why the outcome turned out in the way it did.

ACTIVITIES

2 Describe what actions you and your family take that are environmentally friendly. What else do you think you and your family could do?

3 a) From what you have learned in this section, list the three most important environmental issues that you feel must be solved. Explain why you chose these.

b) Choose one issue and plan a campaign to persuade the rest of the world to do something about it.

Examination questions and advice

Exam questions in both papers can be divided into two groups.

1 *Source-based questions* testing your ability to apply your studies to the stimulus material.

2 Questions testing your *recall and understanding* of the examples and cases you have studied.

There are lots of source-based questions of different levels of difficulty running right throughout the book, so in this section we are going to practise the second type of question – all of which are for 8 marks maximum.

You need to practise so that you can write about 160–200 words in fifteen minutes for a top answer.

There are both questions for you to try and candidates' answers to some of the question for you to discuss in groups.

Culture and beliefs

1 People have different views about the importance of nature and nurture in shaping who we are. Write a short essay about the nature/nurture debate. In your answer you should:

- explain the meaning of the terms
- use examples from your studies
- give your own conclusion on the debate.

AQA, 2003

Candidate Naomi writes:

Some people say that it is nature that makes you who you are because you get your genes from your parents. The way they act is the way you will act at the same age.

Other people say it is nurture because most young kids have role models and they copy the way they do things and learn from them.

Also, if you are brought up in a tough area, you will be tough yourself.

We looked at how adverts for toys use colours to show which toys were for boys and which were for girls. This is socialisation. There is primary

socialisation, which is your parents, and there is secondary socialisation.

I think primary socialisation is the most important because then parents can keep more control over the child. After this, when a child has learned its roles, norms and beliefs, it can socialise itself from media and friends.

ACTIVITIES

1 a) Read candidate Naomi's answer to question 1.

 b) In groups, discuss the strengths of the answer and ways in which it could be improved. Consider the following marking guidelines when discussing the answer:
 - Is there evidence of understanding of the key concepts?
 - Has the candidate used examples from her own studies?
 - Have specialist words/language been used?
 - Has the candidate covered the three bullet points?

2 Now try the question yourself.
 a) First, talk your answer through in small groups/pairs.
 b) Then write down some bullet points or draw a concept map to help you plan your answer.
 c) When you are ready, complete your written answer in about fifteen minutes. You will speed up with practise.

A grade guide and comments on the candidate's answer is given on page 115.

Now try the following questions.

2 Choose a moral issue you have studied. Write about the issue using the following guidelines:

- Explain clearly what the issue is.
- Give examples of the people (individual groups) who hold these views.
- Explain in detail how the views are different.
- Explain why it is difficult for people to agree or compromise about the issue.

3 Explain why people might develop different beliefs and values in different cultures. Use examples from your studies to support your answer.

4 Which of the following have the most influence on teenagers' values and behaviour?

- Parents
- Mass media
- Other

Use examples from your studies to support your answer.

Conflict and co-operation

5 What approaches might help resolve international or national conflict? Use an example from your studies to explain why attempts might succeed or fail.

Candidate Sam writes:

You always have to have a compromise. One attempt to resolve conflict was the United Nations in 1948. The conflict was about Israel. Lots of Jews had been coming from Europe because of Hitler and the Nazis who persecuted them. The UN wanted to split the land up, but the Arabs would not accept it. This is known as the partition. So there was fighting and the Jews won, so they set up the state of Israel. Then there were four wars. The first was the Suez War in the 1950s, which the Israelis won. Then there was the six-day war, which the Israelis also won. Each time they got more land.

There is still fighting today because the UN partition plan failed.

ACTIVITIES

3 a) Read candidate Sam's answer to question 5.

b) In groups, discuss the strengths of the answer and ways in which it could be improved. Consider the following marking guidelines when discussing the answer:
- How many approaches has Sam mentioned and explained?
- Has an example from his studies been used?
- Have reasons for success or failure been discussed?
- Have any specialist terms been used?

4 Now try the question yourself.

a) First, talk your answer through in small groups/pairs.

b) Then write down some bullet points or draw a concept map to help you plan your answer.

c) When you are ready, complete your written answer in about 15 minutes.

A grade guide and comments on the candidate's answer is given on page 115.

Now try the following questions.

6 Using an example from your own studies, explain how conflict may arise between individuals/small groups.

7 From your own studies, explain how conflict can affect individuals. In your answer you should write about the following:

- Personal effects.
- Social effects.
- Economic effects.

8 Identify a national or international conflict you have studied and explain the economic and social effects on the people involved.

Environmental issues

9 Using your own knowledge, explain why some people have taken action over an environmental issue. In your answer you should:

- identify and explain the environmental issue
- explain the concerns that people have about the issue
- describe the method(s) used.

Candidate Tom writes:

Environmental groups such as Greenpeace affect environmental issues in many ways. Whale hunting is a good example. When this came to the attention of Greenpeace in the 1970s, they found evidence that whales were in danger of becoming extinct and decided to take non-violent direct action. This means they tried to disrupt the whale hunters peacefully and legally.

They got their own ship, Rainbow Warrior, *and used inflatables to get in the way of the harpoon gun, all the while videoing what was going on. They influenced people's attitudes towards whale hunting by sending the video to TV channels and using pictures on their own publicity leaflets. They explained how whales have become an endangered species and how this affects the rest of the marine ecosystem. Whales control the numbers of krill, which feed on plankton. Plankton put oxygen in the water, which other fish need to live.*

So Greenpeace helped to change people's attitudes. By seeing the video and finding out about how important whales are, the public became concerned. Greenpeace also showed the public that something could be done, so politicians were afraid of losing votes and made an agreement to ban whale hunting.

ACTIVITIES

5 a) Read Tom's answer to question 9.

b) In groups, discuss the strengths of the answer and ways in which it could be improved. Consider the following marking guidelines when discussing the answer:

- Have the three bullet points in the question been covered?
- Has the environmental issue been explained in detail?
- Has the question been answered?
- Is there evidence of own studies and specialist words/language being used?

6 Now try the question yourself.

a) First, talk your answer through in small groups/pairs.

b) Then write down some bullet points or draw a concept map to help you plan your answer.

c) When you are ready, complete your written answer in about 15 minutes.

A grade guide and comments on the candidate's answer is given on page 115.

A grade guide and comments on the candidate's answer is given on page 115.

Now try the following questions.

10 How do people's culture and beliefs affect the way they treat the natural environment? Use information and examples from your studies in your answer to this question.

11 Using an example or examples from your studies, explain how tourism can have both positive and negative effects on the people and environment in tourist destinations.

12 Why are environmental pressure groups campaigning for a reduction in the burning of fossil fuels?

Commentary and grade guide

For question 1
The candidate has a fairly sound grasp of the main concepts. Genes are associated with nature, but not explained very fully. Nurture is linked to the way you are brought up, but this could be explained more clearly. Socialisation is included and reference to own studies is made. It is implied that gender roles are learned, but this is not spelled out. All three bullet points are covered, although reasoning for conclusion is suspect. Answer jumps around a little. Some specialist language used.

Grade and mark guide: C 5/8

For question 5
Strengths:
- One valid approach has been mentioned (compromise).
- Reason for failure suggested.
- Own studies have been recalled.

Areas for improvement – answer should have included:

- an explanation of compromise and what might be used to achieve this, for example, negotiation, use of intermediaries, arbitration

- an explanation of how the case study shows failure of the UN's attempt to resolve conflict due to lack of negotiation. Compromise not seen as fair.

Second half of answer does not focus on the question. Could have explained how bitterness due to wars and killings has caused the failure of other attempts to negotiate a solution, for example, Oslo accords in 1990s.

Grade guide and mark: E 3/8

For question 9
This is a comprehensive answer that addresses all the requirements of the question. Good use of specialist language and study of Greenpeace. Good detail in the explanation of importance of whales in marine ecosystem. Could have:

- explained how much scientists believe we have yet to learn from whales – we cannot if they are extinct.
- added that some key countries like Norway and Japan are ignoring the ban.

There will always be something to improve, even though grade and mark guide for this is: A 8/8

4.1 What is a family?

- Do we mean the same thing when we talk about families?
- Why is the FAMILY important to SOCIETY?

A society is made up of individuals, but it is not just a large collection of people living in one area of the world. Section 1 on Culture and Beliefs has shown that a society works as a unit only if it has a shared culture (see page 6). People have to understand how to communicate and co-operate with each other if they want to live together. But how do people learn to live together? In most people's view, it is the family that takes on the job of teaching babies and children how to live and survive in society.

But what exactly is a family? Are all families the same?

This topic examines these questions.

Do we mean the same thing when we talk about families?

Read the activity below. You can see that a family is not easily defined, but most people have an image of what a 'proper' family is. This image is not the same in different parts of the world, but in most societies 'a family' is seen as the best form of SOCIAL ORGANISATION for raising children and supporting people, both economically and emotionally.

It is not hard to see why families are so widespread and popular across the world. Babies are completely dependent on adults, and children take a long time to develop the skills of survival. They need someone to look after them and teach them the culture and how to fit in. This is called PRIMARY SOCIALISATION (see Topic 1.4, page 15). If this did not happen, the child would have none of the skills needed to survive in society.

ACTIVITIES

1 a) Before you read any further, write down your definition of a family.

b) Discuss your answer in a group. Is your definition the same as everybody else's in the group?

2 Which of the examples below would you consider to be a family? Organise your answer into two columns – one with the title 'A family', the other with the title 'Not a family'.

- Man and woman married for twenty years without children.
- Two males COHABITING with an adopted son.
- Man and woman cohabiting with an adopted son.
- Man and woman married, both children away working in a different town.
- Man and woman cohabiting with the children from the woman's previous marriage.
- Woman living with her children after her husband has died.
- Man and woman married, children living with mother, father living separately but seeing children regularly.
- Man and woman married, living together and looking after the 80-year-old mother of the man.
- Woman living with her sister and her sister's husband.
- Man and woman married and living with their three children.
- Man and woman cohabiting with their three children for fifteen years.
- A woman living with her daughter and the daughter's baby.

3 From your answers and discussion, work out your new definition of a family, for example, 'A family is a group made up of …'.

The mother and the father usually bond with their baby, and the social pattern of the father and mother living with their child or children, and sharing the work and responsibilities of raising the children, is very common across the world.

Human beings also have social and emotional needs. With very few exceptions, people want companionship, affection and social acceptance. Family life can provide all this, which may account for the existence of family groups across all cultures.

Do not forget we use the word 'family' to mean different things. A family can be parents and children that live together, or a wider group of people linked by marriage and blood relationships, who recognise that they are related but live apart, and may not even have much to do with each other. Think of family gatherings like weddings and Christmas when relatives who rarely see each other get together.

And, of course, groups of people living together are not all families. To distinguish these groups from families we call them 'HOUSEHOLDS'. Because we use the word 'family' in so many different ways, you need to make it clear what you are talking about.

> ### Two definitions
> The family: the family is a group of persons directly linked by KIN connections, the adult members of which assume responsibility for caring for children.
>
> A household: a group of people who live together in shared accommodation.

Why is the family important to society?

A SOCIOLOGIST said this:

'There is no definition of the family that everyone accepts, but there is agreement about the role of the family in society and what it should do. It should be responsible for reproduction (producing the next generation), SOCIALISATION, and providing affection and personal support. In particular, the family has a central role in the education, socialisation and care of children.'

Adapted from *O'Connell*, 1994

This is what many people across the world accept as the main social value of families. They keep society going by producing and training the next generation.

Families can and often do a lot more. Many adults look after their elderly parents. Parents often help their grown-up children with money, advice, babysitting or full-time childcare. These activities can be called SOCIAL ROLES.

ACTIVITIES

4 'A household can be a family, but not all households are families, and not all families are households.'
   a) Explain why the statement above is true. Describe a household that is not a family, and describe a family that is not a household.
   b) Describe two other forms of household that are not families.

5 Make a list of the social roles a family might play in the lives of their relatives. Use the ideas above to start your list, then add roles from your own experience and knowledge.

4.2 What are the different types of family?

- Have families changed over time?
- What recent changes in family structure (types) have taken place?

We know from historical accounts that the way families live and are organised changes over time. New ways of living become possible as knowledge, TECHNOLOGY and opportunities increase. We also know that at any one time families can be different: some are richer than others, some are living in different ENVIRONMENTS and some have different priorities. The next topic examines some of these different types of family.

The traditional extended family

In societies that are based around agriculture rather than industry, such as many societies in LEDCs (for example, countries in central Africa), families tend to be much more connected to their wider relatives.

This was also the situation in the UK for many families until the eighteenth century and later. One reason for this was that the families relied on each other to share the work. Everyone – children, uncles, cousins and grandparents – would work together in order to survive. As a result, the family operated as a big network, often living together and doing all the jobs needing to be done to help the family survive. This was not only farm work, but also building, making clothes, looking after the sick and elderly, selling goods they had made or grown and teaching the children. These families were sometimes made up of three or four generations working together to support everyone. This type of family organisation is called the extended family.

This type of family still exists in many parts of the world. It can still be found in several communities in the UK, such as some farming communities and especially amongst recent IMMIGRANT communities who rely on family members to help them get established in a new country.

A family can survive best by getting all its members of all ages to work together.

The Industrial Age

However, when countries became industrialised, the new kind of work available in factories meant that people could move away to the new towns and set up smaller family units. They could earn money to buy or rent houses, and it made more sense to live in smaller (nuclear) families. As modern industrial societies developed, it became more and more usual for people to move to where they could find work, and they had to leave their families to do so. Towns and cities grew larger, and most housing that was built was designed for smaller families. Of course, richer people lived in bigger houses, but they often lived in households made up of just parents and their children, and sometimes one or two elderly relatives.

These changes produced a worldwide trend towards NUCLEAR FAMILY types, and extended families became more rare.

This meant that family life changed in many ways.

The nuclear family

If you ask most people in the UK to describe a family, they would probably say: 'Mum, dad and the kids.' This arrangement is often called the 'nuclear family', which means the family is stripped down to its basic components: parents and children.

The nuclear family is different from extended families because of the close emotional bonds that are formed in this small group. In the extended family, relationships would be wider and often based on working together rather than on personal emotions. In the nuclear family, there is a high degree of family-centred privacy. The members of the nuclear family are likely to be very close to each other emotionally. Parents are often mainly concerned with raising their children and making a comfortable home.

Children's marriages are mostly based on their own choices, guided by sexual attraction or romantic love, rather than arranged by their parents for the benefit of the whole family, as was often the case in earlier (extended) types of family.

But the classic nuclear family of 'mum, dad, and the kids' is not the most common household in the UK or in most countries of the world.

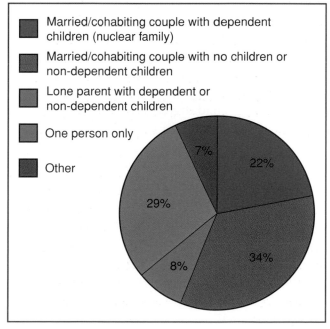

Married/cohabiting couple with dependent children (nuclear family)

Married/cohabiting couple with no children or non-dependent children

Lone parent with dependent or non-dependent children

One person only

Other

A summary of types of households in the UK in 2003.

ACTIVITY

1 From the pie chart, answer the following questions:
   a) Which is the most common type of household in the UK?
   b) What does 'non-dependent children' mean?
   c) What other type of household is more common than the nuclear family?
   d) What is meant by 'lone parent'?
   e) Give two examples of types of household that could be described as 'other'.

A note of caution!

Many people think that the pattern of family life was a clear-cut change from the extended family farming the land, several generations all living together and working for each other. Then along came the Industrial Revolution and everyone ran off to the towns and set up little nuclear families and the relatives were forgotten.

This is not how it was. The core of the nuclear family (two parents bringing up their children) has always been around. The extended family was more a description of how families shared responsibilities, often living nearby, sometimes living in the same house, but, importantly, playing a big part in the daily lives of other members of the extended family.

Nowadays, there is evidence that in many families the role of the relatives is still very important: they are involved in childcare, family businesses and share holidays, leisure and social activities.

Single (lone) parent families

One very big change in recent family types has been the rise in numbers of single-parent families living in the UK and across the world.

Between 1972 and 2002, the percentage of children living in single-parent families in the UK rose from seven per cent to 25 per cent. This is the second highest rate in Europe (Denmark has a higher rate). In some countries, it is much lower (Greece, Portugal, France), but in most of Europe and the USA there is a similar rising trend.

Many children only spend part of their life in a SINGLE-PARENT FAMILY, until the parent finds a new partner and marries, or cohabits, with them. Often, children in single-parent families spend time with the other parent.

Single-parent Families

- People who were married can become single parents through:
  - divorce
  - separation
  - death of a spouse (either husband or wife).
- Some single parents have never been married or cohabited.
- About 88 per cent of single parents raising children are mothers.

How and why has there been this big increase in single-parent families?

There have always been single-parent families throughout history. Before the mid-twentieth century, this was usually the result of one parent dying, but nowadays it is likely to be for one of two reasons:

- an increase in marital breakdown (separation or divorce)
- a rise in births to unmarried mothers.

Divorce and unmarried mothers

Why has there been an increase in divorce and an increase in the number of unmarried mothers?

The most common answer is that people's ATTITUDES to relationships and marriage have changed. Up until the 1950s, divorce was rare and people thought it was shameful to break up a marriage. Up until this time, it was accepted in most of the Western world that the 'proper' role for a woman was as a wife and mother.

Many women did work, but the approved family pattern was for the man to work and the woman to raise children and maintain the house. Women's work outside the home was seen as less important (though in poorer families it was often vital extra income). Marriage was the respectable way for men and women to live together, anything else was scandalous.

Getting a divorce was difficult and expensive, and to be divorced was a source of shame, especially for women.

Changing attitudes to marriage and divorce

After the Second World War (1939–45), attitudes to marriage changed in the UK. During the war, many women had lived without a man in the house and worked in jobs usually done by men. They had gained independence and confidence. Both men and women increasingly believed that marriage was not about being respectable; it was about finding happiness and romance.

During and after the war, many marriages fell apart because of long separations and people finding they no longer had much in common with the person they married.

During the 1950s and 1960s, divorce laws were changed and it became easier and cheaper to get divorced. Numbers of divorces rose rapidly and, because it was so common, divorce was accepted and the shame gradually disappeared

The bigger shame attached to having a child 'out of wedlock' had driven many couples into a marriage that they did not want.

Cohabitation is no longer seen as a 'sin'. Many people think it is sensible to live together before getting married so that the couple can learn about each other. Older generations were less accepting at first, but because parents had less power to control children's lives and choices, they were unable to do much about it. Gradually, cohabitation has gained acceptance in developed societies, where the BELIEF that people's private life is their own business has gained popularity.

The Christian Church had always said that people should marry before having sexual relations, but in recent years in the Western world, RELIGION and the Christian Church have had less influence on people's VALUES and beliefs.

Many people now believe that you should only marry if you expect it to be happy and fulfilling, so nowadays, forced weddings (SHOTGUN WEDDINGS) because of pregnancy are rare.

Changing opportunities, especially for women
• Women have realised that they can support themselves through work, and this freedom means they do not have to depend on marriage to a man.
• There are more opportunities for both men and women to meet other people through work and leisure.
• More access to contraceptives has taken away some of the risk of unwanted pregnancy, so it is less risky to have a sexual relationship outside marriage.
• More people have the money to start a new life if they want to end a marriage.

Reconstituted families

The number of divorces has produced another form of family called the RECONSTITUTED FAMILY. This describes families that are made up from people who have divorced or separated from an earlier partnership and formed another family, bringing up children from one or both previous relationships. This form of family will be discussed on pages 122–123.

ACTIVITIES

2 Look at the cartoon (left) and say what it tells us about attitudes to marriage in the past.

3 Look at the poster (below) and discuss why images like this during the Second World War may have changed women's self-confidence.

A Second World War poster depicting 'Rosie the Riveter' encourages American women to show their abilities and go to work for the war effort.

Other family forms

There has been a growth of same-sex couples (gay and lesbian) living together. This has created some controversy, especially amongst some religious groups, but several governments have brought in legislation that gives same-sex couples the same legal rights as other couples.

There are also various forms of COMMUNES, where several couples and individuals live together in a COMMUNITY and share the responsibilities for raising children and running the household between them. This form was briefly popular during the 1960s and continues to exist, sometimes as religious-based groups such as the Moonies (the Unification Church of Reverend Moon) or as large households made up of friends with similar interests and values.

People working in the gardens at the Findhorn Foundation, a community based in the north of Scotland.

Investigation

Use the Internet to find out more about communes. On the basis of what you find out, write about:

- the advantages a commune might have for its members compared to life in a nuclear family
- the reasons why you think communes were not more popular. (Think about why might it be difficult to keep a commune going.)

Increasingly, in affluent countries, families are headed by the mother and father both doing full-time work and using paid help such as child-carers, tutors, house staff or other assistants to look after the children and maintain the home. Some affluent families see little of their children because they are at boarding schools, and much of the socialisation process is carried on there rather than in the home.

In many other countries, particularly in African countries, it is common for children to live and be brought up by relatives who have enough room in their homes, or enough money for food and care that the parents cannot provide.

Ethnicity and family diversity

In the UK, different ETHNIC GROUPS have introduced different family forms. Many immigrants into the UK bring their culture and values with them and this influences the way their families are organised. Of course, there are variations within the ethnic groups, but some patterns are revealed in surveys and research.

South Asian families

Numerous migrants from the Punjab, Gujarat and Bengal who have come to the UK over the last 50 years have continued to organise their families according to their cultural TRADITIONS. Traditionally, these families are extended families, often dominated by the MALE members. In the first years as immigrants, it was common to live and work together in a large household that contained several generations. Many businesses were started using family members to keep costs down. This strategy was often successful and many now own successful businesses.

Recently, some of these families have become more distant from their relatives, and women are more likely to work outside the home. The older people try to keep the traditional extended family form and keep links with their villages of origin. Some families try to maintain the practice of ARRANGED MARRIAGES and obligations to the kinfolk both in the UK and in their country of origin. The children, especially girls, are often strictly controlled.

The younger generations, educated and working in the UK, often try to challenge this.

Traditional Hindu weddings are very elaborate ceremonies, which are a highlight of Hindu family life. It would be regarded as a betrayal of the culture if a wedding did not follow the traditions, and young people may feel they cannot ignore these pressures.

Recent films such as *Bend it like Beckham*, and *Bhaji on the Beach*, and soaps such as *Coronation Street* and *Eastenders* have all had plots that explore these CONFLICTS. What they often show is that the traditional family pattern is hard to break.

West Indian families

West Indian families in the UK, and in the Caribbean, have a range of different forms. Some are nuclear families, some are common-law families, where an unmarried couple lives together and looks after children who may not be their own, and some are 'MOTHER HOUSEHOLDS', where there is no permanent adult male. In such families, the mother or grandmother is the head of a household. Often, these families in the Caribbean rely on a network of FEMALE relatives to survive. In Britain, this is harder to do as there are fewer relatives living nearby.

There are many other ethnic groups in the UK who have brought their traditional culture with them.

Investigation

Use the Internet to investigate the family structure and customs of other immigrant groups who have come to the UK. For example, you could find out about families from Cyprus or immigrant families from African countries.

Summary

It is wrong to suggest that any one of these groups will all have the same family structure, and talking about Asian or West Indian families as if they were all the same is misleading. This is also true of families from all cultures and ethnic groups. They vary according to WEALTH and class, age group and place of origin. Research shows that there are fewer divorces or single-parent families in the South Asian communities, and more divorces and children outside marriages, in the Afro-Caribbean communities in the UK compared with the overall pattern in the UK.

However, these patterns are changing over time, and what this research shows is that across the UK (and across much of the Europe and the USA) there is a wide range of family forms and that these are generally part of an accepted culture.

The idea of the 'modern family' as being 'a breadwinning-father and child-rearing mother' is being replaced by many new family forms. These include single mothers, reconstituted families, cohabiting couples, lesbian and gay partners, communes and two-worker families.

4 PATTERNS OF FAMILY LIFE

4.3 How is the family important to an individual?

- What social and economic changes (external factors) have influenced modern family life?
- How does your family influence you as an individual?

The family has gone through many changes in recent times. This topic examines how and why families have changed over the last century.

It is important that you understand how your family influences your future life. Your primary socialisation does not only teach you how to eat and speak a language, it gives you your values, your attitudes and your expectations. The family is also your starting point in society. The wealth, power and social status that your family holds in society will be a major influence on your life chances in the future. This wealth, power and status is called SOCIAL CLASS. This topic also looks at the many ways in which you are the product of your family life.

What social and economic changes have influenced family life?

The 'traditional family' was based on strict values and attitudes and the need to survive.

Men and women had fixed roles based around their GENDER (whether they were male or female). Women had no real status unless they were married. Men controlled the family. They owned the property and passed it on to their sons. Women worked but their work was usually domestic: child rearing and domestic chores. The men were the breadwinners and the family did as they were told. For most people, the education they received was very limited and prepared you to live in the same way as your parents.

You were born into a social class and generally stayed there. In other words, if your parents were factory workers, there was little chance that you could be anything different. Most people believed that you were born into a certain social class and this dictated your future lifestyle. Few people broke free from this pressure until after the First World War (1914–18).

But, at the same time, the changes brought by the Industrial Revolution, which gave rise to the 'nuclear family' (see Topic 4.2, page 119), meant that family life has changed and attitudes to marriage and male control have changed alongside it.

The 'nuclear family' could not rely on relatives to help them do all the jobs a family has to do, so gradually the government has taken on many of these jobs.

The social role of the government
- ✓ Education of children
- ✓ Health care
- ✓ Training people and helping them get jobs
- ✓ Supporting people who need help with money or with guidance
- ✓ Looking after elderly people

Some people say these things are not done very well by the government, but together they have brought about a revolution in individual lifestyles and opportunities, and modern families now rely on services provided by the state.

Changes in family life in the UK

- Women have gained much greater rights and freedom.
- Women have gained the same legal rights as men. They make decisions within the family and have personal control over their working lives.
- Mostly people choose their own partners, rather than follow their parents' choices. (However, arranged marriages are still common in many Asian families.)
- More distant relatives and KINSHIP GROUPS have less influence on the way individuals choose to live.
- In most modern and developing societies, there is much more sexual freedom than there used to be. Society is less restrictive about personal/private BEHAVIOUR.
- Children have rights to education and protection from exploitation.
- The government provides support for families that have financial and social difficulties.

Recent changes in social life in Britain (since 1945)

ACTIVITIES

1 Working in small groups, discuss why the changes listed a–e (below) have taken place.

   a) In Britain, there is an increasing number of women in paid work.

   b) The average age at marriage is rising.

   c) More and more young people are cohabiting instead of marrying or before they marry.

   d) Family size is smaller, people have fewer children.

   e) People live longer.

Here are some points to help you.

   • Women have gained greater equality under the law.

   • More women are staying on in education and they expect to work, have a career and earn money.

   • In the past, most women had to rely on a man's wages to survive.

   • Modern attitudes to SEXUALITY and individual freedom mean that marriage is seen as less important.

   • The Church and religion are less influential than they used to be.

   • Families have less influence over their children's lifestyles.

   • Modern society needs a wide range of special work skills to function.

   • The range and opportunities for work and lifestyle are much wider.

   • Overall, people have much greater wealth than in previous years.

2 On your own, use the information in this section to describe what effects these social and economic changes may have had on families and marriage. Copy and complete the table below.

Social and economic changes	How this affects family life and marriage
Women have more independence and rights	Example: Women can make the decision to end a marriage if they are not happy with the situation. They have equal rights to family property. Extended families and parents have less influence
Women earn money and want careers	
The Church and society have less influence	
More people cohabit	
People spend more time in full-time education	
Families have less children	
People are wealthier	
People live longer	

Your family and you

Family 1
Diana (14)

My family lives in a big house in Solihull. We have five bedrooms and three bathrooms and a paddock

My dad (he's really my step-dad) works in London three days a week, and spends a lot of time on the phone and working online

My mum teaches at the university and gets tons of free time

School is sometimes boring but I like it because the teachers are nice and I've got loads of friends there. I like languages especially Italian, because I want to live in Italy when I'm older. I try hard at school because my parents say 'without a good education you'll get nowhere'

The family go abroad on holiday at least twice every year. Last year we went to Austria and Barbados

I go riding most weekends, and I sing in the choir at the church

I get on with my parents, but they are always going on about homework, and 'making the most of myself'. They are old-fashioned about clothes, and wouldn't let me get my eyebrow pierced, but my mum says that when I'm 15, I can have a clothes allowance. My dad says I can have a car when I go to university. I want to get married and have children, but not too soon because I want to have a career in the media first

ACTIVITY

3 Although a modern family does not have as much power over the children, the family does have a big influence on your future. Read these two accounts of family life and compare the differences in lifestyle, values and opportunities of Diana and Liam. Then answer the following questions:

I live with my mum and Derek, my step-dad, and my three sisters in a three-bedroom house on an estate in Nottingham. There's not much to do round here, just a corner shop and a pub on the main road

My mum works in a shop, and Derek works for a builder when he's got a big job on. We have a car, but it needs a new clutch so we don't get much use out of it

I work at the chip shop three nights a week, so I've got a bit of money

It's alright at home, but it's noisy and we argue about what to watch on TV. There's nowhere to be on your own to listen to music or just think

I go to a school in the estate and it's not bad. When I was at the junior school I liked it, but at this school I am struggling because I don't do the homework so I sometimes get into trouble. I can't do the homework because there's nowhere to do it in the house, my sisters have their stuff everywhere. I'd like to do A levels, but I don't think I'll do well enough at GCSE. Derek says school is a waste of time because the stuff they teach is useless. He's going to teach me plastering when I leave. My mum wants me to stay on, but they can't afford to keep me until I'm 18, so I'll have to get a job

I don't think I will get married, married people are always rowing about money or something. I'm going to have a good time. When I'm 16, me and my mates are going to have two weeks in Ibiza. It's brilliant out there, dead cheap and you can have a laugh. My mum says that when we all leave home she's off on a cruise. Hope she does, she needs a break

4 PATTERNS OF FAMILY LIFE

a) How are Diana and Liam's lives at home different?

b) What differences are there in their attitudes to school?

c) How are their plans for their futures different?

d) How would you explain these differences in attitude and ambition?

4.4 Why are there different attitudes to the family?

- Is the family in crisis?
- Why are there differences in attitudes to divorce, marriage, GENDER ROLES, child rearing and the care of the elderly?

We have looked at the way the family has changed over time. These changes have not always been welcomed by everyone. Many people feel that the family is in crisis. They say that the increase in the number of divorces and separations, the large numbers of people cohabiting rather than marrying, and the large number of single mothers have all resulted in major problems in society. This topic will look at the different views on whether this is a crisis or a natural development over time.

Look at the table below. Three changes in particular have caused major disagreements in society. These are changes in attitudes to:

- divorce and marriage
- gender roles and child rearing
- the care of the elderly.

Divorce and marriage

The number of divorces in the UK has risen from 5,000 in 1935 to 166,700 in 2003. There was a massive increase from 1938 until 1970, then the increase in the number of divorces rose more slowly. In 2003, for example, the number of divorces rose by 3.7 per cent from 2002.

Is the family in crisis?

	ARGUMENTS THAT THE FAMILY IS IN CRISIS	ARGUMENTS THAT THE FAMILY IS NOT IN CRISIS
In the past	**Family** Kept people together **Parents** Supported each other and had clear roles in the family **Children** Were looked after and taught to be caring and law-abiding adults **Elderly** Looked after by their family	**Family** • Oppressed its members and made them feel miserable, but they could not escape family pressures • Restricted opportunities to change • Treated people who challenged its rules as SOCIAL OUTCASTS **Women** Were second-class citizens, dominated by men
Nowadays	**Children** • Broken marriages and lone parenting mean that children are not brought up properly • Do not learn to follow the rules and cause problems in schools • Become disruptive adults **Elderly** Adults do not look after each other or the elderly **Society** Because parents are not providing discipline in the home, the rules of society are ignored or not understood, causing unhappiness and problems such as antisocial behaviour, drug abuse, a rising crime rate, and many students failing in school	**Family** People have greater freedom to live as they wish without being social outcasts **Children** • Have rights and wider opportunities • Get a better education **Women** • Are not second-class citizens • Are more equal • Are able to follow careers and be independent **Elderly** Are looked after better than they used to be, with good medical treatment

So, in the UK today, more than 40 per cent of marriages will end in divorce. The rate is higher in the USA and similar to the UK in non-Catholic European countries.

For some people, being able to get divorced and start a new life without being criticised as a failure is a major improvement in SOCIAL VALUES and has produced a better society. Divorce is a way of escaping from an intolerable life and has given people the freedom to find a new, happier way of life.

Other people see divorce as a major social problem and as a SOCIAL EVIL because it results in broken families, causes unhappiness, and disrupts the raising of children.

The problems caused by divorce

- Children: lives are disrupted and it probably causes real grief and misery for children. They may find it hard to cope with new relationships in the family, and it may affect their self-confidence. Schoolwork often suffers.
- Parenting: it is often difficult for a single parent to earn a living and look after the children. Many say that broken families give rise to juvenile delinquency, and blame divorces for much social disorder because the children are not brought up properly.
- Costs: the break-up of households is distressing. A divorce usually means that the family income is lower and somebody has to move out of the family home.
- Culture: there are still many cultures where divorce is seen as shameful.

The positive side of divorce

However, some people believe that being able to get divorced is a major advantage in modern society. In the past, when a divorce was almost impossible to get, there were many sad marriages. Unhappy couples had to stay together. Many people think that being able to leave an unhappy marriage is essential to people's well-being.

Below are three case studies to illustrate why divorce can be good.

Yvette (34), Sheffield
'When we first met, we went out drinking a lot. We both liked being sociable. After we got married and had kids, I knew we had to change. But Dave couldn't get used to staying in and we had rows. Dave got drunk often and sometimes got violent. In the end, I left him and took the kids because I was scared for our safety.'

Keith (27), London
'We were childhood sweethearts. A year after we got married, I was offered a brilliant job in London, but Jane didn't want to move. The job and money were so good, we agreed that I should live in London in the week and come home at weekends. It was fine at first, but soon we were like strangers. In the end, we agreed to part. We were different people than when we were kids.'

Sarah (54), Dorking
'I stayed at home to bring the children up and Simon worked hard in the City making pots of money. We had fantastic holidays and he bought us a beautiful house. He couldn't spend much time with the children because of work, but he said it was for their future.

'When the children left home, there seemed to be nothing left for me. Simon was at work or the golf club. It was an empty shell marriage. I had an affair and Simon went berserk. The divorce was difficult but at last I feel like a person.'

ACTIVITIES

1 From the information in this topic and your own knowledge and experiences, list the problems divorce can cause.

2 Why might a religious person object to divorce?

3 Suggest reasons why there are fewer divorces in Asian families in the UK.

4 Explain in your own words why divorce often creates poverty.

5 Read the three case studies. Explain what is meant by:
   a) 'an abusive marriage'
   b) 'to move on'
   c) 'an empty shell marriage'.

6 Apart from the explanations in the three case studies, discuss other reasons there might be for supporting the right to get divorced.

Gender roles and child rearing

Gender roles are the jobs and responsibilities that people are expected to take on based on their gender (whether they are male or female).

In the UK, during the first half of the twentieth century, gender roles were fixed. Women were responsible for looking after the children and for taking care of the household duties such as washing, cleaning and cooking. This was true of all social classes. Even in wealthy families, the woman was expected to supervise the housework and the raising of children, though servants often did this work. The men's role was to provide for the family by working and earning money.

These roles were generally accepted across much of the world, and the division of labour seemed to work well. The family was housed, fed and clothed, and the children were kept clean and raised to know their future roles.

However, during the late twentieth century in the UK and the DEVELOPED WORLD, gender roles in the family have been changing rapidly.

There are several linked reasons for this as shown in the table below.

REASON FOR CHANGES IN GENDER ROLES IN THE FAMILY	EFFECT OF CHANGES IN GENDER ROLES IN THE FAMILY
Women have rejected being treated as second-class citizens and gained greater equality in the home and at work	Traditional gender roles have faded and men and women share more household tasks, including childcare
The cost of living has risen	People still have to work hard to earn enough money
Women have become a major part of the workforce	Greater equality for women means they have more opportunities to earn money. At the same time, the cost of living means both parents have to work
It is more expensive to bring up children	People want their children to have a good life, so they have fewer children
Wealth and wages have been increasing for most people	People can have a better quality of life, for example, comfortable houses, cars, holidays

ACTIVITY

7 a) Copy and fill out the chart below to show who mostly does what household job in your family.

b) In class or groups, compare your family division of labour with others. What are the common patterns?

c) If you can, do the same chart with relatives or friends from an earlier generation and identify any changes in family life over time.

Household task	Done mostly by male	Done mostly by female	Done mostly by you	Shared equally
Washing and ironing				
Preparing meals				
Cleaning the house				
Household shopping				
Organising money and bills				
Maintaining and repairing household equipment				
Raising children				
Looking after sick members of family				
Disciplining children				
Decides on big expenses (for example, holidays, car, building patio)				

The role of children in the family

During the nineteenth century, most children would be expected to work from an early age. Nowadays, children stay in education at least until they are 16, and many stay longer. This means that their roles have changed. Although many teenagers have part-time work, usually the money from this is for them, not the family in general.

Having children is expensive. Many parents try to provide their children with financial and practical support until they leave school. However, for many families, this is not easy to achieve. Single-parent families are often poor. Children in these families often have to earn money and look after younger children.

In single-parent and reconstituted families, the children have to provide emotional support for their parent, who may be struggling to cope with a divorce or simply be exhausted.

Attitudes to changing gender roles

For many men and women, the changes in relationships within the family are a good thing. Many women are happy to have lost the secondary role of helping the man and are glad that they have more power in the home and in the outside world. Being able to earn a living, having their own money and property, and being treated with respect has made their lives much better. Sharing the work of raising the children and maintaining the home has made the family closer.

Men have also gained by being able to share the responsibility of providing for the family and having a better relationship with their partner. They have become much more involved in raising children, and an equal relationship is closer and more satisfying for many people.

But some people are less happy about these changes in gender roles.

- There is a lot of evidence from sociological research that although both parents go out to work, many women are still responsible for the housework and most of the childcare.
- Some experts in child development feel that when both parents are at work, they are not able to provide the children with enough attention and care.
- Some people believe that women are better at child-rearing and that men are better as wage-earners.

ACTIVITIES

8 Read the two extracts from recent newspaper articles. What criticisms of modern gender roles are expressed in them?

9 Using the material in this topic and your own experiences, what advantages have come about as a result of modern gender roles in the family?

Problem students of working parents

The head of a secondary school in the west of England has caused a row in education circles by claiming that some students were not doing well in school because both parents were working and were too tired to get involved in their children's education. Parents need to make sure they can devote enough time to encouraging and teaching children, or they may find that their children lack a sense of direction.'

Mothers working double shifts

A recent survey revealed that many women now do two jobs. There are now as many women as men in the British labour force. This has brought financial independence to many women, but at a cost.

The survey reveals that 68 per cent of women do 'most of the housework', and 76 per cent of women are 'mainly responsible for childcare'.

More than half the women responding to the survey said they were exhausted at the end of the day. 43 per cent of the mothers responding to the survey said they felt their 'quality of life had declined' since they returned to work.

The care of the elderly

In the UK and in the developed world, life expectancy has risen dramatically over the last hundred years.

In 1901, males born in the UK could expect to live to around 45 years of age and females to around 49. By 2003, male life expectancy at birth had risen to almost 76 years, and for females to just over 80 years.

There are several reasons for this. Despite all the worries about pollution, obesity, smoking and stress, our modern lifestyle is much healthier than it was 100 years ago. In Britain, we have adequate clean water and healthy food. People have access to much better medical care. We are wealthier so we have warmer, drier houses; our working conditions are much safer. We are better educated so we know more about how to take care of ourselves.

But because people live longer, there are many more elderly people than there used to be. The older people are, the more they need care and help. Elderly people often have health problems or difficulties in looking after themselves. They may have difficulties with mobility, with vision or hearing, or with memory and understanding the world.

The need to care for the elderly presents many problems for the modern family. Most people over 65 live away from their children. When elderly people can no longer look after themselves, the job of caring usually becomes the work of female family members. Most people want to look after their ageing parents and feel it is their responsibility. Many families try to bring their parent into their home or move so they live near enough to provide care.

This can cause difficulties.

- Many elderly people need full-time care.
- Most houses are too small to provide a home for an elderly person.
- It is difficult to move home for both the carer family and the elderly relative (because of work, friends, money, etc.).
- Many women who might have been carers in the past are now working outside the home.
- Looking after an elderly relative can cause stress in the household.
- Many elderly people do not want to cause difficulties for their family.

Life can be lonely for elderly people, especially when their partner has died.

- Outside care (for example, in a nursing home) is expensive.
- Many elderly people do not want to live in a nursing home.

Different attitudes to the care of the elderly

1 Family responsibility

Some people argue that a family should look after their relatives because:

- they have a MORAL duty
- care in nursing homes is not always good
- the elderly deserve to be repaid for caring for their children
- the family will provide better care than a stranger.

2 Government responsibility

Other people argue that when an elderly person needs care, they should be cared for by the National Health Service (NHS) or by social services (the government should provide the funding) because:

- the elderly have paid taxes all their life
- many people do not have the resources to look after their parents
- they have the skills and facilities to do a better job (for example, 24-hour nursing, medical skills and treatments).

ACTIVITY

10 Read the two accounts (right) of caring for the elderly and answer the following questions using the information in this topic and your own ideas.

    a) Using Janice's account, explain the difficulties that occur when an elderly relative moves in with the family.

    b) From the same account, explain why moving in might be good for both the elderly person and the family.

    c) From Fred's account, explain why a residential home can be a good place for an elderly person to spend their days.

Companionship is what most people want out of life.

Janice, Wolverhampton

'My mother was fine until she fell and broke a hip. When she came out of hospital, she found it impossible to look after herself at home. We decided that we should move her in with us, but we were very worried because our house only has three bedrooms and we have two boys aged nine and seven.

'We struggled at first because we were so crowded. The boys felt pushed out and I was so tired I thought I'd have to give up my job. My mother gave us some money for an extension, and once we got used to having her around things got much better. She is the best babysitter and she can look after herself with our help. It's actually better now. My husband and I get out more often, and now she's settled in she's good company.'

Fred (83), Leeds

'When my eyesight got really bad, I could just about see enough to cook my tea, and I could do the shopping, but that was all. I couldn't read or watch TV so I spent all day listening to the radio and talking books. It was really boring. I had nobody to talk to and I forgot how to talk, nearly. My daughter comes over once a week, but she lives 130 km (80 miles) away and it is too far. Her visit is the big event of the week.

'She wanted me to move in with her family, but I didn't want to get in the way. They have their own life to live. So when my eyes got worse, I decided to go to this residential home. I checked it out and it didn't seem too bad, but I wasn't keen. It just seemed the best option.

'I must say, it's been a lot better than I expected. The food is good, they look after me well. I like my room, but the real benefit is that I can talk to people again. They're all about my age so we can talk easily, and the days go much more quickly. I'm glad I moved.'

4.5 *Is there an ideal family?*

- Why is there still one dominant view of the family?
- What does the government think of the family?
- Do British people think there is an 'ideal' family?

This section has been about how families have changed over time and it has shown that there are many different types of family organisation in the UK and elsewhere. These types of family organisations range from lone parents to extended families. Marriage is no longer regarded as essential if couples want to live together or have children. Divorce is common, and having children outside marriage is not regarded as a scandal.

However, there is still lots of evidence that for many people there is an 'ideal' family type. We see it in the media, in TV shows, in newspaper articles and documentaries about the 'decline' of the family, in advertisements and in government statements. This topic looks at this evidence and examines the arguments about what families should be like.

At one time, people got married for life. Now, people decide whether they will live together, live in a group, marry, have children, have children and live alone, be MONOGAMOUS, divorced, separated and so on. People have more choices.

There are disagreements about whether this freedom of choice should be accepted. The disagreement comes down to two basic arguments.

Argument 1

There are many people who say that this range of different households and family types is right for a modern society. People are different and have different values and ambitions. Most modern societies are made up of a mixture of different cultural groups. There are differences in religious beliefs and in family traditions. These people say that trying to make all these people live in the same way is pointless and would cause great conflict. They say that how we live together is a personal decision and should stay that way. They say there is no such thing as an 'ideal' family.

Argument 2

Other people look at society today and believe that it is going wrong. They say that young people do not respect authority. They say that the crime rate is rising, and that the streets are not safe. They say the main reason for this social crisis is the breakdown of the traditional nuclear family.

Divorce, single parents, and broken marriages and relationships have resulted in a breakdown of discipline and values across society. They say that to heal society we need to get back to the 'ideal family', which is the traditional nuclear family that used to exist in the past.

1 What are the two views about changes in family and household structure? Explain them in your own words.

What does the government think about families?

During the 1990s, the government made many criticisms of the changes in families. They were particularly concerned about the growing numbers of single-parent families. Politicians at the Conservative Party conference in 1993 made speeches that suggested that girls were getting pregnant so that the state could support them and find them homes.

The press took this story up and there were headlines like:

TEENAGERS GET PREGNANT AND WE PAY

Unmarried Mothers Damage Society

Some politicians and psychologists said that children without fathers in the home are more likely to become criminals and truants, and end up being a burden on the social services. They argued that when children are not looked after by two parents, they do not get enough discipline, and that boys living with just their mothers do not learn the male role.

John Major, the Prime Minister at the time, launched a 'Back to Basics' campaign, which said that conventional family life was the best way to put society on the right track again.

What happened to these campaigns?

The campaigns backfired. Many people sprang to the defence of single parents, saying there was no evidence that girls got pregnant to get a council house and benefits, and that most single parents' biggest problem was poverty, not the absence of men in the household. It was poverty that caused crime and truancy. They found in research that most single parents wanted a conventional family life but were not able to find suitable partners.

The three Williams sisters who are from Allington. They were all under the age of sixteen when they gave birth to their children.

Where does the government stand now?

The government in 2005 seems to have mixed feelings about the contemporary family. In 1997, Tony Blair made a speech where he said that teenage pregnancies, families not caring for the elderly members, poor parental ROLE MODELS, truancy and poor educational achievement could all be explained by failures in family life. When he said this, most people believed he meant that a strong family was a heterosexual couple living together in a permanent relationship with an employed male breadwinner.

However, when it comes to policies, the Labour government has done much to support all types of family life. It is gradually giving all families and couples equal rights, whether they are married or not, or whether they are heterosexual or homosexual. Single parents are given both practical and financial help.

The government is trying to cut teenage pregnancies by education, not by punishment. In 1998, it wrote a Green Paper (outlining government policy), which said:

'We also acknowledge just how much families have changed. Family structures have become more complicated, with many more children living with stepparents or in single-parent households. They may face extra difficulties and we have designed practical support with these parents in mind.'

Recently, the government has made it possible for homosexual couples to adopt children, and has increased the rights of both men and women to have maternity and paternity leave from work.

ACTIVITIES

2 Why do some politicians seem to think that families that aren't traditional nuclear families are a problem for society?

3 Do governments seem to think there is an 'ideal' family? Explain your answer using the information on pages 135–136.

4 What evidence is there that the people of Britain and the government accept that these changes in family and household life are likely to be permanent?

Do the British people think there is an 'ideal' family?

Most people in Britain have shown that they accept new family and household structures by adopting them, or being tolerant of them. Unmarried mothers and single parents, divorcees and reconstituted families are a familiar part of British life.

People seem to accept that how people choose to live is up to them. There is much less public criticism of lifestyles that used to be seen as shameful, such as having children outside marriage or living together without getting married, or putting an elderly relative into residential care. Most people seem to accept that things have changed.

But we still seem to hang on to the idea that the traditional family is the 'ideal'. There is much evidence for this.

Statistical evidence

- Many people who get divorced remarry. They obviously think that marriage is good; they made a mistake but want to try again.
- Most people who cohabit for longer than two years either stay together as if they were married or do eventually marry.
- In 2004, the *Guardian* newspaper ran a poll of 16-year-olds to find out their views:

Do you believe in marriage?
YES 74% (boys 68%, girls 79%)
Do you want to have children?
YES 94% (boys 91%, girls 97%)
Do you have to love someone before having sex with them?
YES 43% (boys 32%, girls 54%)

- The average cost of a wedding in Britain is said to be £25,000. This figure includes the cost of the wedding and reception, and the cost of transport and accommodation that the guests pay for (according to research done by Cahoot (a bank)).

Evidence from the media

Even more evidence that we still think of the traditional family as the ideal is the amount of attention families and their relationships get in the media. Here are some examples to illustrate this:

- *Coronation Street* and *Eastenders* are the most widely watched programmes on British TV. Their plots and storylines are based around families and their relationships. Weddings are a regular big event.
- Many advertisements for products, especially food and household goods, are centred on family scenes. The family is usually the traditional type: mum, dad and the kids.
- Other programmes, such as sitcoms, are often based around a happy family life.
- Many magazines aimed at women, such as *Hello*, either concentrate on the marriages and families of celebrities or run articles that assume all families are traditional in structure.

The reason this media image of families is important is that the media play a big part in our understanding of what is normal and what is desirable. Our attitudes to lifestyle and family life are influenced by what we see in the media.

Investigations

Analyse the way families are portrayed in the media.

1 Watch TV for an evening and for each programme, including news and documentaries, keep a record of each time a family is featured or discussed and what type of family it is. Check your results and see which type of family is most commonly shown or referred to.

2 Watch a soap opera for a week and do the same exercise as in investigation 1.

3 Read four women's magazines and cut out stories/articles/photographs that include or mention families (there will be a lot!). Collect your cuttings and sort into groups according to what types of family they are, for example, nuclear family, extended family, single-parent family, reconstituted family, gay family.

For each of these projects, try to identify whether the family is depicted as normal or unusual.

ACTIVITY

5 Look at the advert and the magazine on this page and say what image of family life they represent. For example, who do they show as being members of the family? What kind of activities are the men/women/children doing? What do you infer from this about media attitudes?

Not quite a conventional wedding, but everyone is beautiful and the wedding was 'magical'.

An advert for Kingsmill bread, with the comedy duo Mel and Sue, and a family setting.

5.1 What are prejudice and persecution?

- What do prejudice and PERSECUTION mean and what form do they take?
- How do people become prejudiced (NATURE or NURTURE)?
- How can prejudice lead to DISCRIMINATION and persecution?

Prejudice and persecution exist in all societies despite efforts to get rid of them. It is important to learn about their causes – both now and in the past – in order to understand why you should fight against them. This section starts by looking at what prejudice and persecution actually are. It aims to give you an understanding that it is human BEHAVIOUR – an ATTITUDE – which causes others to experience prejudice and persecution.

ACTIVITY

1 List three advantages to SOCIETY of young people learning about the dangers of prejudice.

Prejudice

Prejudice is an attitude about a person or group that is formed without having all the facts – that is, pre-judging someone. It usually involves disliking someone because of their GENDER, ETHNICITY, SEXUALITY, RELIGION, etc. rather than because of their personality.

Prejudiced attitudes are learned. We are not born with them. We develop them through SOCIALISATION (see Topic 1.4, pages 11–18). For example, children in Nazi Germany were taught to hate Jews (anti-Semitism) (see Topic 5.4, pages 143–47).

Discrimination

Prejudice often influences our behaviour and leads to discrimination. Discrimination is treating someone differently, usually less well, because they belong to a particular group. The examples in activity 2 should help you build up a better understanding of the word 'discrimination'.

ACTIVITY

2 a) Study the drawings opposite and match the captions below to the pictures.
   i) By law, organisations do not have to provide a prayer room. But if you request use of a quiet place that is available and are refused, this could amount to discrimination.
   ii) 'I can't even go out for a night on the tiles – just because pubs, clubs and venues don't think about their disabled customers.'
   iii) 1.8 million people between the ages of 55 and 64 have experienced AGEISM in their job.
   iv) In 2004, a black woman was turned away from a hotel in Chorley. She was suspicious and asked a friend to phone them. The friend was told there were three free rooms.
   v) Every year, in England and Wales alone, around 1,000 women take legal action against their employer claiming they were sacked because of their pregnancy.
   vi) Private members' clubs, such as golf clubs, can choose to be men-only or have men-only areas – such as the clubhouse – as they are exempt from the Sexual Discrimination Act.
   b) What do we learn from these examples about discrimination in Britain?
   c) What have all the victims of discrimination got in common?
   d) What attitude is held towards each of the victims of discrimination?

A

B

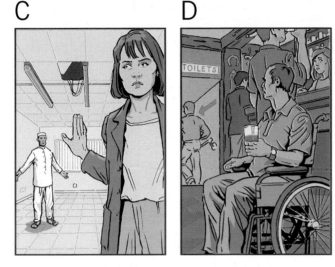

C

D

E

F

There are different forms of prejudice and discrimination. Activity 2 should have started you thinking about some of these such as disability,

gender, religion, age and ethnicity. The drawings also show that it is not just individuals who can be prejudiced, but that quite often there is INSTITUTIONAL DISCRIMINATION. This is where prejudiced behaviour exists (not necessarily knowingly) throughout an institution such as in employment, housing, education, the police force, etc. So, for example, racist or sexist language or stereotyping might be part of the accepted CULTURE of an institution.

Moreover, governments can also be prejudiced against certain groups so they are treated unequally in law. A good example of this in the past was the Jim Crow laws in the southern states of the USA (see Topic 2.4, pages 50–60).

Persecution

Persecution is the HARASSMENT and mistreatment of an individual or group. It can take different forms, such as:

- OSTRACISM – for example, not inviting a child to a party when the rest of the class has been invited.
- Violence – for example, in 2003 in the UK, 20,000 people were physically attacked, 40,000 had property damaged and 230,000 were racially abused.
- Murder – for example, Stephen Lawrence, a black teenager, was stabbed to death by a gang of white youths while waiting at a bus stop in London in 1993.
- GHETTOISATION – for example, from October 1941, German Jews were transported to GHETTOES in Poland.
- GENOCIDE – for example, between April and June 1994, an estimated 800,000 Tutsis in Rwanda were massacred by the ruling Hutus in the space of 100 days.

Denial of rights

Prejudice, discrimination and persecution all involve the denial of human rights. Everyone has the right to education, to life, to freedom of expression, etc., and to be treated equally under these rights regardless of race, religion, sex, political views, etc.

5.2 What are stereotypes and scapegoats?

This topic explores the role of individuals, groups and government in forming prejudices in society. It shows you how prejudice can lead to discrimination and persecution. It should help you understand how fixed attitudes about certain groups (stereotyping) can lead to individuals experiencing prejudice and becoming scapegoats.

Stereotyping

Stereotyping is one way of expressing prejudice. It means labelling a group of people with the same characteristics – as if all the people in the group were exactly the same. Stereotyping can be expressed in different forms such as national stereotypes (for example, labelling all Scotsmen as mean), sexist stereotypes (for example, labelling all blonde women as 'bimbos'), and ageist stereotypes (for example, labelling all old people as grumpy), etc.

Many individuals who form stereotyping attitudes would say they are not intended to cause offence and are only meant to be funny. Some groups, such as parts of the media, would say the same.

The media often use stereotypes for comic effect or to create a good headline. This, however, could lead to the stereotype becoming more common, as it makes it seem normal, and therefore influences

ACTIVITY

1 Sort out the statements below into either fact or stereotype.

   a) Tennis players usually wear white.
   b) All girls are obsessed with clothes.
   c) All Americans are overweight.
   d) Many French people eat garlic.
   e) All England football fans are troublemakers.
   f) Elderly people sometimes enjoy pop music.
   g) Kids today are always noisy.
   h) Some teenage girls drink more than boys.

Are there any particular words in the statements that helped you to decide which was a fact and which was a stereotype?

attitudes. For example, do headlines about teenagers being violent, rude, lazy, drug-takers and heavy drinkers affect the attitudes and actions of adults you do not know towards you?

However unintended, stereotyping can cause offence. More seriously, stereotyping can lead to persecution and scapegoating by groups and governments. This is because it is often easier to create scapegoats if the person or group that is being blamed can all be labelled the same.

Scapegoating

Scapegoating is where a group is blamed for something because of the stereotypes attached to them. Pressures in society such as unemployment, inflation, depression, defeat in war, etc. usually cause this. Examples are:

- Blaming IMMIGRANTS for a rise in unemployment by saying they are taking 'our' jobs.
- Trying to get rid of a local gypsy encampment by calling them all dirty and dishonest.
- Blaming a football team's lack of success on the foreign players being only interested in the money and uncommitted.

On a larger scale, scapegoating can be an excuse for ETHNIC CLEANSING. For example, in 1998, Serbians accused Muslims of holding back the development of Bosnia and proceeded to drive out as many of them as possible.

As a group, the press quite often uses scapegoats to help sell newspapers. For example, some newspapers talk about the UK being swamped with 'bogus ASYLUM SEEKERS' taking advantage of its benefit system.

Although scapegoating can be started by individuals or groups, such as the media, it is something governments might encourage:

- so that they are not blamed instead
- to win support by being 'tough on immigration' or 'cracking down on yob culture', etc.

Insiders and outsiders

Scapegoating is usually carried out by the dominant social or cultural group in society. They are in control of the media, the top jobs and the government, and are referred to as the 'insider group'. An example of an insider group is white settlers in Australia, the timber companies in the Amazonian rainforest (see Topic 3.2, pages 72–76),

or company directors in the UK. Victims of scapegoating are the less dominant social or cultural group. They are often unwelcome, poorer and disadvantaged in education, housing and jobs. They are the 'outsider group'. Examples are the native Aborigines in Australia, the Yanomani in the rainforest, or asylum seekers in the UK.

Source A

Police stop march

Police in riot gear halted a march by the National Front yesterday … which could have taken them past rival protestors.

'We demand the right to put forward our views', shouted one member of the National Front …

A spokesman for a local trade union … said: 'These people are racist and homophobic, spreading a message of hatred and division. There should be no voice for people who are racist and homophobic.'

ACTIVITIES

2 **a)** How do the cartoons opposite stereotype the person they portray? For example, the first cartoon suggests all FEMALE librarians are plain and wear glasses. Can you complete the rest?

   b) Can you think of three people who do not conform to these stereotypes?

3 **a)** List six characters from TV soaps, programmes or films and suggest the stereotypes they represent.

   b) Was it easy to compile the list? What does this tell you about the influence of the media in creating stereotypes?

4 The following quotes are from Source A:

   'We demand the right to put forward our views.'
   'There should be no voice for people who are racist and homophobic.'

   Should racists who wish to organise events that encourage hatred and fear have the right to put their views across? Set out the arguments for each of the points of view. Conclude with your own views, with reasons.

5.3 *What are the causes of prejudice and persecution?*

- How can the following factors cause prejudice?
  - NORMS and VALUES
  - Political IDEOLOGY
  - Religious differences
  - Economic conditions

This topic explains the various causes of prejudice and persecution.

There are many ways individuals, groups and societies can become prejudiced towards each other.

Norms and values

Norms and values are the standard of behaviour and MORAL principles that a group regards as important (see Topic 1.7, page 32). When a group comes across individuals or groups with different norms and values, it can lead to prejudice, discrimination and persecution. This prejudice is caused by fear and IGNORANCE of the unknown or outsiders, SUPERSTITION or TRIBALISM. So, for example, someone might shun or treat differently someone who is HIV positive and mistakenly believe and fear that any contact can lead to catching the disease themselves.

Political ideologies

Prejudice is often a part of a political ideology – that is, it can form part of the body of ideas that a particular political group have.

An example of tribalism is the supporters of one football team hating another just because they support a different team.

Many societies' political ideologies have been built on racial prejudices. Examples include the African–American slave trade, APARTHEID in South Africa and Nazism in Germany (see Topic 5.4, pages 143–47).

Religious differences

Religion can also encourage prejudice and persecution. For example, persecution can occur where the religion of the state does not tolerate other BELIEFS, such as the Romans persecuting the early Christians. Another example might be the growth of Islamaphobia (the fear and dislike of Islam) in some Western countries.

Economic conditions

Economic pressures, perhaps above all, can foster prejudice. Difficult economic situations where there are high levels of unemployment and inflation can encourage people to turn to extreme political parties for the answers to their problems as these parties tend to blame scapegoats (see Topic 5.2, page 140). For example, the Nazi Party blamed Jewish people for the harsh economic conditions that Germany faced in the 1930s (see Topic 5.4, pages 143–47).

ACTIVITIES

1 'This town is turning into a foreign land … They are all illegal migrants.' These are the words of a BNP candidate in Sunderland, 2003. Why do you think he held these views? How are views like these examples of prejudice? Discuss this in groups.

2 Choose three of the causes of prejudice discussed in this topic and provide an example of your own for each one.

5.4 What were the causes of the Holocaust?

- How does the Holocaust show that the causes of prejudice can lead to the persecution of a whole group?

This case study on the Holocaust illustrates and explains how prejudice can lead to discrimination and persecution in a modern, civilised society. It is an example of the continuum theory – where one action leads to another increasingly worse action.

The Holocaust is the name given to the slaughter of six million people, mostly Jews, during the Second World War. By learning about it, you might understand how racial prejudice can lead to the most horrendous events and how ordinary people can play their part.

The case study also provides a warning about what can happen and how it is important to act against prejudice. This is shown in the words of Pastor Martin Niemoller, a Christian minister who survived a Nazi concentration camp:

'First they arrested the COMMUNISTS – but I was not a communist, so I did nothing … Then they arrested the trade unionists – and I did nothing because I was not one. And then they came for the Jews and then the Catholics, but I was neither a Jew nor a Catholic and I did nothing. At last they came and arrested me – and there was no one left to do anything about it.'

The persecution of the Jews

Source A

'If I am ever in power, the destruction of the Jews will be my first and most important job.'

Adolf Hitler, 1922

Source B

'We were ordered to dispose of about two hundred Jews. I could see fear in their eyes as we began to unload cans of petrol and forced them into the house … We moved back and threw grenades through the windows.
We listened to the screams as the flames spread from room to room. Dense smoke poured out and some of the Jews jumped out through the windows only to be shot by our troops. Later, many of us were disturbed by what we had done but were told by our commander that Jews were not human.'

A German soldier remembering, from *The Sunflower* by Simon Wiesental

Source C

'I saw a great collection of bodies, perhaps 150, flung down on each other, all naked, all so thin, their yellow skin glistened like stretched rubber on their bones.'

Richard Dimbleby describing the scene as the British army liberated the concentration camp at Belsen, 19 April 1945

ACTIVITY

1 What do the sources tell you about the Holocaust? List four things.

The Treaty of Versailles

To understand why the Holocaust took place, we must go back to the period immediately after the First World War. Germany had lost the war and had been forced to accept humiliating terms in the Treaty of Versailles, 1919:

- It had to accept the blame for the war.
- It lost 13 per cent of its territories.
- Its armed forces were drastically reduced.
- It had to pay £6.6 million reparations (compensation).

This caused many Germans to feel as Hitler did in Source D.

Hyperinflation

Partly because of the huge reparations bill, Germany was hit by HYPERINFLATION in 1923. Bank notes became worthless and savings were wiped out. People blamed the new democratic government of the Weimar REPUBLIC for having accepted the Treaty. Many turned to new EXTREMIST parties. Source E shows what hyperinflation meant in practice for people trying to buy basic necessities such as food.

Hyperinflation meant the German mark became worthless. This photo shows German children playing with stacks of banknotes in the street in 1923.

Source E

The cost of a loaf of bread in marks (the old unit of currency in Germany).

Date	Cost of bread
1918	1 mark
1922	163 marks
January 1923	250 marks
July 1923	3,500 marks
September 1923	1,500,000 marks
November 1923	200,000,000,000 marks

Hitler and the rise of the Nazis

Between 1924 and 1929, Germany recovered economically as the USA lent it money. The new extreme parties lost support as the German people became better off. In October 1929, the collapse of the US stock exchange on Wall Street led the USA to demand back the money borrowed and Germany was plunged into depression. Thousands of businesses collapsed, unemployment rose dramatically and living standards plummeted. Many lost their homes and lived on the streets. People were now ready to support alternative parties who promised a solution. The largest of these were the communists and the Nazi Party led by Adolf Hitler.

There were street battles between the parties, supporters as Germany was plunged into political chaos. It was the Nazis who gained most support because Hitler deliberately appealed to many groups.

Who supported Hitler?

- The working class who were promised jobs.
- Farmers who were promised higher food prices.
- The MIDDLE CLASS who were afraid of a communist revolution.
- The upper classes who resented the Treaty of Versailles.
- Women who were promised a vital role as wives and mothers.
- The military who wanted a bigger army.
- Racists who hated the Jews.
- Young people who found the Nazi methods and military style exciting.

The Nazis became expert at putting across their ideas. Hitler toured all over the country and spoke to huge crowds in halls and sports stadiums. This was very important when radio was still new and TV did not exist. Dramatic marches, music, searchlights, etc. added to the occasion. Hitler made the most of the economic crisis and appealed to German NATIONALISM. He said things many wanted to hear as he was in tune with people's anger and frustration. The audience were ready to accept the Hitler myth of him as a strong leader or 'superman' who would save their country.

Source F

'I met a poor FAMILY – a couple and their nine children who had to survive on £1.50 a week. They lived on cabbages.'

Reporter for *The Spectator*, 1932

Source G

In such circumstances (the depression), people no longer listened to reason. The German people had fantastic fears, extravagant hatreds and extravagant hopes. In such circumstances, the speeches of Hitler began to attract a mass following.

Alan Bullock, *A Study in Tyranny*, 1962

Source H

'I was held under a hypnotic spell. The will of the man seemed to flow into me. It was like a religious conversion.'

An admirer of Hitler, quoted in Ian Kershaw, *Hitler*, 1991

In January 1933, the political situation had become so desperate that President Hindenburg decided to appoint Hitler as Chancellor. This was because the Nazi Party was the largest in the Reichstag (parliament). The first thing Hitler did was to call for an election in March 1933. Before it took place, the Reichstag fire occurred (possibly started deliberately by the Nazis themselves). A communist was blamed, so Hitler asked Hindenburg to declare

Source I

A Nazi election poster that reads: 'Our last hope'.

a state of emergency and the communists were prevented from taking part in the election.

The Nazis won but only managed to get 44 per cent of the votes. Because of the economic and political crisis, Hitler persuaded the Reichstag to pass the Enabling Bill, which allowed him to rule without parliament. Within a few months he banned all other parties and trade unions and closed down all anti-Nazi newspapers. Hitler was now a dictator with total control. When Hindenburg died in 1934, he combined the jobs of Chancellor and President and became known as the Führer (leader). The army swore an oath of personal loyalty to him.

Source J

Growth of the Nazi Party

Date	No. of unemployed (millions)	Nazi votes in Reichstag	Nazi seats
1928	1.8	800,000	12
1930	3.2	6,400,000	107
1932	5	13,700,000	230

ACTIVITIES

Look at Sources D–J on pages 144–145 and the information on pages 143–147 and answer the following questions.

2 a) What is meant by 'scapegoating'?

b) What factors in Germany in the early 1930s led many people to look for scapegoats? Consider norms and values, IDEOLOGY and economic pressure (see Topic 5.2, pages 140–141).

3 What factors explain the rise of Hitler to power?

4 Make a large copy of the chart below and complete it.

Group	What Hitler promised
Working class	Employment
Farmers	
Middle class	
Upper class	
Women	
Military	
Racists	
Young people	

The Nazis in power

The Nazis were racists. They believed that the German or 'Aryan' race was the 'master race' (blonde hair and blue eyes). They believed that all Jews belonged to an 'inferior race'.

There were half a million Jews living in Germany, and they made valuable contributions to the economy, science and the arts. Many had fought for their country in the First World War. However, they were undeservedly made 'scapegoats' for the country's woes. The reasons for this are outlined in the box above right. It is an example of how racial prejudice can exaggerate a 'threat'.

Persecution

As soon as they were in power, the Nazis began to persecute the Jews. They were not the only ones to suffer – communists, gypsies, homosexuals, homeless people, the disabled and mentally ill were other victims. Not all Germans were Nazis, but their control of the state meant there was little resistance or opposition. Hitler used two methods to gain that control: PROPAGANDA and terror.

Why Jews became scapegoats in Germany

- There was a TRADITION in Europe of persecuting the Jews.
- Jewish people looked, dressed and spoke differently. They had their own CUSTOMS and religion.
- Many Jews were successful and wealthy, which led to jealousy.
- Poor Jews were often immigrants and were seen as a threat to jobs.

1 Propaganda

The Nazis established a Ministry for Propaganda under Dr Joseph Goebbels in an attempt to make every German think the same way by controlling the information they were allowed to see and hear. He was one of the first to realise the importance of radios. They were deliberately made cheap so that every home would have one. Thus millions of people could be brainwashed. The radio, newspapers, books, plays and films were also censored and squeezed out all other ideas.

Young people were also forced to join youth movements. Boys enlisted in Hitler Youth and were taught to march and fight. Girls joined the League of German Maidens and taught to become mothers and have babies for Germany. The activities were fun and exciting and meant that they were not aware that they were being brainwashed to believe in Nazi ideas.

2 Terror

Not all Germans would succumb to Nazi methods of social control. Those who would not were either intimidated into submission, sent to concentration camps or killed. The SS (Schutzstaffel or Hitler's bodyguards) and the Gestapo (Secret Police) crushed all opposition.

By these means, the Nazis gained freedom to persecute the Jews. The level of persecution increased gradually in proportion to growing Nazi control.

Today it is difficult to understand how the Holocaust could have happened, in the same way that more recent genocide in Rwanda, Yugoslavia and Sudan is almost impossible to explain. Jews were told they were being re-settled to a new home

This Nazi painting of 1939 by Adolf Wissle shows the ideal 'Aryan' family.

and were even under the impression they were being taken to the showers as they were led to the gas chambers and their death. Twenty thousand people a day were murdered in Auschwitz alone.

There were Germans who were horrified and brave enough to protest. Some took enormous risks to hide Jews. Many of the SS who carried out the murders later committed suicide, unable to live with what they had done. On the other hand, there were also Germans who knew or guessed the truth, but were too afraid to protest or ignored the situation. Many must have even approved – as far as they were concerned, the Nazi 'New Order' was better than the misery of the Weimar Republic. Germans now felt pride in their NATION – they had jobs, food and security.

During the Allied occupation after the war, all German citizens were forced to watch a film that had been made by the Allies of the concentration camp in Belsen. Many watched in silence, whilst others wept.

ACTIVITIES

5   Why did Hitler personally hate the Jews?

6   Why were the Jews persecuted in Germany in the 1930s?

7   List the different methods used by the Nazis to spread their racist ideas.

8   a) Explain what an 'outsider group' is.
    b) How had the Jews in Germany become outsiders by 1941?

9   Using the sources throughout this case study, design a chart that gives examples of different stages in the escalating persecution of the Jews. You could construct your chart by dividing events into the following date ranges:

   • 1935–38
   • 1938–41
   • 1941–45.

   This will help you see how the situation got progressively worse.

10 In groups, discuss who should be held responsible for the Holocaust:

   • Hitler.
   • The Nazis, many of whom claimed to be only obeying orders.
   • The whole of Germany.

11 Why do you think German citizens were forced to watch the films shown by the Allies?

12 Can the persecution of ethnic or religious groups be avoided in the future? Use the following questions as guidance:

   • What lessons can be learned?
   • Are things different today?
   • Are the Race Relations Act (see page 149) and the Universal Declaration of Human Rights enough (see page 164)?
   • What else needs to be done?
   • What can *you* do?

5.5 How can we challenge prejudice and persecution?

- How can individuals and groups act to reduce prejudice and persecution?
- How can nations and international organisations act to resolve prejudice and persecution?

This topic focuses on preventing, reducing and resolving prejudice and persecution. In other words, it considers what can be done.

In Topic 5.3 (pages 140–41), we established that prejudice comes from badly formed attitudes. Reducing prejudice therefore depends on changing people's attitudes and also on challenging the prejudice and discrimination wherever it exists. Individuals, groups, nations and international organisations have throughout history acted to reduce or resolve persecution and prejudice as can be seen in the examples in the table opposite.

ACTIVITY

1 With a partner discuss:
  a) What point is the poster below making?
  b) How effective do you think it is?

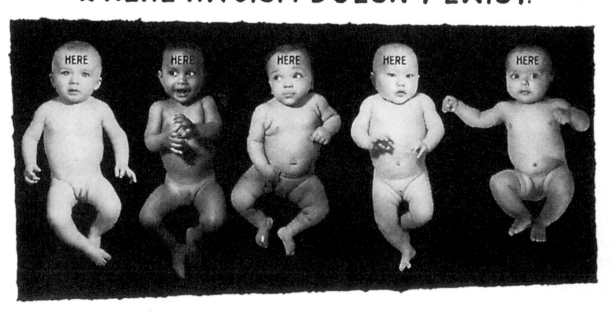

'Babies' poster from the Commission for Racial Equality, 1997.

EXAMPLE	
Individual action	• Becoming a school governor to influence decision making on bullying policies in a school. • Socialising your children so they learn prejudice is unacceptable (see Topic 1.4, pages 11–18).
Local action	• Local government introducing policies such as providing school meals that take into account everyone's dietary needs. • Employers introducing positive employment policies – for example, B&Q have decided on a positive policy of employing people over 50. Such policies are lawful, while positive discrimination is not.
National action	• In the early twentieth century, the Suffragette Movement campaigned to gain women the vote. • In the USA, Martin Luther King led the Civil Rights Movement to gain freedom for blacks. • The Commission for Racial Equality started a campaign to tackle racism in soccer, which now runs as a separate organisation – 'Kick it Out' – supported by national football organisations. • The British government has passed legislation to protect minorities, for example, the Women's Suffrage Act 1918, Equal Pay and Sex Discrimination Act 1970 (which led to the setting up of the Equal Opportunities Commission 1976) and the Race Relations Act 1976.
International action	• The Human Rights Convention (see Topic 2.3, page 46) and the International Court of Human Rights promote justice and equality of treatment for all. • The European Union introduced measures and campaigns to fight prejudice. For example, 1997 was made European Year Against Racism as a response to the growth of extreme political parties on the continent, such as the Neo-Nazis.

'Show Racism the Red Card' is part of the campaign against racism in sport. Here, England player David Beckham wears the logo on his shirt for the game against Holland in February 2005.

The Race Relations Act 1976
The Race Relations Act 1976 makes it illegal to discriminate on racial grounds in a range of areas including pay, job applications and housing. The Act also set up the Commission for Racial Equality with powers to examine cases of unfair dismissal and allegations of racial discrimination.

ACTIVITIES

2 Discuss the best ways of challenging prejudice and persecution at either school or work.

3 Most football clubs are taking action against racism. Make a list of six actions individual clubs could take to deal with things such as racist chanting, graffiti, throwing things, etc.

4 Draw a poster or design a website for the 'Kick it Out' campaign.

5 'It is easier to stop discrimination than it is to stop prejudice.' Do you agree with this statement? Discuss it in groups.

6.1 What do we mean by 'power' and 'democracy'?

- How do democracies work?
- What types of power are there?

In this section we are going to study two important ideas: 'power' and 'democracy'. It is important to understand the need for democracy so that power can be shared and controlled. It is also important to learn that democracy brings rights and freedoms but also responsibilities – individuals need to participate in democracy in order for it to work.

Democracy is a system of government that began in Ancient Greece. The term 'democracy' is taken from two words: *demos*, meaning 'the people', and *ocracy*, meaning 'rule by'. 'Democracy' therefore means 'rule by the people'.

The Greeks developed a system of direct democracy where all the MALE citizens would come together in an assembly to decide on important issues by voting.

Democracy is based on certain freedoms and rights that act to balance power and influence, and the authority power can bring. For example, the police have the power to arrest a citizen. However, the citizen has certain rights that the police must not ignore.

There have been societies in the recent past where such rights and freedoms have not existed. These societies have also tended to concentrate all political and other forms of power into the hands of one individual or group. These are called DICTATORSHIPS.

For example, Hitler in Germany (see Topic 5.4, pages 143–47), Stalin in COMMUNIST Russia and Pinochet in Chile (see Topic 6.4, pages 160–63) were called dictators because all power was concentrated in their hands. This system is the opposite of a democracy. This system of government is called totalitarianism.

Political power in the UK

The UK is a representative democracy. This means people vote for representatives (called Members of Parliament (MPs)) who sit in an assembly (called Parliament) and make decisions on behalf of the people. As the people do not make the decisions themselves, this is a system of indirect democracy.

MPs are usually members of a political party. The UK has many political parties, the largest of which are the Labour, Conservative and Liberal Democrat Parties. Parliament is made up of two chambers. MPs sit in the House of Commons. The other chamber, the House of Lords, is not elected. The political party with the largest number of MPs in the House of Commons forms the government, and its leader becomes prime minister of the UK.

ACTIVITY

1 Study the photographs opposite and think of possible answers to the questions below. Discuss your answer with a partner and then the rest of the class.
   a) What kind of power is shown in each of the photos?
   b) What makes them powerful?
   c) The prime minister is said to have a lot of political power. How far do you think these four examples are more or less powerful than the prime minister and why?
   d) Which might be said to have more influence over everyday life than the government?
   e) Rank the four pictures according to which one you think is the *most* powerful. Be prepared to explain your decision.

1 Richard Branson is a chairman of several national and international businesses including Virgin Airways.

2 Rowan Williams as Archbishop of Canterbury is leader of the Church of England and an international leader of the Anglican Church.

3 Justin Timberlake is a rich and famous pop star who has sold millions of CDs and has many fans across the world.

4 The BBC is an important media organisation (radio, terrestrial, satellite and cable TV) not just in the UK but also across the world.

Before an election, political parties produce a list of things they would wish to achieve if they were to become the government. This is called a 'manifesto'. Governments can only carry out their manifesto because they have the power to do so. This is called political power. Governments use their political power and the authority it gives them to make important decisions on behalf of the country such as on the economy, taxation, spending on education, etc.

Other forms of power

There are other forms of power in addition to political power. The photos above show examples of economic, religious, cultural and social power. In a democracy, different types and levels of power are held by individuals and groups at the same time. Different types of power might CONFLICT. For example, in the 1970s, trade union power conflicted with the government (political power), and, in 2004, people power conflicted with the government over the decision to invade Iraq.

ACTIVITY

2 Political power also operates at different levels of SOCIETY – local (local councils), national, European (European Parliament) and international (UNITED NATIONS).
   a) Which level do you think has the most political power and why?
   b) Which do you think affects you and your FAMILY most and why?
   c) In what ways do you think each of these centres of political power can be influenced in their decision making?
   d) Which do you think you could influence most in their decision making and why?

6.2 How are decisions made?

- In a democracy, at what level are decisions made and who is responsible for making them?
- How far can competing BELIEFS and attitudes be fairly addressed?
- What happens when decision-making processes fail to resolve a controversial issue?

There are many different ways to make a decision. In this topic we are going to evaluate how a decision about a controversial issue might be made and how the decision-making process works by looking at a case study about Stonehenge.

ACTIVITY

1 A decision has to be taken about a new school uniform for your school. Divide into small groups to discuss questions a–e and record your conclusions in a table.
   a) Who should take this decision and why (the head teacher, parents, governors, students)?
   b) What is the most effective and efficient way of making this decision and why?
   c) What is the fairest way of making this decision and why?
   d) What is the most democratic way of making this decision and why?
   e) What is the best method to take this decision and why?

Activity 1 encourages you to think about the best way to make a particular decision in a school community. The following case study of Stonehenge now goes on to develop your understanding of decision making by looking at how the decision-making process can work at a local community level. At Stonehenge there is a conflicting need. On the one hand there is a need to improve the A303 through Wiltshire. On the other hand, the A303 passes very close to the ancient and important site of Stonehenge. How then can the A303 be improved so that it does not damage Stonehenge? This is 'the Stonehenge challenge'.

- What are the issues at stake in this decision?
- Which individuals and groups have an interest in the outcome of this decision?
- At what level should this decision be taken?
- How should this decision be taken?
- Who should take this decision?

1 Why is Stonehenge so important?

Stonehenge is the UK's most important ancient monument. The ENVIRONMENT around Stonehenge is considered to be internationally important. To protect the monument and its surrounding landscape, the United Nations (UN) classified Stonehenge as a World Heritage Site, giving it the same status as the Pyramids and the Great Wall of China. The Stonehenge Management Plan, the key document that lays out how the monument is to be conserved and managed, recognises that the stones have had great 'spiritual' importance for many centuries and that this is still true today. For many visitors, Stonehenge is an astronomical wonder, a mystical and sacred place, with a strong sense of history stretching back over 5,000 years.

Stonehenge is a unique and special landscape. 450 archaeological monuments of various sizes surround the central stones. The future of Stonehenge concerns not just the massive stones but also its surrounding environment. Under the WORLD HERITAGE CONVENTION, the UK government has a duty to conserve and preserve the whole site, not just the stones. This is a huge challenge for the government, as Stonehenge is a very sensitive area and could easily be damaged.

English Heritage runs Stonehenge, but the National Trust (NT) owns thousands of hectares of land around the site. (They can be looked up on the Internet.)

2 What is the problem?

The A303 is a major trunk road (not a motorway) going from the M3 through Wiltshire, past Stonehenge and down to Cornwall. The HIGHWAYS AGENCY (HA) has long wanted to make significant

Problem 1:
The central area around the stone circle has been damaged by agriculture over many years.

Problem 4:
The Stonehenge landscape has been badly affected by the building of a number of smaller roads across or near to the site.

Problem 2: There are a huge number of visitors to Stonehenge every year. These visitors have to be efficiently managed. Tourism increases the pressure on the local road system and especially the A303.

Problem 3: The present visitor centre is old, small and considered inadequate to cope effectively with tourist numbers.

improvements to the A303 because it is a major communication route for industry, business and tourism. However, HA has identified four main problems concerning the Stonehenge site (see above).

3 What improvements were proposed and why?

Following a detailed inspection of the site, the government announced in December 2002 the basis of the Stonehenge Scheme. The HA would be responsible for implementing this scheme.

- To restore the site to its prehistoric setting.
- To tackle congestion and safety issues on the A303.
- To develop the A303 as a dual carriageway.
- To build a by-pass around a local village.
- The A344 to be closed to traffic and grassed over.
- The HA to build a 2.1 km (1.3 mile) bored tunnel (that is, a tunnel cut by a machine under the ground) as part of the A303 Stonehenge improvement south of the stones.

The diagram below illustrates these proposals.

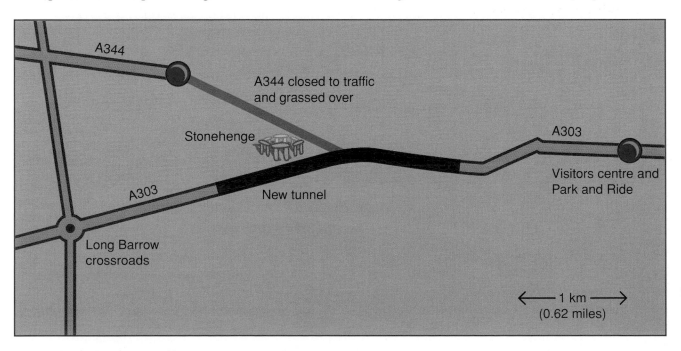

The government recognised that because these were controversial proposals affecting a very sensitive site, the decision could only be made after all the arguments for and against the proposals had been heard. They appointed an inspector who, as an expert in planning, building and the environment, would:

- investigate all aspects of the Stonehenge Scheme, especially the environmental and archaeological effects of the scheme
- consider the advantages and disadvantages of the scheme

- hold a public inquiry or investigation into the Stonehenge Scheme to which interested individuals, groups and organisations could come and put across their point of view about the proposed scheme.

The Stonehenge public inquiry was held in Salisbury between February and March 2004.

> The total cost of the Stonehenge Scheme was estimated by the government to be £192 million, with work starting in 2005 and open to traffic in 2008.

4 What were the different views on the Stonehenge Scheme?

GROUP	PURPOSE	LEVEL	VIEWPOINTS ON THE PROPOSAL
English Heritage	A government funded organisation set up to protect and conserve sites of historical and environmental importance.	National	• In 2002, proposed a new £57 million visitor centre to cope with the one million visitors. The centre will be away from the existing site. • Supports the Highways Agency proposals for Stonehenge.
The Highways Agency	A government funded agency. The HA builds and manages all motorways and major roads in England.	National	• The bored tunnel will remove the traffic from the centre of the World Heritage Site and will minimise damage to the landscape and the surface archaeology. • The scheme would help to ease congestion and improve safety along the route, and protect Stonehenge from noise and air pollution.
National Trust	An independent organisation that seeks to conserve and preserve the natural and historical environment.	National but with county and regional offices	• The international importance and unique quality of Stonehenge has to be preserved. • Human activity through agriculture, road building and the thousands of visitors meant that action had to be taken but in a way that safeguarded the spirit of the stones. • However, the NT disagreed with the location of the tunnel, fearing that its construction would damage the site. • The NT also wanted a longer 2.9 km (1.8 mile) tunnel to reduce the impact of traffic on the Stonehenge site.
Salisbury District Council	The local council.	Local	• Proposed to build a new visitor centre – but there is no agreed site.
Wiltshire County Council	The county council.	Local	• Supported the HA scheme.
The Pagan Federation	An interest group representing a religion.	National with local groups	• The whole of the archaeology of Stonehenge and its spiritual and religious importance has to be protected. • Opposed the shorter tunnel proposed by the HA and favoured the long bored tunnel to avoid damage to the archaeology and the sacred landscape.
Campaign for the Protection of Rural England (CPRE)	An organisation set up to protect the countryside.	National with local groups	• Concerned that the scale and impact of the scheme would seriously damage the visual character of Stonehenge. • Wanted a longer tunnel than that proposed by the government to protect the archaeology.

GROUP	PURPOSE	LEVEL	VIEWPOINTS ON THE PROPOSAL
Stonehenge Alliance (CPRE, Transport 2000, The Pagan Federation, UK Rivers Network)	A group of environmental and archaeological organisations opposed to the road proposals.	Local – created once the Stonehenge Scheme was announced in detail – supported by national organisations	• Wanted to protect the whole of the World Heritage Site and all the archaeology of Stonehenge. • Concerned about the type and length of the proposed tunnel – suggesting a 4.5 km (2.8 mile) toll tunnel instead, which would remove traffic from the Stonehenge site. • Concerned about the extra traffic the new road improvements would make in the long term.
The local Salisbury Green Party	Political party promoting environmental solutions.	Local but supported by the national UK Green Party	• Wanted to restore the landscape of Stonehenge and all the archaeology without new roads cutting into the World Heritage Site. • Did not support road construction scheme at Stonehenge, especially developing the A303 as dual carriageway. • Supports a long bored tunnel to ensure the minimum of pollution. • Against by-pass around local villages. • Doubtful about the visitor centre because extra visitors would increase road congestion and pollution. • Wants the whole scheme to be an environmentally sustainable project.

The HA recognised that finding a solution to the Stonehenge challenge would be limited by a number of factors:

Land use: the land around Stonehenge is used either for agriculture or tourist purposes. There is also a large military presence in the area. This limits the amount of land for building large roads or developing the Stonehenge site.	**The cost:** to build a major new road with a tunnel to preserve the Stonehenge site would be very expensive.	**Geology:** the rock and soil surrounding the Stonehenge site may not be helpful to road and tunnel builders – the more difficult the geology, the greater the cost would be to construct the tunnel.
Archaeology: Stonehenge is a World Heritage Site, which means that the monument is internationally important and could not be damaged in any way. This might limit what road builders might be able to do near the site.	**Water resources:** the local rivers, streams, water table and drainage all have to be taken into consideration when planning and constructing a new road or tunnel. Poor drainage might increase the cost of the project.	**Planning laws:** the new road and tunnel would have to meet strict existing planning laws. If the project did not meet these laws, then this could cause delay and increase the cost of the project.
Nature conservation: the Stonehenge site is itself an area of natural beauty. Protecting the environment might increase the overall cost of the project.	**Existing highway network:** the proposed improvements must link into existing roads in and around Stonehenge. The existing roads system must not be made worse.	**Ecology:** the immediate Stonehenge site is itself a small-scale ecosystem. In building the road and tunnel, the project must not damage the ecology of the local area.
Landscape: the Stonehenge site is a unique landscape – and of international value. The proposed changes to the traffic system around Stonehenge must not damage this landscape. The project may even improve the Stonehenge landscape.	**Local community:** this might be affected by the building of the road and tunnel. Parts of the community will support the new road and parts will not. The project will be a source of stress, concern and possible inconvenience for local people.	**Noise, vibration and air quality:** every effort would have to be made to ensure that in the building and managing of the new road and tunnel, noise and air pollution were kept to a minimum. This would require a major environmental protection scheme.

2 Draw a circle in the middle of a piece of A4 paper. Label the circle 'The Stonehenge Challenge'. From the information on pages 152–55, produce a concept map to show the key parts of the Stonehenge problem. You might include the following issues – and any other issues you think are important.

Local; National; Historical; Political; Environmental; Transport

Share your map with another person in the class to see how far you agree on the key parts of this problem.

3 There are a number of interested parties to the Stonehenge problem, as shown in the tables on pages 154–55.

Look at the line at the bottom of the page. On this line, mark where you think each interested party is in terms of its power and influence in relation to the Stonehenge problem.

4 The various parties with an interest in the future of Stonehenge have very different viewpoints and interests. Prepare a class presentation from the point of view of one of the interested parties. In your presentation you might outline:

• your attitude towards the proposals for Stonehenge

• the audience for your viewpoints
• the methods you might use to influence decision makers
• the methods you might use to influence the general public and why
• the evidence you might present at the Stonehenge public inquiry.

5 The decision on whether to have the Stonehenge Scheme went to a public inquiry.
   a) Identify the advantages and disadvantages of a public inquiry in order to make a decision on the Stonehenge proposals.
   b) A public inquiry was one way to reach a decision about the future of Stonehenge.
      • What alternative ways could have been used to reach a decision on Stonehenge?
      • For each alternative, explain their advantages and disadvantages.
      • Having evaluated alternative approaches, how far were these better or worse than a public inquiry and for what reasons?

6 Organise a class debate with different groups of students representing different points of view. Then, as a class, come to your own decision about the future of the Stonehenge site.

Most powerful and influential to the making of the final decision on Stonehenge

Least powerful and influential to the making of the final decision on Stonehenge

6.3 How can democracy resolve a local difference?

- How far should local communities be involved in decisions affecting national organisations?
- What is the best way for local communities to be involved in key decision-making processes?
- What happens when local communities disagree with decisions taken at national level?

In this topic we shall investigate what can happen when decisions taken at the national level affect a local community through a case study about the NHS. It looks at whether a local community can influence decision makers who may be many miles away and what it can do when it disagrees with decisions taken at national level.

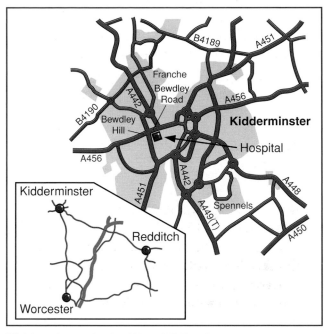

Kidderminster in the West Midlands.

Case Study
Dr Richard Taylor and Kidderminster Hospital

Kidderminster is in the West Midlands close to Worcester, and there has been a hospital there since 1920. In 1999, it was announced by the government that the 192-bed casualty unit at the hospital was to be closed as part of a national re-organisation of the National Health Service (NHS). Instead, a new hospital was to be built in Worcester.

Kidderminster Hospital was a medium-sized district general hospital, which, under the re-organisation, would no longer take critically ill patients. The hospital would become a centre for patients with less serious illnesses who would not need to stay in the hospital. Those with serious illnesses or injuries would have to go to Worcester or elsewhere – Worcester is about 24 km (15 miles) away and Redditch (the nearest hospital) is 25.5 km (16 miles) away.

The population of the Kidderminster area is around 100,000. There were local concerns that having to drive 30 minutes to reach the nearest

ACTIVITY

1 Study the map carefully. What problems do you think closing the casualty unit might cause for the area around Kidderminster?

casualty department might place some patients at risk. Many towns with a population of 100,000 have casualty departments – why not Kidderminster?

Some people said that the only reason why Kidderminster casualty department was to be closed was because too much money had been spent on the new hospital in Worcester.

Not everybody was against the decision. Supporters of the government's proposals said:

- Kidderminster Hospital did not have the number of medical staff needed for a modern accident and emergency department
- a bigger regional medical centre would offer patients a wider choice of specialists
- the new facilities in Worcester would be better and safer than the old Kidderminster Hospital.

Protest

Dr Richard Taylor

Dr Richard Taylor thought the decision to close the hospital was wrong. Dr Taylor, aged 66 and a retired consultant, decided to start a campaign to save the casualty department at the Kidderminster Hospital. There were:

- petitions of 66,000 and 44,000 signatures
- marches of 5,000 and 12,000 people
- thousands of letters
- demonstrations
- deputations (documents) to the Prime Minister and the House of Commons.

All these protests failed to stop the decision to close the hospital. Dr Taylor decided that the strength of local feeling over the hospital closure had to be shown to the whole country.

In 2001 Dr Taylor decided to stand for Parliament in the general election against the local Labour MP, David Lock, in protest against the government's proposals. David Lock was a government minister with a MAJORITY of 7,000 at the 1997 general election. Dr Taylor formed the Independent Kidderminster Hospital and Health

Concern Party to fight the election and raise publicity to save the hospital from closure.

- 1999 – the opponents to the closure gained eleven councillors on local councils.
- 2000 – this was increased to nineteen councillors.

The 2001 general election

Dr Taylor used the general election to campaign on the single issue of the future of hospital services in Kidderminster and nothing else. David Lock said that the general election should 'not be a referendum (submitting a vote to the ELECTORATE) on Kidderminster Hospital. The voters need an MP who is going to represent them on benefit issues, defence, on the whole issues of government.'

However, Dr Taylor's campaign was well supported by the local people and he defeated David Lock with a majority of 17,630. 'I'm absolutely thrilled, honoured and delighted that the people have had faith in me,' he said when his victory was announced.

This is Worcestershire (a local newspaper) quoted Dr Taylor as saying that 'the seething anger and resentment is something that nobody on the other side bargained for. The public support was utterly amazing.' Whereas national newspapers had headlines such as these:

DR TAYLOR PUTS REST TO SHAME

Man of the Year!

Sensational!

HUMILIATING DEFEAT FOR GOVERNMENT MINISTER

Following the general election

✓ Dr Taylor became a member of the PARLIAMENTARY HEALTH SELECT COMMITTEE and sat on the committee overseeing Labour's NHS reforms.

✓ Health Concern went on to become the largest political group on Wyre Forest District Council who, working with other parties, replaced Labour in controlling the council.

✓ The government agreed to give back twenty beds to Kidderminster Hospital and install a new surgery unit costing £14 million.

ACTIVITIES

2 How fair and balanced are the newspaper headlines opposite? Do you agree with them?

3 'It is not right for people who disagree with government policy to use a general election to campaign on a single issue.' How far do you think Dr Taylor was right to stand for Parliament and campaign just about the Kidderminster Hospital?

4 Produce a leaflet or script for an advert broadcast by Health Concern on a local radio station during the 2001 general election.

 • Plan carefully the content of the script.
 • What are the key messages you need to get across as an organisation?
 • How will you ensure Dr Taylor is well known?
 • Who is the audience for this piece of campaigning and why?

Investigations

1 Visit the Health Concern website. Evaluate the content of the website in relation to the following:

 • What do you learn about Health Concern as a campaigning organisation?
 • In what ways was Health Concern a local campaigning organisation focusing on a single issue?
 • How is the website organised?
 • How has Health Concern organised the website in order to put across its message?

List and evaluate the strengths and weaknesses of the website as a campaigning device for Dr Taylor.

2 Investigate the website of one of the other major political parties in the UK.
 a) Using examples from the website you have investigated, explain why websites and other forms of electronic media have become important resources for campaigners, pressure groups and political parties in a democracy.
 b) How far do you think the development of e-campaigning has been a good or bad thing for democracy?

3 Look through your local newspaper or listen to your local radio station. Find three or four issues that seem important locally, for example, the building of a new road.
 a) In a group of four, choose one local issue you have found.
 b) Plan and carry out further detailed investigation into this issue: this might include Internet research, letter writing, fieldwork, the taking of photographs.
 c) Design and complete an opinion poll for this local issue and analyse the results.
 d) From the information you have collected, produce a report or PowerPoint presentation identifying and evaluating the key points of this issue:

 • What is the issue?
 • Why is this an issue?
 • How important is this issue?
 • Why might individuals and groups have differing attitudes on this issue?
 • Are there local groups publicising these views?

 e) What conclusions do you come to about this issue – are you in favour or against it? Provide several detailed reasons why.
 f) Following your investigation and evaluation, write a letter or article on your views about the local issue and send it to your local newspaper.

6.4 *What happens when democracy is replaced by dictatorship?*

- What are the strengths and weaknesses of democracy?
- What are the consequences for democracy when a) society is divided by conflicting interests, and b) powerful interests, such as the military or big business, conflict with the government?

The case study in this topic raises some important questions about how safe and secure democracy is as a system of government. It shows what can happen when strong and powerful interests within a country disagree with the policies of the democratically elected government.

ACTIVITY

1 As part of a whole-school charity event, each tutor group has been asked to raise money for a charity of its choice. Your tutor group has elected four students to research a charity and to organise the fundraising activity. You were one of the four students elected to this organising committee. However, even though you and the other three members were elected, you are not happy about their choice of charity or the ideas they have come up with for fundraising.

- What can you do to raise your concerns about the fundraising event?
- Who should you discuss your concerns with?
- The whole tutor group democratically and fairly elected the four members of the organising committee – how can your concerns about the fundraising be resolved to everyone's satisfaction?
- What might happen if your concerns are not in some way resolved?

Case Study
Chile, 1970–90

Chile in 1970 was a country with deep divisions between poor and rich parts of society. A new government was elected which promised to help the poor and make Chilean society fairer. The rich therefore felt threatened and angry with the new government – but what could they do if Chile was a democracy?

The new government in Chile was not popular with other governments around the world. The Chilean situation raised the issue of how far governments of one country have the right to alter the way another – democratic – country is governed.

1 The government of Salvador Allende, 1970–73

In September 1970, Salvador Allende, a SOCIALIST politician and leader of the Popular Unity (UP) was elected President of Chile. The UP wanted to modernise Chile by:

- improving Chilean farming, education, housing and social care
- bringing industry under the control of the government (nationalisation).

Allende wanted to help the poorest in Chile and to create a democratic socialist country. He also promised to rule Chile in a constitutional way, respecting everyone's human rights.

Right from the start, Allende knew that ruling Chile would be very difficult. In 1970, when Chile was suffering a severe economic crisis, Allende's election frightened many businesspeople, industrialists and wealthy Chileans. Many ordinary Chileans withdrew their savings from the banks. There was a lot of unemployment. The USA did not like Allende's left wing ideas for how Chile should be modernised and openly criticised his government.

In response to Allende's plea for working-class support for 'the people's government', industrial workers increased output by 14 per cent during 1970. In September 1970, the Chilean unemployment rate had stood by 8.4 per cent; by September of 1971, it had dropped to 4.8 per cent.

ACTIVITY

2 Using the spider diagram below, produce an initial response to the following questions: how far might Allende's policies make Chile:
  • a more or less fair society – and why?
  • a more or less democratic society – and why?
  • a more or less peaceful society – and why?

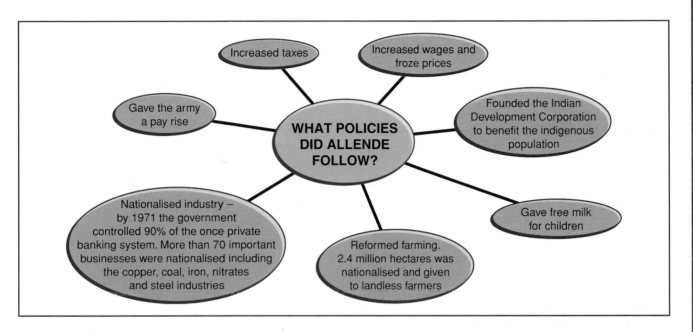

Increased taxes

Increased wages and froze prices

Gave the army a pay rise

WHAT POLICIES DID ALLENDE FOLLOW?

Founded the Indian Development Corporation to benefit the indigenous population

Nationalised industry – by 1971 the government controlled 90% of the once private banking system. More than 70 important businesses were nationalised including the copper, coal, iron, nitrates and steel industries

Reformed farming. 2.4 million hectares was nationalised and given to landless farmers

Gave free milk for children

Pinochet's dictatorship

After some success in 1970, things went badly for Allende and Chile.

This photo shows Chile's presidential palace on fire after being bombed during the *coup d'état* in 1973. How did things get so bad for Allende? The timeline on the next page explains what happened.

Chile, 1971–90

1971	The Chilean economy was in an even worse condition. • There were shortages of goods and food in the shops. • Businesspeople hated government controls on prices as this reduced the amount of profits they could make. • The value of the Chilean currency fell strongly. • Copper represented 70 per cent of the Chilean exports, but international copper prices were also falling after 1970 and this made things even worse for the Chilean economy. • The nationalisation of American and other foreign-owned companies increased tensions with the USA. President Nixon reacted by encouraging other countries and international banks to reduce their lending to Chile. This further weakened the Chilean economy. • The USA now gave support to Chilean political parties and the media opposing President Allende.
1972	The Allende government was in crisis. The economic situation worsened, unemployment and inflation increased, and this led to rioting on the streets. Allende tried to get support from other political parties and from the military by appointing some generals to his government. However, there was virtually no support for Allende from the rich or the military, while the poor and unemployed were suffering and angry. Chile was in chaos. In these conditions, it was clear that the military would remove his government by force.
1973	General Augusto Pinochet was made Chief Major-General in the army. On 11 September 1973, there was a military rebellion led by Pinochet. Allende's Presidential Palace was surrounded and Salvador Allende is believed to have killed himself before soldiers loyal to Augusto Pinochet could take him alive. Allende's officials were arrested, taken to military bases and many were executed. A new military government (or Junta) was formed and led by General Pinochet and the commanders of the army, navy, air force and police. General Pinochet ruled Chile for 17 years during which thousands of political opponents were killed or disappeared, and many more Chileans had their human rights violated by this military dictatorship.
1977	The United Nations Human Rights Commission criticised the Pinochet regime for its human rights violations including torture.
1980	Pinochet introduced a new constitution that made him President until 1989, and it secured the role of the military in the government. Basic human rights were limited under this Constitution. Opponents of the government continued to be arrested and mistreated. The Constitution could not be amended without the approval of the government.
1987	There was a referendum to decide whether Pinochet should stay in government. The political opposition parties joined together to campaign against Pinochet. They demanded the return of democracy to Chile.
1988	Fifty-five per cent of the electorate voted to end Pinochet's rule. The opposition parties gained a majority in the Chilean parliament. Pinochet resigned as president, but was allowed to stay as Commander-in-Chief of the army until 1998 when he finally retired.
1990	Chile returned to full democracy.

ACTIVITIES

3 Copy the following chart and complete a 'living graph' to show the respect for individual rights in Chile between 1970 and 1990. Label the key dates when important changes took place in Chile that might have affected individual rights either for the better or for the worse.

Respect for individual rights

1970	1972	1974	1976	1980	1984	1990

No respect for individual rights

General Augusto Pinochet.

4 Which groups in Chilean society supported Allende and which supported Pinochet – and why?

5 Explain how the rights and responsibilities of Chilean citizens to participate in society and politics changed between 1970 and 1990.

6 Allende was said to have been a 'constitutional' leader whilst Pinochet was said to have been an 'UNCONSTITUTIONAL' leader. Explain what this means.

7 Chile had experienced a number of problems in 1970:

- A weak economy from 1968–73 creating unemployment and inflation.
- A society divided between rich and poor.
- A weak democracy with powerful interests such as landowners, businesspeople and the military – all critical of politicians.

a) In what ways was the 1973 military rebellion in Chile an appropriate method for solving Chile's problems at that time?

b) What alternatives might have been tried by the Chileans to solve the country's problems?

c) How far should the international community or organisations become involved with events in other countries, especially when they face problems as Chile did in 1970?

8 From studying the example of Chile and its democracy, and any other examples you may have studied, copy and complete the table below.

a) What are the advantages of a democratic system of government and society?	b) What are the disadvantages of a democratic system of government and society?
c) What are the strengths of a democratic system of government and society?	d) What are the weaknesses of a democratic system of government and society?
e) Which factors strengthened and supported a democratic system of government and society?	f) Which factors weakened and undermined a democratic system of government and society?

6.5 *What is the role of pressure groups in democracy?*

- What are the aims and methods of pressure groups?
- How do pressure groups help to resolve differences in society?
- How do pressure groups benefit democracy?

In Topic 3.9 (page 107), you looked at the methods of environmental pressure groups. This topic looks at a case study about Amnesty International to help further your understanding of how pressure groups work.

Pressure groups are organisations that seek to influence policy and decision makers, such as councillors, MPs, government ministers and government leaders, both in the UK and abroad. There are two types of pressure groups.

1 Interest groups: these are pressure groups that represent a particular group or section of society. Examples of such groups would be trade unions (representing the interests of particular groups of workers), the AA (representing the interests of motorists) and the Child Poverty Action Group (representing the interests of poor families).

2 Promotional or issue groups: these are pressure groups that gain support from all parts of society, but are concerned with a particular issue. Examples of such groups would be Friends of the Earth (promoting issues relating to the environment), Transport 2000 (promoting the issue of public transport) and Amnesty International (promoting the respect for human rights across the world).

ACTIVITY

1 Make a list of pressure groups you have heard about in the media or from the Internet. What methods have these groups used to make you aware of them?

Case Study
Amnesty International

What is Amnesty International?
Amnesty International (AI) is an example of a 'promotional or issue pressure group'. It is a worldwide movement of people who campaign for human rights.

AI was launched in 1961 with a newspaper article by a British lawyer, Peter Benenson, calling on people to work independently and peacefully for the release of men and women across the world imprisoned for their political and religious beliefs.

What are human rights?
In 1945, the United Nations was created. The world was shocked when it discovered the truth of Hitler's Holocaust. World leaders wanted to define and defend the rights of all people. In 1948, the United Nations created the UNIVERSAL DECLARATION OF HUMAN RIGHTS (UDHR), which all members of the UN signed and agreed to respect.

The UDHR covers legal and political rights (such as free speech, movement and association), economic, social and cultural rights. The UDHR is universal because it is said to cover all people on the earth regardless of the age, GENDER, nationality, SEXUALITY or RELIGION. Every human being is said to be entitled to health care, education, employment, housing and welfare benefits. This Declaration is the basic standard for human rights. Countries now have their own standards. Europe has its own Convention on Human Rights and in 2000 the UK passed the HUMAN RIGHTS ACT.

AI began its campaigning life working for:

- the release of prisoners of conscience – individuals imprisoned solely for their beliefs, colour, gender, ethnic origin, sexuality, language or religion, who had not used or argued for the use of violence
- fair trials for prisoners
- an end to the use of the death penalty, torture and all cruel, inhuman or degrading treatment or punishment of prisoners
- an end to extra judicial executions and 'disappearances'.

Today, AI now campaigns for all parts of the UDHR, whether political, social, economic or cultural rights.

What methods does AI use?

- AI as a campaigning organisation needs to be impartial. Therefore AI is independent of any government, political IDEOLOGY, economic interest or religion. AI is only interested in promoting and defending human rights and can only do this if it is independent of governments.
- AI has to inform the public, governments and other organisations about human rights violations. AI carries out research into these violations by visiting countries, prisons or observing trials. AI produces reports listing human rights violations and suggesting ways in which human rights can be respected in the future.
- AI has websites to inform its members and the public of human rights violations. AI publishes leaflets, posters, videos and campaigning materials for members and supporters to act upon. AI members and supporters receive information about human rights violations and they write letters to presidents, prime ministers and ministers asking politely that their government respects human rights and brings to justice those who might be violating the rights of people in their country. This material is all part of a process to create an atmosphere where human rights are respected.
- AI has many networks of members and supporters around the world. At the latest count, AI had more than 1.8 million members, supporters and subscribers in over 150 countries.
- AI organises campaigns to inform the public of human rights violations, for example, in Russia or in Africa, to improve the rights of specific groups such as women or ASYLUM SEEKERS, or ensure that the human rights of vulnerable groups such as refugees are respected by governments.
- AI lobbies government officials across the world to encourage them to respect human rights.

Example of an Amnesty campaign

VIOLENCE AGAINST WOMEN IS THE GREATEST HUMAN RIGHTS SCANDAL OF OUR TIMES

From birth to death, in times of peace as well as war, women face DISCRIMINATION and violence at the hands of the state, the community and the family.

- At least one out of every three women has been beaten, coerced into sex, or abused in her lifetime. This figure comes from a study based on 50 surveys from around the world.
- More than 60 million women are 'missing' from the world today as a result of sex-selective abortions and FEMALE INFANTICIDE.
- Every year, millions of women are raped by partners, relatives, friends and strangers, by employers and colleagues, soldiers and members of armed groups.
- Violence in the family is endemic all over the world; the overwhelming majority of victims are women and girls. In the USA, for example, women account for around 85 per cent of the victims of domestic violence.
- The WORLD HEALTH ORGANISATION has reported that up to 70 per cent of female murder victims are killed by their male partners.
- Small arms and light weapons are the main tools of almost every conflict. Women and children account for nearly 80 per cent of the casualties, according to the UN Secretary-General.

All over the world, women have led brave and inspiring campaigns against this violence. They have achieved dramatic changes in laws, policies and practices. But the violence persists.

Amnesty International

2 Why would Amnesty campaign on issues such as those shown in the photos below and opposite, and in the example on page 165?

Amnesty International demonstrators protest in Brighton, UK, against Egypt's PERSECUTION of gay men in 2003.

Investigations

1 a) Using Amnesty International's website, research the different kinds of human rights violations identified by AI and where these occur. Copy and complete the table below to record the results of your research.

b) From your investigation, select one type of human rights violation, for example, torture, or one area of the world, for example, Africa, and produce a detailed evaluation on your findings. Your findings could be reported back to the whole class in a presentation.

Human rights violation	Africa	Europe	North America	Asia/Pacific	South America
Women					
Refugee and asylum seekers					
Death penalty					
Arms sales					
Disappearances					
Torture					
Ethnic violence					

Chelsea pensioner, Doug Woolford, from the Royal Hospital Chelsea, walks among fake gravestones placed in Trafalgar Square to launch the 'Control Arms' campaign to control the international arms trade in October 2003. The campaign, launched by three charities – Amnesty International, Oxfam and IANSA (International Action Network on Small Arms) – is aimed at the world's most powerful governments who are also the world's biggest arms suppliers: France, Russia, China, the UK and the USA.

2 Working with a number of other students, select one area of AI's work on human rights. You are now going to form a campaign team.

a) To help you plan your campaign, think about the following issues:

- What is the main human rights issue you are going to campaign about?
- Who is the target audience for your campaign (for example, the government of the UK, a foreign government, the prime minister or minister of the UK or of another country, the media or the general public)?
- What methods are you going to choose to bring to the attention of your target audience that there is a human rights issue to be resolved?
- How will you monitor your campaign?
- How will you know how effective or successful your campaign has been?

b) Having thought through these issues, plan a campaign for your chosen human rights issue. You will need to be as specific as possible to ensure that your campaigning action plan will be effective.

c) Plan and produce a letter to a relevant decision maker – prime minister or president – highlighting the human rights concern you have and what steps you are seeking from this official to have this human rights concern resolved. (There are hints on the AI websites on how to write such letters.)

4 Explain why it is more effective to campaign through a group than to campaign as an individual.

5 From your work on AI, produce a list of strengths and weaknesses of pressure group activity for democracy.

6.6 How can local democracy be developed and extended?

- In what ways can democracy be extended in society?
- What are the arguments for and against the extension of democracy?

Democracy has been defined as 'rule by the people'. This suggests that the people somehow actually govern society. In a country of 60 million people this seems a strange form of government. This topic looks at how democratic methods can be used at a local level. It asks you to think about whether democracy should be extended to younger people in the UK. It then asks you to think about which type of democracy would be best for school councils.

What are school councils?

School councils have been set up in many schools over the last ten years. It is argued that school councils encourage students to participate in the key decisions affecting their school and education and so have some ownership of not just the decision-making process but also of the final decision. Participation in decision making encourages students to value their school as partners with other key groups such as teachers, governors and parents.

What do school councils achieve?

School councils, it is argued, can make a positive contribution to a school community. Through the school council students can have:

• a ROLE in developing aspects of school life
• a say in how subjects are taught and in some cases assessed
• a role to play in reducing bullying or vandalism
• a role to play in improving teacher–student relations
• a role to play in whole-school issues such as uniform, homework or the catering.

School councils differ from school to school, but there are some similarities. The key issue is how to involve students in the decision-making process of the school. This is often achieved through year councils as well as whole-school councils. In addition, schools may operate class councils, circle time, charters of BEHAVIOUR and peer MEDIATION where conflict exists betweens students (see Topic 2.3, pages 44–49).

School councils are encouraging students to participate in the affairs of their own community. As such, an important objective is helping students to develop life skills such as speaking and listening skills, teamwork, emotional literacy, problem solving, MORAL reasoning skills, SELF-ESTEEM and self-confidence. These skills are important for learning about CITIZENSHIP.

Above all, it is argued that school and class councils enable pupils to have a voice and to understand that their opinions count.

An example:
A High School, Surrey
• The school senate was established in 2000.
• Two representatives from each form are elected to the year council, and each year council elects two 'senators' (one boy, one girl).
• Councillors have job descriptions, and the senate are involved in functions around the school, for example, speeches at the parents' evenings.
• The senate has a budget of £3,500 per term to invest in school improvements.

ACTIVITIES

4   Are school councils a good idea? Copy out and complete the table below from the point of view of:
    a) a student in a school
    b) the head teacher
    c) a parent.

Strengths	Weaknesses
Opportunities	Threats

5   What is the best way to select the members of your school council and why?

6   What sort of issues should and should not be brought to a school council and why?

7   School councils are an example of representative democracy. What do you think are the main difficulties in developing such a 'democratic principle' in a school or college? Would a 'direct' form of democracy be more appropriate? (See Topic 6.1, page 150.)

8   Why might many students ignore the school council? What practical steps could be taken to ensure high support for the school council amongst students?

9   Individually, or in groups, prepare a manifesto for a candidate to your school council.

10 Why is a school council rather than a whole-school assembly the most effective way of making decisions for students?

11 Should teachers, parents or governors have a voice on the school council?

One of the main features of a LIBERAL DEMOCRACY is the right of the people living in a particular country to freely participate in the political process. This usually means the right to vote in elections, though this now means the right to join political parties or pressure groups, or to have certain freedoms of speech, thought and belief.

Democracy in the UK was very limited in 1800. The vote was given to men over 21 who had a certain amount of WEALTH. This excluded the vast majority of the population from the political system. The Reform Act 1832 did make some changes and extended the right to vote to more men, though to only a few and, again, wealth was the key factor. The right to vote was extended again in 1868 and 1885. In 1918, all men over the age of 21 were given the right to vote. Some women were also given the vote in 1918. All women over 21 were given the right to vote in 1928. In 1969, the age of voting was lowered to those over the age of 18. There has been some discussion on extending the vote to everyone over the age of 16. However, is this a good idea?

It is said that lowering the voting age would encourage more young people to become involved in politics. This is what two MPs think:

A government minister said:

'I think it is a very important issue. We expect more and more of people in relation to personal participation and social responsibility, in my view rightly, particularly young people.

'If we want to both engage young people and make them discharge their responsibilities, then I think there's got to be a quid pro quo of letting them see greater influence in the political process.'

Tony Blair has said:

'There is obviously a case for saying: "Look, people grow up a lot more quickly ... so why shouldn't you be able to vote?"'

- At present, a 16-year-old can get married and join the army, but he or she cannot vote in elections and has to wait until reaching the age of 21 to stand as a candidate.
- At the general election in 2005, only 37 per cent of 18–24-year-olds bothered to vote, according to the pollsters MORI.
- A survey by the British HOUSEHOLD Panel that suggested nearly 30 per cent of 15–17-year-olds said they were either very interested or fairly interested in politics – a higher figure than 18–20-year-olds.

The Electoral Commission, which advises the government on how elections can be modernised, has been consulting on the voting age following concern over falling turnouts among young voters in general and local government elections.

The Commission sought views from people attending party political conferences, the annual sitting of the UK Youth Parliament and youth interest groups.

The Commission found that just 16 per cent of voters aged under 25 voted in the May 2001 elections to the Welsh assembly.

Not only did the under-25s fail to vote in significant numbers, but only 21 per cent of the next age group, 25–34-year-olds, exercised their democratic rights.

Liberal Democrat youth spokesman Matthew Green backed changing the voting age to 16: 'Denying 16-year-olds the vote because some consider them politically immature is trite nonsense,' he said. 'If 16-year-olds can marry, have children of their own, pay taxes and join the army, why should they not be able to vote for the government they want?'

But Conservative shadow cabinet member David Willetts was cautious over the idea. He told *Sky News*: 'I personally think that 18 has been a reasonable age – I don't particularly see any need to lower it. It is important to engage younger people in the political process but I'm not sure that lowering the age to 16 would be the right way to do it.'

What do young people think about issues such as crime, tax, health and foreign policy? Should people, many of whom are still at school, have the right to vote? Do the quotes below from young people, interviewed by the *Guardian* newspaper, show they are informed enough to vote?

ACTIVITIES

12 What are the arguments for and against the lowering of the voting age to 16?

13 Produce a leaflet or an article for your school newspaper on the issue of lowering the voting age to 16. To help you:
- design a survey to test the opinion of students in your school on this issue
- extend your survey to include the views of adults
- ensure that you have a reasonably large sample to make the result an accurate reflection of opinion
- you might invite your local MP or councillor into school to discuss this issue
- produce graphs of the data collected and evaluate them thoroughly.

7.1 *What do you see, what do you know?*

- What inequalities do you think exist between people living in Africa and the USA?
- How do you know about these inequalities?

In the first topic in this section, you will start by examining how stereotypes can be formed about inequalities that exist between different countries. This will help you start to think about inequalities that exist within the same country as well as inequalities between countries.

ACTIVITY

1 **a)** What images would come to your mind if someone started to talk to you about a country in Africa? Make a list of five things.

b) What images come to your mind when you think about the United States? Again, make a list of five things.

c) Study the photos A–H opposite. Select those which you think are closest to the images you described in activity 1 and note them down.

d) Now study the photos again and note down which ones are closest to the images you described in activity b.

e) Compare your results in small groups. How similar were your answers?

f) You should have a few pictures left over which do not fit with your images of either a country in Africa or the US. Discuss why this is so.

g) As a class, discuss what has made you form these images of people in other countries.

Well done! From doing activity 1, you have probably established that we form different images of African countries and the USA and that the media is a powerful influence on the way we 'see' people we have not met in these countries.

This is all part of our socialisation, as discussed in Section 1. The revolution over the past 100 years in the ways we can communicate sound and images around the world means that it is the mass media that provide us with the information and images which shape the way we come to 'know' and 'understand' people in other countries. But how reliable is this information and these images?

Pictures B and H are of scenes in Africa and are probably the ones you chose. These are images most frequently seen on TV and in the newspapers when they cover the latest disaster. Images of African countries are mostly associated with a disaster story. We rarely see programmes about daily life which help redress the balance. Pictures D and E were taken in the USA and, again, probably the ones you chose. Images we associate with the USA are heavily influenced by the huge output of TV programmes and films highlighting the wealth and power of people in that country.

Pictures C and F are also pictures from African countries and pictures A and G were taken in the United States. Does this surprise you?

All these pictures remind us that when we divide the world into rich and poor countries there is a danger of stereotyping. Not all people in either group are rich or poor. Despite the basic truth that there is much poverty in the African continent and much wealth in the USA, there are also many success stories to be found in Africa just as there is much evidence of poverty and failure in the USA. This section goes on to look at why these inequalities exist in the world today and what can be done to address them.

A

B

C

D

E

F

G

H

7.2 What do we mean by 'global inequality'?

- How can we compare the quality of life in different countries?
- How great is global inequality?

Feeling that we have been treated unfairly is one of the main causes of CONFLICT in our lives. For example, we might feel angry if we are blamed for something we have not done. Imagine how much greater might be the sense of INJUSTICE if we were condemned to struggle every single day to stay alive, just because of chance: the chance of where we were born.

This section will help you to consider these ideas:

- *Is inequality between human beings natural?*
  - *If so, does this mean that inequality is not unjust?*
  - *If not, what are the causes, and what can be done?*
- *Is 'inequality' the same as 'different'?*
- *Is inequality always unjust?*

In this topic, let us remind ourselves what an unequal place our world is.

National inequality

As well as inequality on a global scale, inequality exists within each country, even the wealthiest. This is known as national inequality. For example, in 2004 in the USA, the richest one per cent earned more WEALTH than the bottom 95 per cent, and one child in four lived below the official POVERTY LINE.

There are some people living below the poverty line in all the rich countries (MEDCS). This means their income is less than half the average of the SOCIETY they live in. This type of poverty is known as RELATIVE POVERTY. This is not necessarily life threatening, but it does mean some people are living in a way that excludes them from enjoying the norms of the society in which they live due to their low income.

ACTIVITIES

1 One definition of relative poverty means being excluded from what most people in a society can enjoy (NORMS) due to low income. Look at the drawing below – it shows you that some people live in relative poverty. Make a checklist of the 'norms of society' for researching the extent of relative poverty in the UK in the twenty-first century. (You could refer to Topic 1.7, pages 31–37 to help you). Compare your lists in small groups and attempt to agree on a common list.

2 What do you think might be the problems in measuring the extent of relative poverty in any society?

Inequality in the UK
Imagine that your height was decided by your income.

A pensioner would be 2 cm tall

A person on average income would be 5 cm tall

A cabinet minister would be 40 cm tall

… and a computer company boss would be 74 m tall

Global inequality

There is great inequality between countries too. This is called global inequality. Some idea of the extent of global inequality can be found by studying the evidence that follows.

The gap between the richest countries and the poorest has actually been increasing. For example:

- In 1976, Switzerland (an MEDC) was 52 times richer than Mozambique (an LEDC). In 1997, it was 508 times richer.
- Two hundred and fifty years ago, Europe was only twice as rich India. In 2004, however, the average French person, for example, earned just over ten times as much ($27,000 per year) as the average Indian ($2,700).
- Over recent years, people in sub-Saharan African countries have on average been getting poorer compared to the rest of the world so while living standards in the UK have been rising an average of 2.5 per cent a year over the last 30 years, in sub-Saharan Africa they have remained stagnant or been falling.

This inequality means that millions of people are denied the opportunities enjoyed by those living in the wealthier countries.

In fact, the extent of the inequality is so great that millions of the poorest are actually struggling on the edge of survival in absolute poverty.

People who are absolutely poor are not getting enough nutrition in their diet to avoid MALNUTRITION. Malnutrition causes the body to gradually shut down its functions. Many who suffer from malnutrition contract illnesses that they would be able to shrug off if they were healthy. To avoid malnutrition, the daily food intake required for an adult is about 2,000 calories.

Let us now consider how we can find further evidence to show the extent of global inequality.

An unequal world

- World population: 6.4 billion (in 2004)
- The combined wealth of the 225 richest people was $1,000,000,000,000 in 1999 – one million, million dollars. Compare this with the annual income of the poorest 2.5 billion (2,500 million) people which was the same. That is nearly half the population of the planet.
- 84 per cent of the world receives only 16 per cent of its income.

In what way does this diagram illustrate the points above about the world being unequal?

7.3 *Using development indicators*

- What do DEVELOPMENT INDICATORS tell us about the quality of life in LEDCs and MEDCs?
- How does the POVERTY TRAP work?

The UNITED NATIONS has produced a Human Development Index. This combines social and economic indicators to allow the quality of life between different countries to be compared. These DEVELOPMENT INDICATORS include: gross national product per person, or per capita (GNP pc), LIFE EXPECTANCY, infant mortality and adult literacy. In this topic we examine some of these indicators and how they can help us assess inequality on a global scale.

In 2000, the United Nation's (UN) annual report on human development showed that 100 million children were living on the streets and 1.2 billion people were subsisting on less than $1 a day (50p). Let us look a little closer at these two pieces of information to unravel what life in these conditions close to absolute poverty must be like.

ACTIVITIES

1 Look at the seven measures of child poverty below. Put the areas of deprivation in order of those that you think would be most important for human development, down to those you think would be least important.

2 Discuss your lists in small groups and try to come up with an order that you can all agree with.

The seven measures of child poverty

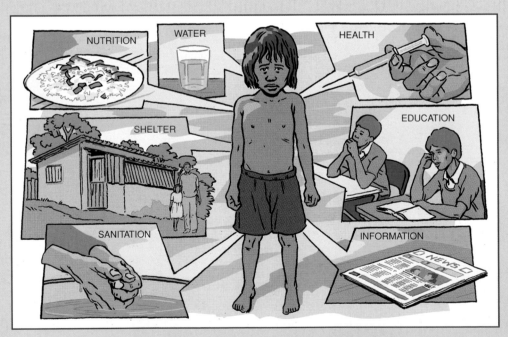

NUTRITION · WATER · HEALTH · SHELTER · EDUCATION · SANITATION · INFORMATION

According to a recent UNICEF report, over 1 billion children suffer serious deprivation in at least one of the following areas:

- 500 million children have no access to SANITATION.
- 400 million children do not have access to safe water.
- 640 million children do not have adequate shelter.
- 300 million children lack access to information.
- 270 million children have no access to health care services.
- 140 million children have never been to school.
- 90 million children are severely deprived of food.

Now let us look at a wider range of data. The UN has produced a UNIVERSAL DECLARATION OF HUMAN RIGHTS and more recently the UN CONVENTION ON THE RIGHTS OF THE CHILD (see Topic 2.3, page 46). The Convention says that all children in the world should be able to enjoy these rights. The following table suggests that unequal development can have a big effect on a child's ability to enjoy his or her human rights. In Section 1 (Culture and Beliefs), we showed the importance of early SOCIALISATION in influencing our development. Consider the real effect on a child of being socialised on the brink of absolute poverty.

Some development indicators for Kenya, India and MEDCs (average)

SELECTED INDICATORS	KENYA	INDIA	MEDCS
% infant mortality (per 100 live births)	7.5	6.9	0.6
% under-five mortality (per 100 live births)	11.7	10.5	0.6
% HIV/AIDS (15–49)	11.6	0.8	0.4
Female literacy as % male rate	84	65	0
Female primary age group enrolment as % of male	105	86	100
Female secondary age group enrolment as % male	89	68	100
Malnourished (underweight children, under five)	22	53	Not available
% with less than $1 per day per person	26	44	0
% with less than $2 per day per person	62	86	0
Calories per person per day as % of high income countries	58	73	100
% with no access to safe water	56	19	0
% with no access to health services	–	25	0
% with no access to sanitation	15	71	0
Number of people per doctor	6700	2100	400
% GDP public expenditure on education	6.5	3.2	5
% GDP spent on health	2.2	0.6	6.4
% not in secondary education	38.9	40.3	4.4
% people per telephone line	111	45	Under 2
% people per television	47	14	Under 2

Source: UNICEF report: 'Child Rights and Child Poverty in Developing Countries', in 2000

UN HUMAN RIGHTS CHARTER – SELECTED ARTICLES
Right to life
Right of equal access to public services
Right to non-discrimination
Right to participate in cultural life
Right to an adequate standard of living
Right to education
Right to social security and economic social and cultural rights

ACTIVITIES

3 In small groups, study the development indicators and the selected articles from the Human Rights Charter. Set out your own table of rights, and for each one match one or more indicator to the relevant right. For example:

Human right	Development indicator
Right to life	Infant mortality

4 Consider this newspaper headline: 'Differences in ECONOMIC DEVELOPMENT do not affect your human rights.' Prepare a speech or a letter in reply using the evidence in the table.

5 a) The G8 is a club of the richest and most powerful countries in the world. The G8 comprises the USA, the UK, France, Germany, Italy, Japan, Canada and Russia. It was the UK's turn to chair a meeting of this powerful group in Edinburgh in 2005. Below are some of the statistics they may have been presented with, but they have become jumbled. Rearrange them so that they are back in order and the statistics match the headings in the first column.

b) In pairs, discuss how such differences in standards of living could affect the ATTITUDES of people towards each other and lead to conflict.

1 Life expectancy (years)	a) DEVELOPED WORLD: 1.5 million	i) Africa: 291 million
2 Access to clean water (%)	b) Developed world: $27,854	ii) Mali: $1
3 Annual spend per person on health ($)	c) G8 countries: 0	iii) Africa: 1 in 13
4 Number of people per doctor	d) G8 countries: 1 in 4,085	iv) Africa: 174
5 People with HIV	e) G8 countries: 77 years	v) Africa: 28 million
6 Number of people who live on less than $1 a day	f) Italy: 169	vi) Africa: $1,690
7 Deaths under five years of age (per 2,000 of population)	g) Canada: $2,534	vii) Africa: 44 years
8 Average annual income ($)	h) G8 countries: 6	viii) Malawi: 50,000
9 Chance of death in pregnancy	i) UK: 100%	ix) Democratic Republic of Congo: 45%

Answers to activity a): 1: e, vii; 2: i, ix; 3: g, ii; 4: f, viii; 5: a, v; 6: c, i; 7: h, iv; 8: b, vi; 9: d, iii

What is the poverty cycle?

The diagram below shows how millions of people become trapped in a life of poverty from which it is difficult to escape.

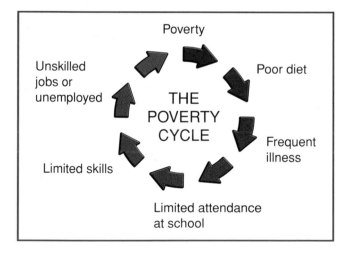

For example, living at or near to absolute poverty will mean living on a poor diet, which will eventually cause malnutrition. This makes people more vulnerable to diseases, especially when they are very young and very old. Illness causes many children to miss school, but many children also do not attend school because the FAMILY needs every child to help in their struggle for survival. So many children spend time working in workshops for very low pay or in the family's field. They help the family to scrape together enough to exist, but when they are older they, too, live on a poor diet and so the next generation continues to struggle. This is the reality of the POVERTY CYCLE.

How can development indicators be used to help explain the poverty cycle?

The poverty cycle can also be used with a table of development indicators to show how they link together in a chain of causes and effects. Complete activity 6 (opposite) to show how they are linked.

ACTIVITIES

6 a) Create a table like the one below. Using appropriate websites (such as the UN's) or books (such as an atlas) with development indicators, select six countries with a wide range of GNP pc. Two should be in Africa, two in Europe and two in Asia.

Add two from South America if you have time. Research each country to complete the following table. In the table, examples of countries have been given but you can choose different ones.

Country (examples given)	Gross national product per capita ($)	Food intake (calories per day)	Life expectancy (years)	Population per doctor (people)	Adult literacy (% of total population)	UN Human Development Index (1.00 = max)	Conclusion: LEDC or MEDC?
Austria							
Bangladesh							
Ethiopia							
Germany							
Japan							
Mozambique							

b) Using the evidence from the countries in your table, select one country that is an MEDC and one that is an LEDC. Explain your decisions using the development indicators.

c) Now draw a poverty cycle (as on page 178) for the LEDC you have chosen. Use the order of the column headings to help you. For example, you might choose to start with the low average income in Ethiopia (GNP per capita). Next, show in your diagram what this low income can directly lead to (for example, a lower CALORIE INTAKE). Complete the diagram showing how each set of statistics can explain a particular feature of the povery cycle. Put the relevant statistics in the relevant stages of the cycle.

7 a) Correlation graphs can be used to show how close the link is between two development indicators. The closer the correlation is, the closer the link between the two indicators. Draw a graph to show the correlation between infant mortality rate and calorie intake for your chosen six

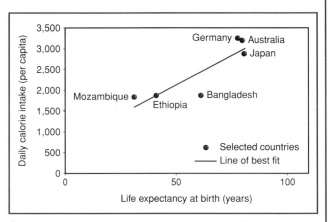

Graph to show correlation between calories per day and infant mortality rate in a country. Life expectancy rises as calorie intake rises.

countries in activity 6. Mark the axes with an appropriate scale. Add a line of best fit. An example of a correlation graph is given above.

b) Explain what your graph shows. How strong is the correlation?

8 Draw another graph to show the correlation between average income (GNP per capita) and literacy rates for your sample of countries. How strong is the correlation?

7.4 *What are the causes of global inequality?*

- How does trade work against LEDCs?
- What is the impact of debt on LEDCs?
- Is COLONIALISM a cause of global inequality?

The main reasons put forward to explain global inequality and poverty in LEDCs are:

- *trade between LEDCs and MEDCs is unfair to LEDCs*
- *colonialism in the sixteenth to the twentieth centuries divided the world into rich and poor countries*
- *LEDCs are so in debt they cannot catch up with MEDCs.*

Each one of these is examined in this topic.

Is trade responsible for global inequality?

ACTIVITY

1 a) Make a list of ten products you own (this could be clothing, electrical products, food, etc.).

b) Find out which countries they were made in and add these to your list.

c) Plot the results on a map of the world to show which products came from MEDCs and which came from LEDCs.

d) How much do you depend on world trade, according to your map?

What is trade?

Trade takes place when people buy and sell products and services. Trade happens when a person or group has a product or service that another person or group wants to buy. The products may have been hunted, grown, mined or made. The services may, for example, be domestic, commercial or technical.

As we showed in Topic 1.2, pages 4–5, human beings are more successful when they live and work in groups. As some groups grew, they developed into the earliest CIVILISATIONS and built cities. The first cities started trading so that goods could be obtained which could not be found locally or because it was not possible to manufacture everything themselves.

Trade works on a local scale, such as trade between villages, and on an international scale when businesses and governments in different countries trade with each other.

Goods and services involved in international trade are called IMPORTS and EXPORTS. International trade has been growing for hundreds of years. Between 1970 and 2005 alone, the value of international trade increased more than tenfold and was worth over £11.5 billion every day in 2005.

The growth in international trade, 1963–2005.

Free trade–fair trade

But is FREE TRADE fair in the way it operates? Ever since the days of colonialism (see page 184), the companies based in the richer, ex-colonial countries have had more power than the farmers and governments of the colonies. So some people argue that this trade, in practice, has never been 'fair' – it has been rigged in favour of the rich and powerful.

7 GLOBAL INEQUALITY

There is a growing belief that in the twenty-first century, international trade will have to be managed differently by representatives of both the rich and poor NATIONS to ensure that no one has an unfair advantage.

What is the argument?

Many argue that trade is not fair. LEDCs lose out because MEDCs control world trade. The 48 poorest countries in the world, for example, only account for 0.4 per cent of world trade, and this share is declining.

What is the cost?

In 2004, the UN estimated that unfair trade rules cost the poorest countries $700 million in lost income. For years these rules have been made by the rich countries for the benefit of the rich. In 2005, there were attempts to get agreement at the conference of the G8 in Edinburgh to make the rules fairer. However, no agreement was made regarding trade.

People who put forward this view argue that MEDCs dominate world trade because:

1 Almost all very large companies (called multi-nationals or transnationals) are based in MEDCs. This is where new product projects and investments around the world are decided on and where profits end up. Nike, MacDonalds, HSBC Bank and Nestlé are examples. The combined effect of these multi-nationals around the world can be to make people feel they are losing control of their own culture. This process is often referred to as 'globalisation'.

2 The governments of the MEDCs are under pressure to make sure the conditions for trading suit the multi-nationals. For example, governments have been using TARIFFS and QUOTAS to block imports, and SUBSIDIES to encourage their own exports. They also use their influence to make it difficult for the LEDCs to use the same methods to protect their industries. The examples of the terms of trade in cotton (right), chocolate and tomatoes (on page 182) illustrate how subsidies and tariffs are used and show how unfair they are to LEDCs.

Case study: Cotton subsidies

How do these two pictures illustrate the differences between LEDC and MEDC producers?

A cotton farm in Jonesville, Louisiana, USA.

A Mali cotton farmer.

In 2003, the USA's 25,000 cotton farmers received more than $3 billion in subsidies. The farmers produced a huge surplus, which could not be sold in the USA, so they sold it on the world market (called 'dumping'). The International Cotton Advisory Committee claims this had the effect of lowering prices of cotton on the world market by about 25 per cent.

This in turn meant that in the countries of West and Central Africa, the 10 million people who are involved in growing cotton, could scarcely make enough to live. Their governments are so poor that they did not receive any subsidies at all. They never do.

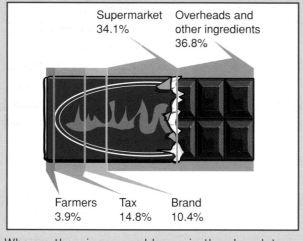
crop is struck by disease, the money they planned to spend on hospitals and schools is no longer available. The case study on page 183 about the Ugandan coffee farmers is an example of this.

5 The two or three products that make up most of the LEDCs' exports tend to be crops such as sugar, cocoa, coffee, tea and raw materials such as timber and cotton. The prices of these crops and raw materials have been declining for a long time compared to the price of exports of manufactured products from MEDCs. Poor countries do not have the TECHNOLOGY to process the crops themselves and sell them at higher prices.

6 Multi-nationals use factories in LEDCs to take advantage of the low wages (see the Teletubbies story opposite).

7 The products and services that LEDCs need for their own development are expensive compared to the low value of their own exports. This keeps the people of these countries trapped, as the country does not have the resources to develop.

3 The banks in MEDCs often make it a condition of their LOANS to the governments of LEDCs that they do not use tariffs, quotas and subsidies to protect their industries. Read the tomato story (right) – what does it illustrate about the possible effects of these conditions?

4 Most LEDCs have to rely heavily on exporting two or three products that may account for 75 per cent or more of their trade. This leaves LEDCs very vulnerable. For example, if the world price of one of these products falls or a

Case Study
A nice cup of coffee?

Uganda's coffee farmers and the world market

Up until 1991, the Ugandan coffee trade was controlled by the Ugandan Coffee Marketing Board (UCBM), which bought the coffee from farmers to sell it on the international market.

In 1991, the World Bank and the IMF made the Ugandan government reorganise its coffee industry. The UCBM was closed, leaving individual farmers to sell their coffee directly to traders and large food companies. Ugandan coffee farmers were happy with this change as they were now paid the global price for coffee rather than accepting what the UCBM gave them.

Investigation
Research the trade in another crop used widely in MEDCs but grown in LEDCs such as cotton, chocolate (cocoa) or bananas. What evidence is there that the trade in these items is unfair/fair?

However, the international coffee price has not been steady. There was a global overproduction in coffee, which pushed coffee prices to an all-time low. Coffee accounts for two-thirds of Uganda's exports and government revenues from coffee fell by 36 per cent. Ugandan coffee farmers no longer protected by the UCBM went out of business.

Whilst the green coffee bean price fell during the 1990s, the price of a jar of instant coffee in supermarkets across the world remained as high as ever. The coffee roasters in the developed countries were blending coffee beans from a number of countries in their jars of coffee. Ugandan producers were at the mercy of the coffee traders and were unable to compete because they did not have the resources to do so.

In addition, the Ugandan government was forbidden by WORLD TRADE ORGANISATION rules to subsidise (support) their coffee farmers to help them compete with the developed countries. Even if Uganda had the money to protect its coffee farmers from unfair competition or when the world price of coffee fell, it would not be allowed to do so under the rules of world trade.

Uganda is a developing country. It has a fragile and vulnerable economy. MEDCs have the wealth to cope with international trade. Ugandan coffee farms are small-scale businesses relying on just one commodity. These farmers therefore have had to suffer the ups and downs of the world coffee trade without any hope of protection.

There are many more examples that illustrate the argument that the terms of trade between LEDCs and MEDCs has been very unfair and keeps LEDCs poor. The next question is, how did it get like this?

ACTIVITIES

2 Why do government subsidies to cotton farmers in the USA affect cotton farmers in Mali?

3 What proportion of the World's cocoa beans are grown in LEDCs?

4 There are two points of view on the Ugandan coffee case study: that of an international company selling instant coffee (the free trade view), and that of a coffee farmer in Uganda producing the raw coffee beans.
   a) Make a list of arguments to support each of the points of view.

b) Which argument do you agree with most? Explain your reasons.

5 'The people of LEDCs must think MEDCs are hypocrites. It is disgraceful, the unfair rules of world trade. We protect our industries but demand free trade rules for them.' Using the evidence in this topic and any further examples of trade between LEDCs and MEDCs, explain whether you agree or disagree with this statement.

Is debt responsible for global inequality?

Most LEDCs have built up a pretty substantial debt to banks in MEDCs. In 2005 at the time of the G8 meeting, the total debt of the 52 poorest countries was $375 billion. Even though they have actually paid back the money they borrowed, the INTEREST payments keep adding to the total bill. This means they still have to pay $30 million a day between them.

The problem goes back to the 1960s and 1970s. Some money was lent for useful purposes such as improving farming methods. Much went to projects that did not benefit the country's people such as putting up luxury buildings, or in some LEDCs the ruling elites stole the money.

Then, in the 1970s and 1980s, interest rates on the loans went up, so many LEDCs ended up still owing more than the original loan, even after years of repayments.

The lenders have also attached unfair conditions to debt relief; for instance, demanding privatisations of industry that benefit big corporations in the rich world, or forcing cuts in public spending, meaning that fewer teachers and health workers can be employed. People in the LEDCs are suffering both from repaying the debts and from these conditions. This is known as the DEBT TRAP.

So why did LEDCs get themselves into so much debt? One explanation links both the unfair terms of trade and LEDC debt to colonialism.

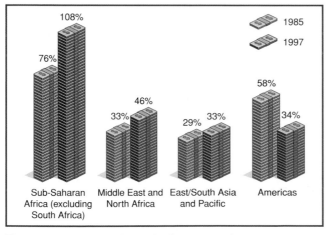

The external debt of developing countries as a percentage of GNP by region.

Case study: Sub-Saharan Africa
For every $1 received in aid grants in 1999, the countries in the region paid back $1.51 in debt service. They owe $231 billion to creditors, that is, $406 for every man, woman and child in Africa. Sub-Saharan countries spend over twice as much on debt service as on basic health care. They spend 6.1 per cent of GNP on education and spend five per cent of GNP on debt service. If Africa's debt were cancelled, it could almost double its spending on education.

Source: Jubilee 2000: The Eye of the Needle

ACTIVITY

6 a) Using the graph (left), explain what has happened to the debt of LEDCs in the different regions.

b) Which region is worst off? Which region owes the least?

c) How does increasing debt affect a country's ability to develop economically and socially?

Is colonialism responsible for global inequality?

What is colonialism?

From the sixteenth century onwards, the leaders of the Western countries of Europe believed it was their right to try to conquer and rule the peoples of other parts of the world and develop EMPIRES. Once a country was conquered, its people were then to be 'civilised' into accepting the control of the conquering power. They lost control of what they grew and made, and were put to work to produce what the colonial power wanted. This process of exploiting the countries in an empire is known as colonialism.

So why does it matter today?

The huge profits made from trade based on cheap imports from the colonies and slavery in America helped Europe and the USA become richer and more industrialised, whilst the countries that became colonies were left behind.

From 1945 onwards, colonies gained their political independence. However, they had lost so much of their former economic independence that it was difficult to recover from the effects of the past. The colonialism argument, many think, is the real reason why international trade is so unfair, leading in turn to other problems like the debt trap. Some say that without drastic reforms throughout the world, sustainable development for both LEDCs and MEDCs will not be achieved.

Some evidence of the impact of colonialism

- Between 1500 and 1750, more than $1,500 million in profits and goods was acquired by Western Europe from its overseas colonies.
- Between 1503 and 1660, 185,000 kgs (408,000 lb) of gold and 16 million kgs (35 million lb) of silver were brought to Spain from the Americas. This fuelled European economic expansion.
- Between 1757 and 1815, Britain helped itself to about £1,000 million from India. This was equal to about seven times Britain's annual GNP.
- In 1789, France exported to her colonies 78 million *livres* (the old unit of currency in France) of food and received sugar, coffee and other products worth 296 *livres* in return.

Case study: India

European traders used to go to India to buy the best cotton cloth in the world. For the technology of the time, India had a very advanced textile industry. By the end of the nineteenth century, India was now part of its empire. In order to help mill owners in Lancashire, the government put a heavy import tax (tariff) on Indian cloth. Raw cotton carried no import tax. This raw cotton was now used in Lancashire to mass-produce cloth at such a low price it was cheaper than cloth made in India.

The result was that people in Lancashire had jobs, the mill owners and shippers made fortunes whilst the Indian textile workers lost their jobs and became poor.

ACTIVITY

7 a) Study the map below. Using an atlas find three countries that were colonies of each of the European countries named and research their GNP pc using an atlas or a website such as the UN's.
   b) Explain why most ex-colonies seem to be LEDCs.

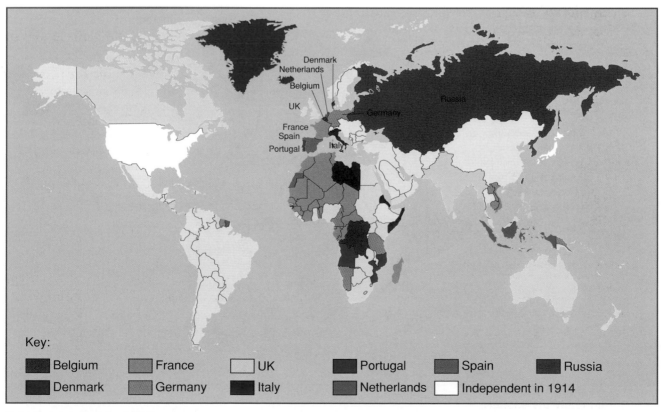

Colonial empires in 1914.

Key:

- Belgium
- Denmark
- France
- Germany
- UK
- Italy
- Portugal
- Netherlands
- Spain
- Independent in 1914
- Russia

7.5 *What can be done about global inequality?*

- What is the best way of reducing global inequality?
  - International aid?
  - Fairer trade?
  - The cancellation of international debt?
  - Greater global interdependence?

This topic considers different views on what should be done to reduce global inequality and poverty. Four possibilities are evaluated: international aid, fair trade, the cancellation of international debt and, finally, increasing international cooperation to recognise our global interdependence.

1 Is international aid the best way of reducing inequality?

Many of the richest countries have given aid to LEDCs to assist them out of poverty. But does such aid work?

Humanitarian aid

This aid is given by governments or raised by non-government organisations (NGOs), such as Christian Aid or Oxfam, to help prevent or deal with the suffering resulting from natural and man-made disasters: for example, aid to the Darfur region of Sudan in 2004–05 or to Sri Lanka, India and South East Asia after the tsunami in December 2004. This aid is a genuine response to

Is more aid really the answer?

human suffering and is in solidarity with those who may have lost their homes, livelihoods and members of their family.

However, some would argue that there are potential long-term problems with such aid. Some of these arguments are outlined in the drawing on page 186.

The tsunami off the coast of Indonesia in December 2004 caused over 150,000 deaths. The response to the appeal for aid in the UK alone was unprecedented – raising tens of millions of pounds. Why do you think that people responded in such a way after seeing images such as these?

Development aid

Development aid is money given to LEDCs to encourage long-term economic growth, aiming to develop their economies through trying to tackle the root causes of poverty (see page 180) such as weaknesses in agriculture, industry, nutrition, health and education. The idea is that long-term development aid encourages economic growth, which enables the LEDC to develop its industry and participate in world trade and so make profits to develop their own society.

However, some would argue that there are potential long-term problems with development aid, such as:

- it leads to the growth of governments and bureaucracies, which use up valuable resources and are slow in giving out the aid. For example, as a result of development aid, the civil service in Zambia grew by twenty per cent
- it can increase inequality within LEDCs. The powerful ruling elites have greater access to aid and its benefits compared to the rest of society
- it tends to create economic inefficiency; it distorts markets and leads to a waste of resources. An example of this is aid given to Nigeria after 1970, which was used to build up military resources.

Is free trade a better way?

Some would argue that a better way of helping LEDCs is by reducing aid and developing more free trade across the world. Why is this?

- If the barriers to trade are lowered, allowing farmers and producers in LEDCs access to global markets, then they would be encouraged to produce more, create larger farms and businesses that would generate more money for LEDCs to spend on developing their own societies.
- Free trade also benefits MEDCs as it would bring competition and new goods into their markets, which would increase choice and lower prices for consumers.
- Free trade increases incentives and opportunities, which an over-reliance on aid does not.
- However, some businesses in MEDCs are afraid their profits would suffer.

ACTIVITIES

1 a) In small groups, research and compare the work of different NGOs. (See also the Investigation on page 191.)

   b) How successful have NGOs been in reducing global inequality?

2 Will there always be a need for humanitarian aid? Use examples to support your answer.

2 Is fair trade the best way of reducing inequality?

The Trade Justice Movement (TJM) argues that trade is not free and fair for the developing world. The Movement is a group of organisations comprising aid agencies, trade unions, fair trade organisations, faith and consumer groups. It is involved with the Make Poverty History Campaign, launched in December 2004, which calls on the UK government to change the rules and practices of unjust trade, cancel poor countries' debts and deliver more and better aid. This is part of a global campaign.

Some of the reasons why the TJM argues trade is not free and fair include the following.

- The global system of trade has rules that allow MEDCs and multi-national companies to make large profits, but prevent LEDCs from developing their economies. It is not fair that MEDCs subsidise their farmers to overproduce goods that are then sold cheaply in LEDCs, forcing poor farmers out of business.
- Companies are out to make profits, which may not be to the advantage of local people in LEDCs.
- MEDCs argue that free trade reduces poverty. But when LEDCs open up their markets to free trade, foreign businesses from MEDCs with huge advantages over businesses in the LEDC

come to take over local markets. Local producers then suffer. When LEDCs do succeed in manufacturing their own goods that do sell well in MEDCs, there is an immediate outcry from threatened businesses in MEDCs. This often leads the governments of MEDCs to put a quota on imports. This is what happened in 2005 when China successfully penetrated the European T-shirt market.

- The World Trade Organisation (WTO) is supposed to ensure that all countries keep the global trading rules and promotes free trade. All 147 members of the WTO are supposed to have an equal say in its work. However, the richest and most powerful countries have a great advantage compared to poor countries because they have greater resources to spare WTO work.
- The IMF and the World Bank give aid to or cancel the debts of LEDCs but often with strict conditions relating to how LEDCs should trade.

ACTIVITY

3 'Fair trade is likely to be more effective than international aid in helping to reduce global inequalities.' Explain how far you agree or disagree with this statement. Remember to provide supporting evidence for your answer.

Nelson Mandela (left) waves to the crowd as he stands next to Bob Geldof at Trafalgar Square in London. Mandela came to London to endorse the Make Poverty History campaign in February 2005.

3 Is the cancellation of international debt the best way of reducing inequality?

A high level of debt amongst LEDCs has long been seen as a major barrier to development, as we saw in Topic 7.4, page 184.

The Jubilee 2000 campaign was started in the UK in the 1980s. Supported by NGOs, churches and individuals, it campaigned for the unsustainable debts of LEDCs to be dropped by the UK government by the year 2000. By freeing such countries from the crippling effects of debt, they would be able to develop their economies and societies in a sustainable way. As this has not happened, it is now called the Jubilee Debt Campaign and is involved with the Make Poverty History Campaign. The Jubilee Debt Campaign and other organisations involved with calling for debt cancellation or reduction argue that the effects would include those shown in the diagram below.

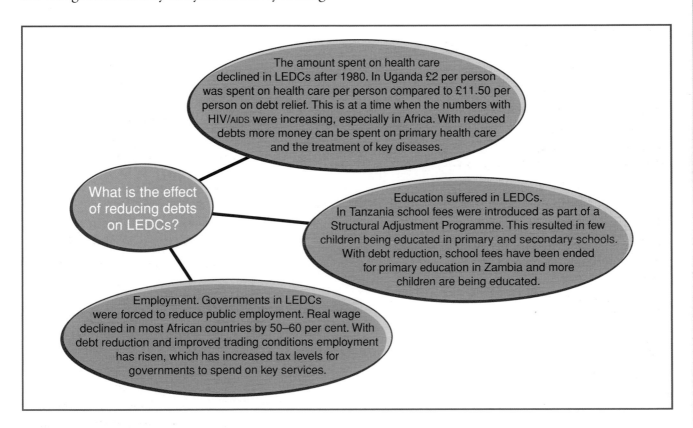

What is the effect of reducing debts on LEDCs?

The amount spent on health care declined in LEDCs after 1980. In Uganda £2 per person was spent on health care per person compared to £11.50 per person on debt relief. This is at a time when the numbers with HIV/AIDS were increasing, especially in Africa. With reduced debts more money can be spent on primary health care and the treatment of key diseases.

Education suffered in LEDCs. In Tanzania school fees were introduced as part of a Structural Adjustment Programme. This resulted in few children being educated in primary and secondary schools. With debt reduction, school fees have been ended for primary education in Zambia and more children are being educated.

Employment. Governments in LEDCs were forced to reduce public employment. Real wage declined in most African countries by 50–60 per cent. With debt reduction and improved trading conditions employment has risen, which has increased tax levels for governments to spend on key services.

ACTIVITIES

4 How could cancelling LEDCs debt to MEDCs help LEDCs to develop? Refer to the poverty cycle in your answer.

5 What could you and your family do to help support producers in LEDCs? Suggest three actions you could take based on information in this topic.

6 Look at the photograph on page 188. What impact do you think high profile people involved in campaigns against global inequality can have on governments?

7 Research the G8 meeting of July 2005. How did the ministers agree to address the LEDCs debt problem? What are the strengths and weaknesses of their decisions?

4 Is greater global interdependence the best way of reducing inequality?

The world is becoming a smaller place. International telecommunications, transport, travel and trade have brought countries closer together. This was demonstrated by the generosity of individuals and governments around the world following the tsunami earthquake disaster in December 2004. Within hours of the launch of an appeal for aid, the British public had pledged £50 million.

Yet the reality is that the world remains an unequal and unfair place. There are countries, international companies and organisations with power and resources, and there are other countries that lack such powers. The chips all look to be stacked in favour of the rich, developed countries.

However, there are powerful arguments for a greater sense of global independence, where countries and cultures increasingly recognise the *necessity* of making rules that allow all human beings the right to life, liberty and justice, irrespecive of the lottery of where they are born.

How might we progress to greater global equality?

1 The UN might be reformed to give a greater say to LEDCs and those countries that are more developed, but not MEDCs, such as India or Brazil.

2 Regional bodies such as the EU could be more open to the needs of LEDCs.

3 Greater openness and democratic accountability of such organisations as the IMF, WTO and World Bank might bring countries together to share resources, knowledge and expertise to the benefit of all.

4 Greater international agreement – there have been moves on environmental issues such as the Kyoto Agreement and on the creation of the International Criminal Court. Might these offer ways in which countries could work together to solve problems such as unfair trading arrangements or the reduction of disease and poverty?

5 There has been a greater interchange of people between the North and the South through travel, employment and MIGRATION. This might bring a greater understanding of the needs of LEDCs and why poverty and inequality have to be reduced.

6 MEDCs rely on resources from LEDCs. Many of these resources will be depleted over the next 100 years. Only through working together will countries find ways of replacing these NON-RENEWABLE RESOURCES.

7 The alternative is conflict and war. The UN has already identified countries and regions of the world where 'water wars' might break out, for example, in East Africa and the Middle East. CO-OPERATION between countries appears even more necessary than ever before.

> ### Water wars
> A UN development report has identified that the main conflicts in Africa over the next 25 years could be over water. Conflicts are likely to occur where water is scarce, and the water sources there, such as the Nile, the Niger, the Volta and the Zambezi river basins, supply more than one country.

8 Copy out the table below. Using all the information in this topic and other information you might have gathered, evaluate which factor might be the most effective in reducing global inequality and poverty in the long term. Remember to provide supporting evidence for your chart.

Factors	Would help to reduce global inequality and poverty because …	Would not help to reduce global inequality and poverty because …
Greater development aid to LEDCs		
Reducing development aid to LEDCs and relying on free trade solutions		
Creating a fairer international trading system		
The complete cancellation of all developing world debt		
Creating greater global interdependence		

Investigation

Choose one example of an NGO and investigate it to answer the questions below:

a) what are its objectives in relation to global poverty and inequality?

b) what does it see as the causes of global poverty and inequality?

c) What methods does it use to get its message across?

d) What campaigns is it currently involved with?

e) What solutions does it offer for global poverty and inequality?

One way of summing up what we have learnt in this section is:

We know that:
- there is significant global ineqality and we can prove this
- our chances in life are decided by where we happen to be born
- millions die or suffer needlessly each year.

And we think we know:
- what the causes of this inequality and poverty are
- what some effective solutions are.

9 So, does this mean that some people are guilty of causing unnecessary suffering? If so, who are these people?

10 a) Consider what part we play in causing unnecessary suffering. Ask yourself, 'Am I part of the problem, or part of the solution?'

b) On your own, gather your thoughts on global inequality and note down your view on the above question.

c) Share your views in small groups.

d) Then consider, again in groups, whether global inequality is a moral issue.

Coursework

Coursework accounts for 25 per cent of the total GCSE grade. Assignments are marked out of 60 marks and there are three assessment strands:

Strand (i)	Investigation	20 marks
Strand (ii)	Evaluation	20 marks
Strand (iii)	Communication	20 marks

There are two options for coursework:

Option 1: A single assignment covering all three assessment strands in 2,500 words.

Option 2: Two assignments where one or two of the assessment strands may be tested in each assignment, where appropriate. Over the two assignments all three strands are assessed. Each assignment would be 1,250 words in length.

The coursework must develop one or more of the key ideas in the Humanities specification.

The word limit for the coursework is 2,500 words regardless of which option is chosen.

Top coursework tips

1 How do I carry out an effective investigation?

● **Do you understand the coursework task?** The task might be set as a hypothesis to test or a key question to answer. You will need to plan your investigation according to the type of task you have been set.

You have to decide what are the best sources of information for the investigation.

● **How will I plan my investigation?** An action plan is a good way to structure your investigation. You need to plan your time carefully in order to design, produce and carry out a questionnaire or survey; photographs have to be taken and developed or downloaded on to your computer, letters have to be written and information obtained from organisations. Your teacher might provide you with some source material. However it is always useful to undertake some additional research yourself.

● **What information will I need for the investigation?** You will need to collect a range of different types of information as part of the investigation:

Primary sources
Your own questionnaires, surveys, interviews, photographs, videos, observations, fieldwork.

Secondary sources
The Internet, books, statistical information, for example, *Social Trends*, articles, video material, TV programmes, information from organisations.

● **How do I use the Internet?** The Internet is a powerful research tool but must be used with care. Try to produce a number of key questions to be used through a search engine. Check the material you find – is it relevant, up to date? Do you understand it? Try to find information from more than one viewpoint. Print off the material, but make sure you have entered each website address on to your bibliography. Internet information, like any source, has to be used to answer your overall coursework question or test the hypothesis. The print-off should not be just cut and pasted into your assignment.

COURSEWORK

Coursework

- **Have I acknowledged my sources of information?** This is important to show from where you have gained information. Taking information from the Internet or a book without giving the source of that information is called 'plagiarism'. Sources of information can be listed in either footnotes/endnotes or a detailed bibliography. All pictures and illustrations taken from secondary sources should also be acknowledged. Quotes should be included in your coursework.

- **Have I found statistics?** These are important and offer you the chance to draw graphs and strengthen your evaluation of issues.

2 How do I carry out an effective evaluation?

- **What is the focus of my evaluation?** You might evaluate the arguments relating to the topic under investigation. You might evaluate the sources of information or the methods of investigation to judge their completeness, balance, consistency, reliability, usefulness or truthfulness.

- **How do I use sources of information in the evaluation?** The evaluation needs to be based on information or evidence. You are drawing conclusions from the information.

- **Where have I evaluated?** Evaluation can take place anywhere in the assignment: as points or issues are raised in the text or at the end of the assignment.

3 How do I communicate effectively in my assignment?

- **Have I structured my coursework assignment?** The assignment needs to be carefully structured using effective sentences, paragraphs, sections, side headings or chapters. All parts of the assignment should be clearly focused on the key question or the hypothesis. This will create a sustained and coherent assignment as all your writing will be relevant to the task.

- **What techniques can I use for communication?** In addition to clear and well-structured sentences and paragraphs, you should plan to use illustrations, diagrams, graphs, quotations or statistics to develop an argument that answers the key question or tests the hypothesis. These various techniques should be integrated into paragraphs.

- **Have I kept to the word limit?** This is very important. You should plan to produce the word limit, not exceed it. There are no extra marks for 5,000 words. Coursework should be edited to keep to the limit. You should draft your paragraphs or chapters to make sure your work is relevant and not overlong.

- **Have I a strong overall conclusion?** Whatever form your coursework takes, the assignment should end with a strong conclusion that answers the key question or draws your conclusion about the hypothesis. The conclusion should be relevant and should link to information found in the assignment.

- **Can I include appendices?** Yes. If you have collected a lot of information, then appendices are a good idea to prevent the assignment from being too long or bulky. Just make sure that you cross-reference facts or opinions in the assignment to the relevant appendices.

GLOSSARY

ACID RAIN Where gases combine with water droplets in clouds and produce acids (sulphuric and nitric), which rains down, killing plants and damaging buildings.

AESTHETICS The study of beauty in art, music, dance, drama, design, architecture, etc.

AGEISM The practice of treating people differently and usually unfairly on the grounds of age only, especially because they are too old.

AIDS Acquired Immune Deficiency Syndrome. A transmitted disease at epidemic proportions in LEDCs, especially in Africa.

ANTHROPOLOGIST Someone who studies humankind, in particular human cultures.

APARTHEID Racial segmentation in South Africa.

APPEASEMENT Policy of granting concessions to enemies to preserve peace.

AQUACULTURE Breeding and raising fish in a controlled environment. Think of it as farming in water (the seas, lakes, rivers or specially built ponds).

ARBITRATION Settling a dispute by a neutral party.

ARRANGED MARRIAGE A marriage where the selection of marriage partners is done by the parents, or other older relatives, and not left to the individuals who are going to marry.

ASYLUM SEEKERS People who flee their own country because they are being persecuted for reasons of race, religion, nationality or membership of a particular social group or political opinion.

ATTITUDE A state of mind or a feeling; a way of thinking, for example, 'He had a positive attitude about work.' Can include the way of positioning one's body.

BALLAST When ships are not fully loaded, they take sea water on board to keep them stable at sea. Often this water contains pollution and oil. When it is pumped out so the boat can be loaded, this pollution ends up back in the water near to a coast.

BEHAVIOUR Manner of acting or conducting yourself.

BELIEF Something accepted as true or valid without actual proof.

BIO-DIVERSITY Wide variety of living things: plants, insects and animals.

BIOLOGICAL Anything related to the way human beings work as living organisms.

BIOMASS An energy resource derived from organic matter. These include wood, agricultural waste and living cell material that can be burned to produce heat energy.

BLACK POWER A movement which believed in the use of force to increase the power of black people in the USA.

BNP British National Party A far right political party. In their 2005 election manifesto they called for an end to immigration and an introduction of incentives to 'encourage immigrants and their descendants to return home'.

BY-CATCH The name given to any fish that is caught unintentionally and thrown back into the water.

CALORIE INTAKE Number of calories consumed per person per day. The survival level is 1500–1800.

CAPITALISM An economic system based on private, rather that state, ownership of businesses allowing free competition and profit.

CIA Central Intelligence Agency in the USA responsible for external security.

CITIZENSHIP The status of a citizen with attendant duties, rights and privileges.

CIVILISATION A society in an advanced state of social development, for example, with complex legal, political and religious organisations.

COHABITING Living together in a long-term relationship without going through a legal marriage.

COLD WAR A state of tension and rivalry between nations, stopping short of actual full-scale war. Usually refers to relationship between the USA and the USSR between 1945 and the late 1980s.

COLONIALISM The conquest and ownership (as colonies) by wealthy countries of other countries around the world as part of their empires.

COLONISE To take over land abroad.

COMMUNES Households where several unrelated individuals and couples live together, sharing responsibilities for maintaining the group economically as if they were an extended family.

COMMUNIST A supporter of Communism, believing in a classless society with all sources of wealth and production owned and controlled by the state.

COMMUNITY 1 A group of people living in the same locality and under the same government; 2 A group of people with a common interest. Includes ideas of sharing, participation and fellowship.

COMPROMISE To settle differences by making concessions.

CONFLICT A state of disharmony between incompatible persons, ideas or interests; a clash. CONFRONTATION A hostile meeting or exchange of words.

CONGRESS The US legislature or parliament.

CONSTITUTION A set of rules governing an organisation; the laws and rights upon which a state is founded.

CONVECTION Describes the movement of gases and liquids caused by heating. For example, air rising as the result of heat from the sun is called convection.

CO-OPERATION People working together towards commonly agreed-upon goals

CULTURAL IDENTITY Knowing who you are through belonging to a group and sharing its values.

CULTURAL RELATIVISM Not putting cultures into a rank order as ethnocentrics do. Judging any culture by its own standards.

CULTURE The shared way of life of a particular society, referring to all aspects of behaviour that are learned and which provide the context in which daily life is lived.

Includes values, norms and beliefs as well as the way these are expressed through actions, words and symbols. The aesthetics, customs and traditions that characterise a particular society or nation.

CUSTOM A generally accepted practice or behaviour developed over time.

DDTA Chemical used to kill mosquitoes and other insects and pests. It is not good for people, birds or other animals.

DEBT TRAP Where LEDCs remain poor because much of the money they earn has to be used to pay off debts to MEDCs rather than to develop their countries.

DEFORESTATION Cutting down or burning most trees and plants over a wide area.

DESERTIFICATION The process where an area becomes very dry (a desert) as a result of low rainfall, rapid evaporation and loss of plants that used to store water.

DÉTENTE A lessening of tension between states.

DEVELOPED WORLD The part of the world where people enjoy a high standard of living as a result of wealth created by industry, services or abundant raw materials.

DEVELOPMENT Process of social and economic improvement that allows people in a country to have an improved standard of living.

DEVELOPMENT INDICATORS Ways of measuring a country's level of economic and social development, for example, life expectancy.

DICTATORSHIP Ruling with complete and unrestricted power.

DISCRIMINATION Discrimination is treating someone differently, usually less well, because they belong to a particular group.

DRAFT Conscription or call-up in to the US army.

DRAFT-DODGING Avoiding conscription or draft.

ECOLOGY The study of the interdependency between different parts of the natural environment.

ECONOMIC DEVELOPMENT To do with increasing the wealth of a country and improving living standards of the people. It usually means expanding trade and developing technology. Tourism may also be a way of starting development.

ECOSYSTEM A range of biological and chemical elements that works together to create an enduring natural environment.

ELECTORATE A body of people entitled to vote.

EMPIRE A group of countries conquered and ruled by a wealthy power, the imperialist country.

ENDANGERED SPECIES Any plant or animal species that is in danger of being wiped out.

ENVIRONMENT The sum of all external conditions and influences affecting survival and development.

ENVIRONMENTALISTS People who are concerned over changes and damage to natural environments and who try to make people aware of what is happening.

ETHICS A system of moral principles, rules or standards that governs the conduct of members of a group.

ETHNIC CLEANSING Genocide or forced removal of an ethnic group or groups by another.

ETHNIC GROUP A group with a distinct cultural identity, for example, own language, traditions, religion.

ETHNICITY Racial status or distinctiveness.

ETHNOCENTRISM An attitude of cultural superiority, which implies that one's own culture is better than some other culture. It is the basis of racism, nationalism and tribalism.

EXPLOIT To make use of for the benefit of individuals or groups. The word can also mean 'use to make a profit'.

EXPORT Sale of goods produced in one country to others.

EXTREMIST Someone who has extreme opinions, especially in politics.

FAMILY The family is a group of persons directly linked by kin connections, the adult members of which assume responsibility for caring for children (Anthony Giddens, 1993).

FEDERAL GOVERNMENT The central government of a group of states such as the USA.

FEMALE Biological characteristics of women.

FEMALE INFANTICIDE The killing of girls at or soon after birth.

FEMININE Behavioural characteristics associated with being a woman in a specific culture.

FERTILISERS Chemicals sprayed or spread on to farmland to help crops grow.

FOOD CHAIN Describes how different species both eat other species and provide food for other species, for example, small fish eat plankton, herrings eat small fish, cod eat herring, seals eat cod, dolphins and whales eat seals.

FOSSIL FUELS Materials found occurring naturally underground. They were produced millions of years ago by organic matter such as trees, plants and animals, which have decayed and been compressed. These are coal, oil and natural gases.

FREE TRADE Trade without artificial protection of prices of goods.

FULLY EXPLOITED This is when a resource, such as a species of fish or a raw material, has been caught, extracted, or used to such an extent that any further exploitation will wipe it out.

GENDER Gender identifies behaviour associated with a specific sex in a specific culture. The term is often used incorrectly as an alternative to the word 'sex'. 'Gender' refers to social or cultural categories whereas 'sex' refers to biological categories.

GENDER ROLES These are the expectations by a culture of the way in which people will behave according to their sex (whether they are male or female). This will include how people participate in social activities, the work they do in the home or in employment, and will usually involve expectations of personal style and manners.

GENES A sequence of DNA that occupies a specific place on a chromosome and determines a particular characteristic in an organism. Genes are hereditary (i.e. passed on from parents biologically).

GENOCIDE The deliberate killing of a whole nation or people.

GHETTO A slum section of a city occupied mainly by a deprived minority group, usually racial.

GHETTOISATION Forcing a certain group of people to live in certain areas.

GLOBAL WARMING The belief that average temperatures around the world are rising steadily.

GUERRILLA CAMPAIGN A method of warfare making use of surprise attacks.

HARASSMENT Pestering or tormenting.

HIGHWAYS AGENCY (HA) The government body that manages, improves and builds all major roads in the UK.

HOUSEHOLD A group of people that lives together in shared accommodation.

HUMAN RIGHTS ACT – 1998 Incorporated the European convention on Human Rights into U.K. law.

HYDROPOWER Makes use of the movement of fresh water in rivers, using the flow of water to generate electricity.

HYPERINFLATION Extraordinary high inflation or increase in prices.

IDEOLOGY Ideas and beliefs which form the basis for a social, economic or political system.

IGNORANCE Lack of knowledge or awareness.

IMMIGRANT Someone who comes to a foreign country to settle.

IMPORT Buying goods into a country.

INDUSTRIAL TRIBUNAL A body set up to hear complaints and make judgments in disputes between employers and employees.

INFRASTRUCTURE The organisation of the services needed to run a community. It would include such things as clean water supply, provision of electricity, rubbish and sewage disposal, roads and transport systems, medical care facilities and some sort of social control to prevent crime and violence.

INJUSTICE Unfairness or lack of justice.

INNATE CHARACTERISTICS A feature of being a human being that is possessed at birth. For example, your sex.

INSTITUTIONAL DISCRIMINATION Discrimination within an organisation, e.g. the police.

INTELLIGENCE The capacity to acquire and apply knowledge. The ability to think and reason.

INTEREST Percentage of money to be repaid in addition to the amount lent. Gives the lender a profit from lending.

INTERMEDIARY Someone who is brought in to settle a dispute or bring both sides into agreement.

INTERNATIONAL MONETARY FUND (IMF) A world financial organisation that guides and/or supports LEDCs.

INTERPERSONAL SKILLS The ability to relate to other people.

KIN AND KINSHIP GROUPS Another word for relatives. This often refers to more distant relatives who play a role in influencing and helping other members of the wider family e.g. uncles, cousins, in-laws and so on. They are connected genetically or through marriage.

LEARNED RESPONSE A reaction to something which has been taught.

LEDCs Less economically developed countries: countries that are significantly less wealthy than MEDCs. They have lower levels of technology and industry, and the population has a lower standard of life. Usually lower life expectancy and lower levels of health care and education. Not all LEDCs are at the same level. Some suffer from famine and widespread diseases, others are better off but still below the wealth level of MEDCs.

LIBERAL DEMOCRACY This is based on two values. 1 That government operates with the freely given consent of the people; 2 Government is somehow responsible to the people who elected it. In a liberal democracy, we would therefore see government chosen through regular and fair elections; that all men and women over a certain age would be entitled to participate in the election process; that elections would be open to a number of political parties to compete in; that the government would be held accountable through a parliament or congress; that the rights of individuals would be respected in society and possibly protected through a constitution, and that the rule of law would be respected.

LIBERALS Those in favour of political and serial reform.

LIFE EXPECTANCY The average age at which members of a country's population die.

LOAN The lending of money: often with interest repayments expected, too.

LYNCHING To kill (a person suspected of crime), especially by hanging, without a proper trial.

MAJORITY The amount by which the greater number of votes cast in an election is more than the total number of remaining votes.

MALE Biological characteristics of men.

MALNUTRITION Inappropriate food intake. The average calorie intake falls below that required to stay healthy (absolute poverty).

MASCULINE Behavioural characteristics associated with being a man in a specific culture.

MEDCs More economically developed countries: countries that have high levels of wealth and well-developed technology and industry. People in these countries have a high standard of living and good services such as health care and education.

MEDIATION An attempt to bring together two sides in a dispute.

MEDIATION TECHNIQUES The skills of mediation.

METEOROLOGIST Someone who studies weather patterns and their causes.

MIDDLE CLASS A description of a section of a population who share similar wealth and influence (power) in society. They are called "middle class" because they are more wealthy and powerful than the "working class", but not as wealthy and powerful as the "upper class". Examples of middle class people could be doctors, senior managers in industry.

MIGRATION Departure from a person's native land to settle in another.

MILITANT Willing to take strong or violent action.

MONOGAMOUS A cultural system which says that people should only marry or have a sexual relationship with one person at a time.

MORAL (adjective/adverb) Virtuous, doing the right thing (opposite: immoral). Personal standards or rules that guide an individual towards making judgements about permissible behaviour with regard to basic human values (for example, individual freedoms, respect for others).

MORALITY Concerned with the distinction between good and evil or right and wrong. Right or good behaviour.

MOTHER HOUSEHOLDS Households where the most significant provider of resources and authority is the mother. In such households husbands and fathers are not present or only play a limited role in family life.

MUTUALLY EXCLUSIVE Incompatible.

NAACP (The National Association for the Advancement of Coloured People) Amercian organization whose goal is the end of racial discrimination and segregation.

NATION A group of people living together in a certain area under the same government; country. Once a synonym for 'ethnic group', designating a single culture sharing a language, religion, history, territory, ancestry and kinship. Now usually a synonym for state or nation-state.

NATIONAL GUARD An organized Force of military reserves in individual American states. They can be called up by the state or by the federal government.

NATIONALISM Loyalty to one's nation.

NATIONALIST Someone who believes in independence for his/her own country.

NATURAL ENVIRONMENT Any part of the planet that has not been altered or much changed by human intervention. It could refer to land, sea or water, or the atmosphere.

NATURAL RESOURCES The raw materials that we take from the natural environment and use to help us live. Sometimes we use natural resources as they are found in nature (for example, we eat berries and fruit, and drink water). Sometimes we use them to make things or energy.

NATURE The charcateristics and behaviour someone inherits, rather than learns.

NEGOTIATE To discuss in order to reach an agreement.

NOBEL PEACE PRIZE A prize given annually for the promotion of world peace; started by Alfred Nobel (1833-96), Swedish discoverer of dynamite.

NON-RENEWABLE RESOURCES Simply explained by saying that once we have used up this type of resource, there will be no more created, for example, coal and oil.

NORMS Rules that define behaviour that is expected, required, or acceptable in particular circumstances. May be written or unwritten.

NUCLEAR FAMILY A description of the basic family group: mother, father, and their children.

NURTURE What a person learns from their experiences, environment or training.

NUTRIENTS Substances that promote growth on plants or animals.

OMBUDSMEN An official appointed to investigate complaints against public authorities or government departments or the people who work for them.

OSTRACISE To refuse to have anything to do with someone.

PACIFISM The belief that violence is unjustified and war is wrong on moral or religious grounds.

PARLIAMENTARY HEALTH SELECT COMMITTEE Appointed by the House of Commons to examine the expenditure, administration and policy of the Department of Health. It has a maximum of eleven members.

PCBs A manufactured chemical used in many products such as lubricants, paints, sealants and many electrical products. Exposure to it causes medical problems in people such as a severe form of acne called chloracne, numbness in the arms and/or legs, muscle spasms, chronic bronchitis and problems with the nervous system.

PEER GROUPS A friendship group with common interests and position, made up of individuals of similar age.

PEER PRESSURE Compulsion to do or obtain the same things as others in one's peer group.

PERSECUTE To ill-treat, oppress, torment or put to death because of religion or politics.

PESTICIDES Chemicals sprayed or spread on to land and crops to kill insects and wildlife that could damage crops or people.

PHOTOCHEMICAL SMOG Petrol and diesel fuels produce many chemical by-products. These chemicals combine with water vapour and sunlight to produce a dangerously polluted atmosphere.

PLANKTON Microscopic plants used by many sea creatures as a basic food source.

POLLUTION Describes a situation where the natural environment is contaminated by harmful substances, often as a result of human activity.

POVERTY CYCLE OR TRAP The results of being poor (like poor health and lack of education) that trap poor people into continuing poverty – a vicious cycle.

POVERTY LINE The level of income below which a person cannot afford to buy all the resources they need to live.

PRIMARY SOCIALISATION Socialisation is the process of teaching people how to fit in to a society. **Primary socialisation** is the first stage of this process and it is usually done by the parents who teach children how to speak, behave with others, and many of the attitudes and values they will live by in later life.

Later in life other groups (such as schools, employers, peer-groups continue the process of teaching people what is expected of them. This is called **secondary socialisation.**

PROPAGANDA The organised circulation by a political group, etc. of ideas, information, misinformation, rumour or opinion by means of the media.

QUOTA The specific quantity of goods that a country's government allows to be imported.

RECONSTITUTED FAMILY A family that is made up of people who have divorced or separated from an earlier partnership and formed another family, bringing up children from one or both previous marriages.

REGENERATED When plants that have been cut down grow again. It can also refer to any natural environment that recovers after it has been damaged.

RELATIVE POVERTY Being poor compared to the average or norms of a country. Poverty moves up or down depending on what the 'average' is. A common measure: relative poverty is less than half the average income (GNP pc).

RELIGION Belief in and reverence for a supernatural power or powers regarded as creator and governor of the universe. May be based on the teachings of a spiritual leader. Includes an organisation and special buildings.

RENEWABLE ENERGY SOURCES Sources of energy that occur naturally and are always available. They do not run out with use.

REPUBLIC A form of government without a monarchy in which supreme power is held by the people or their elected representatives.

RESISTANCE GROUPS Underground organisations fighting for the freedom of a country occupied by an enemy force.

ROLE The behaviour expected of a person with a certain social position or status (for example, child, group leader).

ROLE MODEL Someone whose behaviour and attitudes are imitated by others.

SANCTIONS An economic or military measure taken against a nation as a means of coercion or force, usually to stop aggression.

SANITATION Cleaning, washing, getting rid of rubbish, dirt and sewage.

SEGREGATE To set apart or isolate a race, class or minority from the rest of society.

SELF-ESTEEM Pride in oneself; self-respect.

SEPARATIST A person who wants independence from an established church, organisation or state.

SEX Identifies the biological differences between women and men: male or female.

SEXUALITY A sexual state or condition.

SHOTGUN WEDDINGS Weddings that took place because the woman was pregnant. They were called 'shotgun weddings' because of the stereotype of the father of the pregnant bride going to the wedding with a shotgun to make sure the groom went through with the marriage.

SINGLE-PARENT FAMILY A family where only the mother or father is involved in bringing up the children. The other parent is not generally present.

SMALL-SCALE CONFLICT Conflict at an individual or local level.

SOCIAL CLASS This is a way of dividing up the population of a society into groups which have similar levels of wealth, power and life-styles. [see MIDDLE CLASS]

SOCIAL EVIL 'Social evil' is a term which can be used to define any behaviour, lifestyle, or group which is seen as being a threat to social stability or well-being of society or any accepted group within society.

It is not a precise term and is often used by the media or politicians or the forces of law and order to identify a particular situation which is seen as dangerous and threatening to other members of society. An example could be widespread binge-drinking.

SOCIAL ORGANISATION The way a group of people relates to each other and works together.

SOCIAL OUTCAST This is someone who, as a result of their behaviour or personality or social status, is not accepted by the rest of society. This may result in their exclusion from many events, activities and rights which most people in society enjoy.

SOCIAL ROLES Activities and responsibilities that individuals and groups take on as part of their membership of a social group.

SOCIAL VALUES Social values are what most people in a society think are desirable and acceptable attitudes, beliefs and behaviour.

Some social groups may have different social values and this could cause tension in a society.

SOCIALISATION The process by which human behaviour is shaped through experience with those around them. Through socialisation, the individual learns the values, norms (formal and informal) and beliefs of a society.

SOCIALIST Someone who believes in socialism – the political and economic theory that advocates the state ownership of industry and capital and the distribution of that wealth in the community.

SOCIETY A community of people interacting with each other. May include more than one culture.

SOCIOLOGIST A sociologist is someone who studies the way a society works. They attempt to observe how social organisations operate and how people are influenced by these organisations. They try to look social life in an unbiased way and say what is happening, rather than what should happen.

SOLAR ENERGY Makes use of the heat and light of the sun to produce heat and electricity.

STATE GOVERNMENTS The governments of the individual states of the USA.

STATE LAWS The laws of the individual states of the USA.

STEWARDSHIP Where the people using the natural environment understand what it needs to survive and treat it with respect and concern for the future.

SUBSIDIES Payment of money to producers in your own country so that they can produce their goods more cheaply than foreign competition, for example, Italian tomato growers are subsidised and can sell tomatoes more cheaply than unsubsidised Tanzanian tomato growers.

SUPERSTITION A belief, practice or rite unreasoningly upheld by faith in magic or chance.

SUPREME COURT The highest court in a country or state.

SUSTAINABLE, SUSTAINABLY Methods of working in a natural environment that do not damage the health of the ecosystem and make it possible for the environment to survive and thrive.

SUSTAINABLE TOURISM Also eco-tourism, nature tourism, green travel, environmentally responsible tourism. All these terms describe attempts to organise travel and tourism in ways that minimise the environmental damage that the travel and tourism business could cause.

TARIFF A tax on the goods of another country by the country importing those goods. This forces the price up of the imported produce and protects the home producers.

TECHNOLOGY Any product or process that extends the power of a human being, for example, in terms of survival, comfort level and quality of life.

TRADITION Customs, legends or beliefs that are handed down from generation to generation, often by word of mouth or by example.

TRIBALISM A sense of belonging or loyalty to a tribe.

UN CONVENTION ON THE RIGHTS OF THE CHILD Designed to ensure the survival, development and protection of children.

UNCONSTITUTIONAL Against the principles set forth in the constitution of a nation or state.

UNITED NATIONS (UN) An association of most of the countries in the world, formed in 1945 to promote peace, security and economic development.

UNIVERSAL DECLARATION OF HUMAN RIGHTS A declaration adopted by the United Nations in 1948 which sets out the basic human rights to which everyone is entitled.

USSR Union of Soviet Socialist Republics, i.e. Communist Russia.

VALUES Standards by which members of a culture define what is desirable and undesirable, good or bad, beautiful or ugly, important or unimportant, etc.

WEALTH The accumulation of past income, natural resources and financial resources. According to the rich, it does not bring happiness; according to the poor, it brings something quite closely resembling it.

WMD Weapons of mass destruction.

WOMEN'S LIBERATION MOVEMENT A movement to free women from the disadvantages they suffer in a male-dominated society. Aimed at achieving equality, e.g. with regard to job opportunities and pay.

WORLD BANK A world financial organisation that guides and/or supports LEDCs.

WORLD HEALTH ORGANISATION The United Nations specialised agency for health, established in 1948. It aims to promote the highest level of health for all peoples.

WORLD HERITAGE CONVENTION An international agreement created to protect unique sites such as Stonehenge or the Pyramids.

WORLD TRADE ORGANISATION International organisation that tries to regulate trade between different countries. Sometimes accused of being dominated by MEDCs and looking after them at the expense of LEDCs.

INDEX